We Dissent

We Dissent

Talking Back to the Rehnquist Court

Eight Cases That Subverted
Civil Liberties and Civil Rights

Edited by
Michael Avery

NEW YORK UNIVERSITY PRESS
New York and London

NEW YORK UNIVERSITY PRESS
New York and London
www.nyupress.org

© 2009 by New York University

Library of Congress Cataloging-in-Publication Data

We dissent : talking back to the Rehnquist court :
eight cases that subverted civil liberties and civil rights /
edited by Michael Avery.
p. cm.
Includes bibliographical references and index.
ISBN–13: 978–0–8147–0723–4 (cl : alk. paper)
ISBN–10: 0–8147–0723–8 (cl : alk. paper)
1. Civil rights—United States—Cases. 2. United States. Supreme Court.
3. Rehnquist, William H., 1924–2005. I. Avery, Michael, 1944–
KF4749.A2W4   2008
342.7308'5—dc22   2008031463

New York University Press books are printed on acid-free paper,
and their binding materials are chosen for strength and durability.
We strive to use environmentally responsible suppliers and materials
to the greatest extent possible in publishing our books.

Manufactured in the United States of America
10 9 8 7 6 5 4 3 2 1

This book is dedicated to the memory of Catherine G. ("Katie") Roraback, a Connecticut lawyer and former president of the National Lawyers Guild, who devoted her considerable talents to the representation of ordinary people and the victims of injustice. Among other accomplishments, she wrote the briefs for the plaintiffs in Griswold v. Connecticut. Katie Roraback's legal philosophy and law practice amounted to a lifelong dissent from orthodoxy at the same time that she demonstrated her profound commitment to justice and the Constitution.

Contents

Introduction

Michael Avery

WE DISSENT PRESENTS a vision of constitutional law in the United States that differs considerably from the recent jurisprudence of the United States Supreme Court. It is a vision that takes seriously a commitment to democratic values, social justice, and racial equality and that insists upon governmental accountability to our citizens and others protected by the Constitution. *We Dissent* was provoked by the distance the Supreme Court traveled from these ideals during the tenure of Chief Justice William H. Rehnquist.

The book contains critical essays regarding eight decisions that concern constitutional rights and civil liberties rendered by the Supreme Court between 1984 and 2003. The opinions were handed down during the tenure of Chief Justice Rehnquist, except for *Strickland v. Washington,* which was decided while Justice Rehnquist was on the Supreme Court but before he was named Chief Justice. *Strickland* was typical of the jurisprudence of the "Rehnquist Court" and was followed repeatedly during his tenure as Chief Justice.

The Supreme Court opinions discussed here suggest that the Rehnquist Court was more committed to protecting the government and government officials from the people than it was in protecting the people from the government. The latter, of course, is the principal purpose of the Bill of Rights to the Constitution. Over and over again, the Court narrowed the scope of constitutional rights that protect individual liberty. During the nineteen years of Chief Justice Rehnquist's tenure, the Court, through both procedural and substantive decisions, made it substantially more difficult for individuals to obtain vindication for violations of their rights and compensation for injuries resulting from constitutional violations. At the same time that the Court made it more difficult to hold government officials accountable for constitutional violations, it developed a jurisprudence that encourages officials to guide their conduct by reference to subconstitutional norms. Of overriding concern is the fact that the Rehnquist Court never developed an adequate understanding of racism in the United States.

In the opinions we review, the Court held:

That sovereign immunity affords complete protection for state governments from suits by individuals in state courts for violations of federal statutes;

That government officials who treat white Americans more favorably than black Americans cannot be held liable for their actions unless the victims of unfair treatment can prove a subjective intent to discriminate;

That police who stop motorists on the pretext that they have committed traffic violations have behaved "reasonably" under the Fourth Amendment even where the stop is really for a different reason or is motivated by racial considerations;

That the Fifth Amendment does not protect suspects from interrogation that amounts to torture unless the suspect's statements are later used in evidence in a criminal trial;

That officers who violate the constitution by use of excessive force against civilians are not liable in damages as long as they made a "reasonable" mistake about the amount of force permitted under the circumstances;

That officers whose conduct leads to a death in a high-speed police chase are not liable in damages even where they acted with reckless disregard for human life.

The Court also reduced the likelihood that constitutional rights will be enforced in criminal cases by adopting a very low standard for judging claims that criminal defense attorneys have provided inadequate representation. Finally, the Court has made it difficult to achieve dramatic changes through the political process by protecting the two major parties from electoral challenges by minority party candidates.

Most Americans are unaware of the decisions described in this book and their consequences to our constitutional democracy. Public discussion of the jurisprudence of the Supreme Court tends to focus on a few controversial issues, such as abortion, presidential power, and the rule that illegally seized evidence may be excluded from criminal trials. Even in those instances, there is seldom informative discussion in the mass media about the details of the conservative decisions made by the Rehnquist Court. But the issues the Court resolved in the cases discussed in this volume are crucially important to the maintenance of individual liberty and responsible government.

We have chosen to cast the essays in this book in the form of "dissents" to the majority opinions in the cases for several reasons. First, the Court has moved so far in a conservative direction that it is rare that any of the current Justices writes a dissent that genuinely and passionately defends individual liberty or insists upon government accountability. Indeed, in the eight cases discussed here, there was only one dissent, by Justice Thurgood Marshall, that fits those criteria.

In the past, when the Supreme Court rendered opinions that failed to be true to our constitutional heritage, dissenting Justices often cried out, sometimes laying the groundwork for change in future years. Justice John Marshall Harlan's dissent from the "separate but equal" decision of the Supreme Court in *Plessy v. Ferguson*,[1] the dissent of Justice Oliver Wendell Holmes from the approval of sedition convictions over First Amendment objections during World War I in *Abrams v. United States*,[2] Justice Louis D. Brandeis's dissent from the decision upholding wiretapping in *Olmstead v. United States*,[3] Justice Robert H. Jackson's dissent in the Japanese internment case, *Korematsu v. United States*,[4] and Justice William O. Douglas's dissent in the Smith Act prosecutions, *Dennis v. United States*,[5] are just a few examples of "prophetic" dissents.[6] We do not lay claim to any comparison with such luminaries but do note the absence of similar dissenting voices on today's Court. This brings us to the second reason for writing these essays in the form of dissents.

The law, of course, does not "belong" to the Supreme Court. The Constitution was adopted by We the People of the United States, and constitutional law belongs to all of us. Although it is an important element in our system of separation of powers and checks and balances that the Supreme Court is paramount in the articulation of what the Constitution means, it would be a mistake for ordinary citizens to believe that they have no right to express their views on the law, to "dissent" from decisions by the Court. The dissents in this book are submitted in the spirit of fostering greater public debate about the extent to which the Rehnquist Court strayed from democratic values.

Promoting dissent from the jurisprudence of the Supreme Court is but one element of keeping alive an active tradition of political dissent in the United States. The repressive Alien and Sedition Acts of 1798 were enacted by a Congress that included many of the "framers" who had been delegates to the Constitutional Convention. The Sedition Act was an effort by the Federalist Party to cement its control over the government by criminalizing criticism of government officers and institutions. James Madison and Thomas Jefferson immediately, at their personal peril, organized public opposition, leading to the Kentucky and Virginia Resolutions of 1798 and 1799, which condemned the Sedition Act as unconstitutional.

Madison and Jefferson, of course, were intrepid revolutionaries. In recent years, the members of the opposition political party have grown far more cautious. It has been citizens and public interest groups that have brought legal challenges to constitutional violations committed in the name of the war on terror, not established political leaders. The failure of the House of Representatives even to hold hearings under the constitutional provisions providing for impeachment has left it to individual citizens to argue that the president should be held accountable for his conduct in office. The Bill of Rights Defense Committee, originally organized in private homes in Northampton, Massachusetts, has brought about the enactment of 414 local government resolutions dissenting from the repressive provisions of the Patriot Act, while elected representatives in Washington have remained nearly impotent with respect to protecting constitutional rights.[7] In times of constitutional crisis, informed citizen dissent is essential to maintain the health of our republic.

Given the makeup of the Rehnquist Court and now the Roberts Court, it is particularly important to promote citizen dissent from their decisions. The current Justices poorly represent constituencies that should be heard in constitutional dialogue. It has long been my belief that it would be prudent to require that a nominee to the Supreme Court be the sort of lawyer who had to keep a box of Kleenex on the desk for use by the clients who came to the office frightened and reduced to tears by their legal problems. Only Justice Ruth Bader Ginsburg on the current Court might pass this "Kleenex test." The current Justices who practiced law represented either rich and powerful clients or the government. None were criminal defense lawyers or made their living as civil rights lawyers.[8] None had a career as a staff attorney for a public interest organization. Of the Justices who were academics, only Justice Ginsburg handled civil rights matters as an advocate. The Justices of the Roberts Court have always been reliable members of the Establishment.

The constitutional philosophy of the nine lawyers and law professors who wrote the dissents in this volume has been informed by a different set of experiences. These authors are outstanding constitutional scholars and practitioners, and they pass the "Kleenex test." They have served as the lawyers for victims of constitutional violations and represented criminal defendants. They have a *feeling* for the significance of civil rights protections. They approach the constitutional issues raised by these cases as lawyers familiar, through personal experience, with the perspective of the victims of discrimination and oppression who require the protections afforded by the Bill of Rights and the Fourteenth Amendment. That is, of course, not the only perspective that must be taken into account. But it is one in very short supply among the Justices of the Rehnquist Court and the current Supreme Court.

Consistent with our goal of opening the debate about constitutional law as widely as possible, we have tried to write these essays in a style that is accessible to the nonlawyer reader. The essays are not about abstract constitutional theory, and it is our hope that the reader will not find them to be riddled with legal jargon. Law professors and lawyers are used to making many of their arguments in dense footnotes, but we have tried to avoid that as much as possible here. The endnotes are primarily for the purpose of providing necessary citations to authorities, and there is a brief description of the legal citation system at the beginning of the notes.

In Chapter 1, Professor Erwin Chemerinsky dissents from the decision in *Alden v. Maine*, where the Court held that state governments possess sovereign immunity and cannot be sued in state court without their consent, even on federal claims. The Court had already held that the Eleventh Amendment bars most suits against state governments in federal court. Justice Souter dissented from the decision in *Alden*, joined by Justices Stevens, Ginsburg, and Breyer. Justice Souter made a historical critique of the majority's conclusion that the Tenth Amendment constitutionalized sovereign immunity as inherent in statehood and a reasoned argument about the nature of the division of power between the federal and the state governments that rejects the majority's conclusion that federalism requires this level of respect for state sovereignty. He also expressed concern that the decision leaves citizens without a remedy for state government violations of rights created by federal legislation.

Professor Chemerinsky's critique of *Alden* is more fundamental. He explains that the very notion of sovereign immunity is inconsistent with democratic accountability of the government to the people and has no place in American constitutional law. Professor Chemerinsky relies upon historical sources to demonstrate that the framers had no intent to recognize sovereign immunity in the Constitution. More essentially, he argues, on the basis of close constitutional analysis, that a doctrine premised on the infallibility of a king cannot be squared with democratic principles and the rule of law. Finally, he concludes that sovereign immunity is inconsistent with the guarantees of the Fifth and Fourteenth Amendments that safeguard life, liberty, and property from deprivation by the government without due process of law.

Fundamental democratic principles also motivate Professor Jamin Raskin's dissent to the Court's decision in *Arkansas Educational Television Commission v. Forbes*, in Chapter 2. The Court held that the First Amendment did not protect the right of a minority party candidate to participate in a debate on public television, despite the fact that he had qualified to be on the ballot. There was a dissent by Justice Stevens, joined by Justices Souter and Ginsburg. The essence of the dissenting opinion was that the Arkansas Educational Television Commission (AETC) made the decision to exclude the candidate without using previously established objective criteria to guide its decision. Exercises of discretion without standards that result in the denial of a right to speak are generally held to be unconstitutional.

Professor Raskin's critique of the decision rests upon broader and more fundamental principles. He treats candidate debates on public television as events in a public forum where the full protections of the First Amendment apply. He objects to the fact that the Court has enshrined the two-party system as though it were protected by the Constitution and permitted discrimination against a minority party candidate because his views were unpopular, as though he were *not* protected by the Constitution. Objective standards would not, in Raskin's view, be sufficient to warrant excluding a candidate from a debate. He concludes that all candidates qualified to be on the ballot have a First Amendment right to participate in debates on public television, absent some truly compelling governmental interest in limiting the field. He believes that the self-fulfilling prophecy (made by the government) that a minor candidate has little chance of winning an election is insufficient to exclude him from such a debate. Raskin's view is that the voters decide on Election Day who the winning candidate is and that until that point the government is obliged to treat all candidates who qualify to be on the ballot equally.

In Chapter 3, Eva Paterson and Susan K. Serrano take on the major constitutional doctrine that has kept the Equal Protection Clause from achieving its full promise: the requirement that to make a successful challenge to racial classifications, one must prove that the government intended to discriminate, not merely that the effect of government action resulted in discrimination. In most cases the requirement is extremely difficult, if not impossible, to meet. This doctrine applies to discrimination against other classes, as well. In their dissent to *City of Cuyahoga Falls v. Buckeye Community Hope Foundation,* a housing case, Paterson and Serrano argue that it is time to overrule the Court's 1976 decision in *Washington v. Davis,* which established this rule. There were no dissenting opinions filed by any of the Justices in *Cuyahoga Falls.* Justices Brennan and Marshall dissented from the Court's decision in *Washington v. Davis,* but on other grounds, without reaching the constitutional question regarding the Equal Protection Clause.

Paterson and Serrano dissent not merely from the rule that requires proof of intent to discriminate to prove an equal protection violation but from the Court's basic premises about the nature of racism in the United States. They argue that race discrimination results from institutionalized, historically influenced, and often subconscious processes, rather than from the specific and identifiable intent of decision makers. Rather than understanding race discrimination as the result of blatant or calculated actions by individuals, they explore the historical and contextual explanations for discrimination, specifically institutional structures and subconscious methods of categorization and information processing, through the rich literature in the fields of social psychology and organizational sociology. Paterson and Serrano's dissent provides us with new ways of thinking not only about law but about our society itself.

The Supreme Court's limitations in understanding race are also discussed in Professor Tracey Maclin's dissent, in Chapter 4, to the Court's decision reviewing traffic stops under the Fourth Amendment in *United States v. Whren.* In *Whren,* a unanimous Court held that the constitutionality of a traffic stop is determined by whether the officer has probable cause to believe the driver has violated traffic laws. The Court held that it does not make a stop illegal that the officer is merely using the traffic violation as a pretext to investigate for other reasons, even if he has no probable cause to support the suspicions that actually motivated the stop.

By taking a realistic view of the frequency with which most motorists commit traffic violations, Maclin shows that *Whren* simply gives police officers too much unchecked discretion. His detailed constitutional analysis demonstrates that the Fourth Amendment requires that when there is a departure from standard police procedure during a traffic stop and the stop is a pretext for some other type of investigation, the court has an obligation to determine whether the stop is objectively reasonable in the light of all the circumstances. He concludes that where the stop is arbitrary or discriminatory, the court must find a Fourth Amendment violation.

Professor Maclin's dissent squarely addresses the racial profiling consequences of the decision in *Whren*. He argues that a decision on whether police actions are "reasonable" under the Fourth Amendment should reflect a concern with equality. He would allow motorists to raise an inference of unequal enforcement either by presenting statistical data that show a pattern of race-based enforcement of the traffic laws or by demonstrating that the stop in a given case was arbitrary. Justice Scalia's opinion for the majority in *Whren* blandly asserted that problems of racially discriminatory enforcement of traffic laws could be addressed through challenges under the Equal Protection Clause. Maclin concludes, however, that recognizing such claims under the Fourth Amendment is necessary, because under current law equal protection challenges to traffic enforcement have no realistic chance of success given the requirement that intent to discriminate be proven.

In Chapter 5, Professor Michael Avery dissents from the Court's decision in *County of Sacramento v. Lewis*, where it held that a police officer who acts with reckless disregard for human life does not violate the constitutional rights of a person injured during a high-speed chase. The Court held that the conduct of the officer in this case did not "shock the conscience" because he had not intended to harm the boy killed in the chase. None of the Justices dissented from the decision.

Professor Avery argues that the Court applied the wrong standard to determine whether or not the victim had suffered a deprivation of his substantive rights to due process of law. Avery explains that the "shocks the conscience" test is entirely subjective and allows judges to make decisions on the basis of their personal values with respect to law enforcement practices. He argues that the Court has imposed standards such as the "intent to harm" rule in this case for the very purpose of making constitutional claims difficult to prove in order to reduce the number of suits against government officials, not because the rule is required by constitutional doctrine.

Relying on empirical studies of high-speed pursuits, Avery demonstrates that the Court has an unrealistic view of the harm caused by such chases. On the basis of a review of police training practices, he shows that police administrators have higher expectations of the ability of officers to balance the risk of pursuits against gains than does the Supreme Court.

He concludes that officers should be accountable in damages where they cause injuries by failing to engage in such balancing and by conducting chases with a reckless disregard for life.

In Chapter 6, Professor Marjorie Cohn dissents from the Court's decision in *Chavez v. Martinez*. In a decision fractured by several concurring opinions, a majority of the Justices refused to hold that a man who had been partially paralyzed and blinded when shot by police had a remedy under the Civil Rights Act for a violation of his Fifth Amendment rights after he was questioned against his will in the hospital emergency room while undergoing life-saving medical treatment. Justices Thomas, O'Connor, and Scalia and Chief Justice Rehnquist ruled that the Fifth Amendment guarantee against compelled self-incrimination has no applicability unless a suspect is not only questioned but also prosecuted and his statements are introduced against him at trial. Justice Souter, joined by Justice Breyer, wrote a separate opinion acknowledging that evidence obtained by the questioning would have been "clearly inadmissible" as a violation of the Fifth Amendment in a criminal trial.[9] They concluded, however, that the Fifth Amendment does not require a remedy in damages unless statements are introduced in evidence at a trial. This had the same practical impact as the Thomas opinion, because, in the absence of a criminal prosecution, a suit for damages is the only legal remedy in which the victim of coercive interrogation can attempt to vindicate his rights. Only Justices Kennedy, Stevens, and Ginsburg, who dissented in part from the Court's decision, concluded that coercive interrogation amounts to an immediate constitutional violation under the Fifth Amendment.

Professor Cohn parts company from the Court in two significant ways. First, she concludes that effective protection against coercive interrogation and compelled self-incrimination requires a recognition that a constitutional violation under the Fifth Amendment takes place at the time of the questioning. She also finds that the questioning in this case violated Martinez's rights to substantive due process.

Cohn's analysis is informed by legal principles that none of the Justices in *Chavez* took into account: the Convention against Torture and Other Cruel, Inhuman or Degrading Treatment or Punishment and the International Covenant on Civil and Political Rights. Justice Stevens had described Chavez as using "tortuous methods," and Justice Kennedy wrote that the case involved "torture or its equivalent." Cohn, however, would have decided the case by applying the relevant treaties that had been ratified by the United States and that constitute the supreme law of the land under Article VI of the Constitution. Such treaties are binding on the states as well as on the federal government. Cohn argues that our obligations under these treaties provide specific guideposts that should inform the substantive due process analysis, and she finds that the conduct of Sergeant Chavez in this case constituted torture or, at a minimum, cruel, inhuman, or degrading treatment, also forbidden by the treaties.

David Rudovsky, in Chapter 7, challenges the application of the qualified immunity doctrine to cases alleging that police officers used excessive force. The Court held, in *Saucier v. Katz,* that a police officer may not be held liable under the Civil Rights Act for using excessive force where a reasonable officer might have been mistaken about whether the force used was reasonable. The qualified immunity defense gives a police officer two levels of defense to a constitutional claim for excessive force: first, the force was reasonable and not excessive; second, even if it was excessive, the officer reasonably thought it was permissible. Justices Ginsburg, Stevens, and Breyer wrote a concurring opinion in which they disagreed that qualified immunity is necessary in excessive force cases, because the determination of whether the force was excessive already includes an inquiry into whether it was reasonable.

Rudovsky agrees with the argument that qualified immunity is redundant in excessive force cases, but his dissent articulates a broader challenge to the expansive definition of the qualified immunity doctrine that currently exists in federal courts. The defense provides a version of a "mistake of law" defense to government officials accused of misconduct, a defense not available to ordinary citizens accused of violating the law. Rudovsky warns that this defense drastically curbs the ability of citizens to vindicate their constitutional rights and interferes with the potential of civil rights suits to hold officials accountable for constitutional violations. Even more ominously, by creating a defense from liability for officials whose actions do not conform to constitutional requirements, those officials are encouraged to use subconstitutional norms to guide their conduct. Thus, Rudovsky would limit the qualified immunity defense to situations where a court decision finding official conduct to be unconstitutional was not fairly foreseeable. He would define "fairly foreseeable" to require that officials anticipate most decisions in which constitutional violations are found by applying well-established legal principles, even to novel factual circumstances.

In Chapter 8, Professor Abbe Smith dissents from the Court's decision in *Strickland v. Washington,* a death penalty case in which the Court dramatically watered down the standards to determine whether the criminal defense attorney had afforded his client competent representation. The Court held that in order for a conviction to be affirmed on appeal, it was sufficient if the defense lawyer's representation was "reasonably effective." The Court declined to provide guidelines to flesh out that requirement but held that an appellate court's review of trial counsel's performance should be "highly deferential." Finally, the Court held that even where the defense counsel's representation was deficient, a conviction could be reversed only where there was a reasonable probability that, but for the bad lawyering, the result of the trial would have been different.

Strickland is the one case reviewed in this book where there was a dissent, a lone opinion by Justice Marshall,[10] that took the principles of due process of law and governmental accountability as seriously as do the present authors. Professor Smith, however, paints with an even broader brush. She begins with the proposition that the courts have failed to fulfill the promise of the Supreme Court's landmark decision in Gideon v. Wainwright,[11] holding that indigent criminal defendants are entitled to have a lawyer provided by the Court. The problem of ineffective representation for people financially unable to hire their own attorneys is a national scandal, and the courts have tolerated it. Smith sees the standard in Strickland as responsible for much of the problem.

Smith fundamentally disagrees with the Court's conclusion that prevailing norms of practice are merely "guides" and have no constitutional force in determining whether a lawyer provided effective assistance to the client. She would make such decisions on the basis of established ethical rules and professional standards for criminal defense that are widely accepted, and she rejects the Court's decision to indulge a presumption in favor of finding the defense lawyer's performance "reasonably effective." Of particular relevance to Strickland's defense, she would impose on defense counsel a duty to conduct factual investigation. Smith also rejects the Court's requirement that a defendant demonstrate that a competent performance by counsel would have resulted in a different outcome, in part because of its insensitivity to the fact that even a guilty defendant deserves competent representation.

It must be noted that Justice Marshall was extremely sensitive to criminal justice issues. But Smith's dissent demonstrates the unique value of experience as a criminal defense lawyer, a perspective perennially missing from the Supreme Court and seldom found anywhere on the federal bench. Her discussion of the specific errors made by counsel in this death penalty case gives a strong feeling for the difference a zealous defender can make.

We hope that the reader will find the cases represented here interesting and our dissents provocative. To the extent that *We Dissent* engenders wider discussion and a more critical review of the work of the Supreme Court, we believe it will perform a service to our constitutional democracy.

NOTES

1. Plessy v. Ferguson, 163 U.S. 537, 552 (1896).

2. Abrams v. United States, 250 U.S. 616, 624 (1919)

3. Olmstead v. United States, 277 U.S. 438, 471 (1928).

4. Korematsu v. United States, 323 U.S. 214, 242 (1944).

5. Dennis v. United States, 341 U.S. 494, 581 (1951).

6. For a discussion of the history of dissenting opinions, see ALAN BARTH, PROPHETS WITH HONOR (Alfred A. Knopf, New York, 1974); and William J. Brennan, Jr., *In Defense of Dissents*, 37 HASTINGS L.J. 427 (1986).

7. See the Bill of Rights Defense Committee's Web site for a description of its activities: http://www.bordc.org/.

8. Given his views and his record on civil rights, Justice Clarence Thomas hardly qualifies as one who made his living as a civil rights lawyer, despite his eight years as Chairman of the Equal Employment Opportunity Commission.

9. Those who think of Justices Souter and Breyer as "moderates" would be well advised to consider the deeply conservative impact of their concurring opinion in this case. Had Justices Souter and Breyer joined in Justice Kennedy's opinion, there would have been five votes for the proposition that coercive interrogation itself violates the Fifth Amendment, regardless of whether statements are ever introduced in evidenced at a trial. Absent their votes, there remains only the protection from coercive interrogation afforded by substantive due process, which is a weak alternative remedy because of the fact that conduct must "shock the conscience" to constitute a violation. Moreover, Justice Souter continues in *Chavez* the practice that he began in *County of Sacramento v. Lewis* of claiming that the meaning of constitutional rules in suits against individual government officials differs from the same rules in other contexts. This line of argument constitutes a grave threat to accountability.

10. Justice Brennan dissented from the result in the case because he opposed the death penalty. He joined in the majority opinion, however, with respect to its description of the standard for determining ineffective assistance of counsel.

11. Gideon v. Wainwright, 372 U.S. 335 (1963).

1

Alden v. Maine

Sovereign Immunity—A Vestige of Monarchy
Inconsistent with Democratic Values

Erwin Chemerinsky

Introduction

In *Alden v. Maine* in 1999,[1] the Supreme Court held that state governments possess sovereign immunity and cannot be sued in state court, even on federal claims, without their consent. Justice Anthony Kennedy wrote for the majority in a 5-4 decision, and his opinion was joined by Chief Justice Rehnquist and by Justices O'Connor, Scalia, and Thomas. Justice Souter wrote a dissent, which was joined by Justices Stevens, Ginsburg, and Breyer.

The case involved probation officers in the State of Maine who claimed that they were owed overtime pay by the state under the federal Fair Labor Standards Act.[2] The probation officers initially sued in federal court, but the case was dismissed because of the Eleventh Amendment. They then sued in Maine state court.

By its terms, the Eleventh Amendment applies only in federal court. However, Justice Kennedy's majority opinion concluded that there is a broader principle of sovereign immunity that bars suits against state governments in state courts on federal claims. The Court declared: "We hold that the powers delegated to Congress under Article I of the United States Constitution do not include the power to subject nonconsenting States to private suits for damages in state courts."[3]

Dissent by Erwin Chemerinsky

The majority opinion invents a constitutional principle, sovereign immunity, that has no basis in the text or history of the Constitution. Even worse, it is inconsistent with one of the Constitution's most important commands: no one, especially not the government, is above the law. For the first time in American history, the Court has held that state governments cannot be sued in state court even on federal claims. For petitioners in this case it means that there is no court, federal or state, where they can sue, even though they unquestionably have a right to overtime pay under the federal Fair Labor Standards Act.[4] This violates the command long ago articulated by this Court in *Marbury v. Madison*,[5] that "[t]he very essence of civil liberty certainly consists in the right of every individual to claim the protection of the laws, whenever he receives an injury."

The principle of sovereign immunity is derived from English law, which assumed that "the King can do no wrong."[6] Since the time of Edward the First, the Crown of England has not been suable unless it has specifically consented to suit.

A doctrine derived from the premise "the King can do no wrong" deserves no place in American law. The United States was founded on a rejection of a monarchy and of royal prerogatives.[7] American government is based on the fundamental recognition that the government and government officials can do wrong and must be held accountable. Sovereign immunity undermines that basic notion.

Sovereign immunity is a doctrine based on a *common law* principle borrowed from the English common law. However, Article VI of the Constitution states that the Constitution and laws made pursuant to it are the supreme law of the United States and that, as such, a federal statute should prevail over claims of sovereign immunity. Yet, the Court holds that sovereign immunity, a common law doctrine, trumps even the U.S. Constitution and bars suits against government entities for relief when they violate the Constitution and federal laws.

The fallacy in the majority's approach can be seen first in the absence of any constitutional basis for its holding. Second, the majority's error is evident from the pernicious consequences of its holding, especially in terms of its inconsistency with basic constitutional values. Finally, it is clear that there are not persuasive policy justifications for recognizing sovereign immunity in state courts as the majority does today.

I

The text of the Constitution is silent about sovereign immunity. Not one clause of the first seven articles remotely even hints at the idea that the government has immunity from suits. No constitutional amendment has bestowed sovereign immunity on the federal government.

A claim might be made that the Eleventh Amendment provides sovereign immunity to state governments. Yet, if this is a textual argument, a careful reading of the text does not support the claim. The Eleventh Amendment states, "The Judicial power of the United States shall not be construed to extend to any suit in law or equity, commenced or prosecuted against one of the United States by Citizens of another State, or by Citizens or Subjects of any foreign state." By its very terms, the Eleventh Amendment applies only in federal court; it is a restriction solely on "the judicial power of the United States."

Indeed, the majority in this case expressly recognizes this and bases its holding entirely on the broad principle of state sovereign immunity and not in any way on the text of the Eleventh Amendment. Justice Kennedy, writing for the majority, states: "[S]overeign immunity derives not from the Eleventh Amendment but from the structure of the original Constitution itself."[8] Moreover, the text of the Eleventh Amendment restricts only suits against states that are based on diversity of citizenship; it says that the federal judicial power does not extend to a suit against a state by a citizen of another state or of a foreign country. Nothing within it bars a suit against a state by its own citizens. The prohibition of suits against a state by its own citizens in federal court was the holding of *Hans v. Louisiana*[9] more than a century ago, but it certainly is not based on the text of the Eleventh Amendment.

Justice Kennedy's majority opinion makes a textual argument for sovereign immunity on the basis of the premise that the existence of states is mandated by the Constitution. He writes: "The founding document 'specifically recognizes the States as sovereign entities.' . . . Various textual provisions of the Constitution assume the States' continued existence and active participation in the fundamental processes of governance."[10] Yet, the fact that the Constitution preserves states as entities says absolutely nothing about whether states should have immunity in state court or sovereign immunity more generally. The Constitution, of course, recognizes the existence of state governments, but that does not give any indication of the scope of state power or the existence of state immunity.

Nor can sovereign immunity be justified from an originalist perspective based on framers' intent. The Justices in the majority often describe themselves as originalists.[11] It is important to remember that originalists believe that a right is protected under the Constitution, if the text is silent, only if the framers' intent is clear in justifying protection.[12] If the intent is unclear, the right is not constitutionally protected. With respect to sovereign immunity, we must recognize that, at the very least, the framers' intent is completely ambiguous.

There was no discussion of sovereign immunity at the Constitutional Convention in Philadelphia in 1787. The issue did arise in the state ratifying conventions. The dispute was over whether Article III authorized suits against unconsenting states in federal court. Two of the clauses of Article III, §2, specifically deal with suits against state governments. These provisions permit suits "between a State and Citizens of another state" and "between a State . . . and foreign . . . Citizens." The dispute was over whether the language of Article III quoted earlier was meant to override the sovereign immunity that kept states from being sued in state courts. As Justice Souter recently observed, "[t]he 1787 draft in fact said nothing on the subject and it was this very silence that occasioned some, though apparently not widespread dispute among the framers and others over whether ratification of the Constitution would preclude a state sued in federal court from asserting sovereign immunity as it could have done on any nonfederal matter litigated in its own courts."[13] There is no record of any debate about this issue or these clauses at the Constitutional Convention.

However, at the state ratification conventions, the question of suits against state governments in federal court was raised and received a great deal of attention. States had incurred substantial debts, especially during the Revolutionary War, and there was a great fear that suits would be brought against the states in federal court to collect on these debts. More generally, the concern was expressed that although sovereign immunity was a defense to state law claims in state court, it would be unavailable if the same matter were raised against a state in a diversity suit in federal court.

Thus, at the state ratification conventions, there was a debate over whether states could be sued in federal court without their consent.[14] One group argued that the text of Article III clearly made states subject to suit in federal court. In Virginia, George Mason opposed ratification of the Constitution and particularly disliked the provisions that made the states liable in federal court:

> Claims respecting those lands, every liquidated account, or other claim against this state, will be tried before the federal court. Is not

this disgraceful? Is this state to be brought to the bar of justice like a delinquent individual? Is the sovereignty of the state to be arraigned like a culprit, or private offender?[15]

Mason believed that Article III's explicit provision for suits against the states would have the effect of abrogating the states' sovereign immunity defense.[16] Likewise, Patrick Henry opposed the Constitution at the Virginia convention, in part because of his belief that Article III unmistakably permitted litigation against states in federal court. He labeled as "incomprehensible" the contrary claim that Article III allowed states to be plaintiffs but not defendants.[17] Henry said that "[t]here is nothing to warrant such an assertion. . . . What says the paper? That it shall have cognizance of controversies between a state and citizens of another state, without discriminating between plaintiff and defendant."[18]

Nor was this view that Article III overrides state sovereignty and permits suits against unconsenting states in federal court held only in Virginia or only by opponents of ratification. In Pennsylvania, North Carolina, and New York, there were major objections to this part of the Constitution.[19] Many of the Constitution's supporters also agreed that Article III permitted states to be sued in federal court. In fact, they argued that this lack of immunity was desirable to ensure that states could not escape their liabilities or avoid litigation that was necessary to hold states properly accountable. Edmund Randolph, a member of the Committee of Detail at the Constitutional Convention, argued: "I ask the Convention of the free people of Virginia if there can be honesty in rejecting the government because justice is to be done by it? . . . Are we to say that we shall discard this government because it would make us all honest?"[20] In Pennsylvania, Thomas Pickering argued that it was important for federal courts to be able to give relief against states to citizens of other states or nations who had been wronged and might be unable to receive fair treatment in a state's own courts.[21]

In sharp contrast, many other supporters of the Constitution argued that Article III did not override state sovereignty and that, notwithstanding its provisions, states could be sued in federal court only if they consented to be a party to the litigation. Alexander Hamilton wrote in the *Federalist Papers*:

It is inherent in the nature of sovereignty not to be amenable to the suit of an individual *without its consent*. This is the general sense and

the general practice of mankind; and the exemption, as one of the at-
tributes of sovereignty, is now enjoyed by the government of every
State in the Union. Unless, therefore, there is a surrender of this immunity . . . it will remain with the States.[22]

Similarly, Madison argued that states have sovereign immunity and that
Article III serves only to allow states to come to federal court as plaintiffs,
not that it allows them to be sued as defendants without their consent.[23]
Madison said that "jurisdiction in controversies between a state and citizens of another state is much objected to, and perhaps without reason. It
is not in the power of individuals to call any state into court."[24]

This recounting of the ratification debates reveals that there was no
consensus, even among the Constitution's supporters, about whether state
sovereign immunity survived Article III. Justice Souter, after a detailed
recounting of this history, observed: "[T]he framers and their contem-
poraries did not agree about the place of common-law state sovereign
immunity even as to federal jurisdiction resting on the citizen-state diversity clause."[25] In reviewing the Eleventh Amendment's history, this Court
has rightly observed that "[a]t most, then, the historical materials show
that . . . the intentions of the Framers and Ratifiers were ambiguous."[26]
Justice Souter explains in his dissent:

> There is almost no evidence that the generation of the Framers thought
> sovereign immunity was fundamental in the sense of being unalterable.
> Whether one looks at the period before the framing, to the ratification
> controversies, or to the early republican era, the evidence is the same.
> Some Framers thought sovereign immunity was an obsolete royal pre-
> rogative inapplicable in a republic; some thought sovereign immunity
> was a common-law power defeasible, like other common-law rights,
> by statute; and perhaps a few thought, in keeping with a natural law
> view distinct from the common-law conception, that immunity was
> inherent in a sovereign because the body that made a law could not
> logically be bound by it. Natural law thinking on the part of a doubtful
> few will not, however, support the Court's position.[27]

Nor can sovereign immunity be based on the contemporary practices at the time. The reality is that there was not uniformity among the
states. As Justice Souter explains, "The American Colonies did not enjoy
sovereign immunity, that being a privilege understood in English law to

be reserved for the Crown alone; 'antecedent to the Declaration of Independence, none of the colonies were, or pretended to be, sovereign states.' Several colonial charters, including those of Massachusetts, Connecticut, Rhode Island, and Georgia, expressly specified that the corporate body established thereunder could sue and be sued."[28]

An argument might be made in response that the later ratification of the Eleventh Amendment demonstrated the framers' desire to protect sovereign immunity. Yet, as scholars such as John Gibbons and William Fletcher have persuasively argued, the purpose of the Eleventh Amendment was limited to precluding diversity suits against the states in federal court.[29] The Eleventh Amendment was adopted in order to overrule *Chisholm v. Georgia*.[30] That case involved only the latter part of Article III, which allows the citizens of one state to sue another state in federal court. Therefore, it makes sense to view the Eleventh Amendment as restricting only diversity suits against state governments.

As a result, Justice Kennedy's majority opinion in this case is reduced to defending sovereign immunity as implicit in the framers' silence. Justice Kennedy invokes this silence as key evidence of the framers' intent. He writes:

We believe, however, that the founders' silence is best explained by the simple fact that no one, not even the Constitution's most ardent opponents, suggested the document might strip the States of the immunity. In light of the overriding concern regarding the States' war-time debts, together with the well known creativity, foresight, and vivid imagination of the Constitution's opponents, the silence is most instructive. It suggests the sovereign's right to assert immunity from suit in its own courts was a principle so well established that no one conceived it would be altered by the new Constitution.[31]

The problem with this argument is that silence is inherently ambiguous. Perhaps Justice Kennedy is correct that the framers were silent because they thought it obvious that states could not be sued in state court. Alternatively, maybe they were silent because they thought it clear that states could be sued in state court. Most likely, though, the framers were silent because the issue did not come up and they never thought about it. Silence is inherently uncertain and a highly questionable basis for inferring intent. I am highly skeptical that originalist Justices in the majority such as Chief Justice Rehnquist and Justices Scalia and Thomas would accept the argument that the framers' silence about the right to privacy suggests that they thought it so obvious and clear that it was unnecessary to enumerate.

The point is simply that sovereign immunity cannot be based on the text of the Constitution or its history.

II

Beyond the lack of constitutional basis for sovereign immunity, even worse, the majority's decision is inconsistent with three fundamental constitutional principles: the supremacy of the Constitution and federal laws; the accountability of government; and due process of law.

A. The Supremacy of the Constitution and Federal Laws

Article VI of the Constitution states:

This Constitution, and the Laws of the United States which shall be made in Pursuance thereof; and all treaties made, or which shall be made under the Authority of the United States, shall be the Supreme Law of the Land; and the Judges in every State shall be bound thereby, anything in the Constitution or Laws of any State to the Contrary Notwithstanding.

This is one of the most important provisions in the entire Constitution, for it ensures that the document is not merely aspirational but that it shall trump all other law. Indeed, in *Marbury v. Madison*,[32] Chief Justice John Marshall relied, in part, on the supremacy clause to explain the authority for judicial review. Without judicial review, there is no way to ensure that the Constitution and federal laws are supreme.

In 1819, in *McCulloch v. Maryland*,[33] Chief Justice John Marshall further elaborated on the importance of the supremacy clause: "This great principle is, that the constitution and the laws made in pursuance thereof are supreme; that they control the constitution and laws of the respective states, and cannot be controlled by them." He continued:

If any one proposition could command the universal assent of mankind, we might expect it would be this—that the government of the Union, though limited in its powers, is supreme within its sphere of action. This would seem to result, necessarily, from its nature. It is the government of all; its powers are delegated by all; it represents all, and acts for all. . . . The nation, on those subjects on which it can act, must necessarily bind its component parts. But this question is not left to mere reason: the people have, in express terms, decided it, by saying, 'this constitution, and the laws of the United States, which shall be made in pursuance thereof,' 'shall be the supreme law of the land,' and by requiring that the members of the state legislatures, and the officers of the executive and judicial departments of the states, shall take the oath of fidelity to it. The government of the United States, then, though limited in its powers, is supreme; and its laws, when made in pursuance of the constitution, form the supreme law of the land, 'anything in the constitution or laws of any state to the contrary notwithstanding.'[34]

The doctrine of sovereign immunity is inconsistent with the supremacy clause. Most simply, this is because it allows a nonconstitutional common law doctrine to have primacy over the Constitution and federal laws made pursuant to it. A plaintiff asserting a federal constitutional or statutory claim against the federal or a state government loses because of the defendant's invocation of sovereign immunity. In other words, the common law doctrine is supreme over the Constitution and federal law.

Moreover, sovereign immunity frustrates the supremacy of federal law by preventing the enforcement of the Constitution and federal statutes. How can the supremacy of federal law be assured and vindicated if states can violate the Constitution or federal laws and not be held accountable? The probation officers in this case have a federal right to overtime pay. But there is no way of forcing the states to meet their federal obligation.

At oral argument in this case, the Solicitor General of the United States, Seth Waxman, quoted to the Court from the supremacy clause of Article VI and contended that suits against states are essential to assure the supremacy of federal law. The majority's response to this argument is astounding. The Court states:

The constitutional privilege of a State to assert its sovereign immunity in its own courts does not confer upon the State a concomitant right to disregard the Constitution or valid federal law. The States and their officers are bound by obligations imposed by the Constitution and by federal statutes that comport with the constitutional design. We are unwilling to assume the States will refuse to honor the Constitution or obey the binding laws of the United States. The good faith of the States thus provides an important assurance that ` [t]his Constitution, and the Laws of the United States which shall be made in Pursuance thereof . . . shall be the supreme Law of the Land.' U.S. Const., Art. VI.[35]

What, then, is the assurance that state governments will comply with federal law?: trust in the good faith of state governments. Is it possible to imagine that thirty or forty years ago, at the height of the civil rights movement, the Supreme Court would have issued such a statement that state governments simply could be trusted to voluntarily comply with federal law? James Madison said that if people were angels there would be no need for a Constitution, but there would be no need for a government, either. The reality is that state governments, intentionally or unintentionally, at times will violate federal law. To rely on trust in the good faith of state governments, as the majority does today, is no assurance of the supremacy of federal law at all.

B. Government Accountability

The principle of government accountability is inherent in the structure of the Constitution and embodied in many specific constitutional provisions. Long ago, in *Marbury v. Madison*, Chief Justice John Marshall explained that the central purpose of the Constitution is to limit the actions of government and government officers.[36] This is all about ensuring that the government is accountable for its actions. Chief Justice Marshall declared that "[t]he government of the United States has been emphatically termed a government of laws, and not of men."[37] The sovereign immunity relied on by the majority today is inconsistent with all of these basic principles. Sovereign immunity allows the government to violate the Constitution or laws of the United States and not be held accountable. It obviously means that constitutional and statutory rights can be violated, but individuals are left with no remedies. The probation officers in this case have federal rights but, due to sovereign immunity, no remedies. Sovereign immunity makes the laws of the United States subordinate to the will of the men and women making government decisions.

The principle that the government must be accountable can be found in many parts of the Constitution. Professor Akhil Amar has argued that it is embodied in the first words of the Constitution, "We the People," which makes the people sovereign.[38] Moreover, the Constitution rejects, implicitly and explicitly, royal prerogatives of all sorts. Scholars have shown that sovereign immunity in the United States is very much based on English law and particularly the idea that "the King can do no wrong."[39] Yet, if there is any universally agreed upon proposition about the American Constitution, it is its rejection of a monarchy and royal prerogatives. Article II's simple declaration that the "executive Power shall be vested in a President of the United States," who serves for a limited four-year term, is an emphatic rejection of royalty in the United States. Article I, section 9, prohibits any title of nobility being granted by the United States. This is all about ensuring a government that is accountable to the people.

A constitutional principle of accountability can be found in other constitutional provisions, as well. Professor James Pfander has persuasively argued that the right to petition clause, found in the First Amendment, is inconsistent with the notion of sovereign immunity.[40] Professor Pfander demonstrates that "the Petition Clause guarantees the right of individuals to pursue judicial remedies for government misconduct."[41] In a lengthy and carefully researched article, he shows that "[t]he Petition Clause affirms the right of the individual to seek redress from government wrongdoing in court, a right historically calculated to overcome any threshold government immunity from suit."[42] A constitutional principle of government accountability can be found in many parts of the Constitution. Sovereign immunity is inconsistent with this basic precept because it prevents accountability, even when the government egregiously violates the Constitution and federal laws.

C. Due Process of Law

Even if sovereign immunity were found in the structure of the Constitution, and I have argued that there is no basis for such a conclusion, two constitutional amendments should be seen as modifying and eliminating sovereign immunity: the Fifth and the Fourteenth Amendments' assurance that no person will be deprived of life, liberty, or property without due process of law. The due process clause certainly can be used to strengthen the argument already made as to the Constitution's assurance of government accountability. But, even more specifically, it should be understood as imposing a constitutional mandate that those who suffer a loss of life, liberty, or property at the hands of the government are entitled to redress.

On many occasions, this Court has recognized that the absence of a remedy in court, state or federal, raises a serious due process issue.[43] In a long line of cases, the Court has said that because due process requires a judicial forum, it will interpret federal laws that appear to preclude all jurisdiction as not doing so.[44] The Court has emphasized in these cases the importance of a judicial forum to provide redress when there is a deprivation of life, liberty, or property.[45] However, the Court's decision in this case means that there will be many instances in which individuals will be injured without having any judicial forum available. The probation officers in Maine have a federal property right to overtime pay, but there is no way for them to get due process.

III

Conceptions of tort law have changed dramatically from those that prevailed at the time the United States Constitution was written and ratified. Today, liability is justified primarily on the basis of two rationales: the need to provide compensation to injured individuals and the desire to deter future wrong-doing. In fact, this Court has recognized the importance of these rationales in the context of suits against the government. In 1980, in *Owen v. City of Independence*,[46] this Court held that local governments are liable even when their constitutional violations are a result of actions taken in good faith. The Court stressed that allowing cities good-faith immunity would frustrate the underlying purposes of the civil rights statute §1983 in terms of deterrence and risk spreading.[47] Sovereign immunity frustrates compensation and deterrence. Individuals injured by government wrong-doing are left without a remedy. Moreover, sovereign immunity frustrates deterrence as government knows that it can violate federal law without risking liability.

What, then, are the justifications for sovereign immunity and do they warrant its continued existence? Four primary rationales are discussed here: the importance of protecting government treasuries; separation of powers; the existence of adequate alternative remedies; and tradition. I argue, in turn, that none of these is persuasive or justifies the continued existence of sovereign immunity.

A. Protecting Government Treasuries

Sovereign immunity unquestionably has the virtue of protecting government treasuries from the costs of damage suits. Indeed, that is its main effect. Doctrines exist to facilitate suits for injunctive relief against the government through the ability to sue individual government officers for prospective remedies. Thus, the Court has held that suits against state officers for injunctive relief are not barred by the Eleventh Amendment.[48] But sovereign immunity protects government treasuries from damage judgments.

In his majority opinion today, Justice Kennedy expressly spoke of this justification for sovereign immunity: "Not only must a State defend or default but also it must face the prospect of being thrust, by federal fiat and against its will, into the disfavored status of a debtor, subject to the power of private citizens to levy on its treasury or perhaps even government buildings or property which the State administers on the public's behalf."[49] This concern underlies all of the Court's sovereign immunity decisions. Allowing the government to be sued means that it can be held liable and the ultimate cost is to the taxpayer.

But this argument rests on an unsupported and, I believe, unsupportable assumption: that protecting the government treasury is more important than the benefits of liability in terms of ensuring compensation and deterrence. Sovereign immunity assumes that providing the government immunity so as to safeguard government treasuries is more important than ensuring government accountability. Yet, not in this case, and in none of the sovereign immunity cases, has the Supreme Court ever justified this value choice.

Moreover, it is the wrong value priority under the Constitution. As argued in the prior section, basic constitutional principles such as ensuring the supremacy of federal law, holding the government accountable, and providing due process all make sovereign immunity unacceptable. Although abolishing sovereign immunity would impose financial burdens on the government, it is better to spread the costs of injuries from illegal government actions among the entire citizenry than to make the wronged individual bear the entire loss.

B. Separation of Powers

A separate, though interrelated, argument for sovereign immunity is based on separation of powers. The argument is that the operation of government would be hindered if the United States were liable for every injury it inflicted.[50] The argument is that sovereign immunity is necessary to protect the government from undue interference by the judiciary.[51] As the Fourth Circuit Court of Appeals said, "The rationale for sovereign immunity essentially boils down to substantial bothersome interference with the operation of government."[52] Sovereign immunity preserves the unhampered exercise of discretion and limits the amount of time the government must spend responding to lawsuits. The Supreme Court declared that the "Government, as representative of the community as a whole, cannot be stopped in its tracks by any plaintiff who presents a disputed question of property or contract right."[53] Again, this argument rests on assumptions that are unsupported and seemingly unsupportable. There is no evidence offered that suits against the government would prevent effective governance. In fact, the evidence is to the contrary. The Supreme Court has held that local governments are not protected by sovereign immunity[54] and that they can be sued under section 1983.[55] Yet, there is no evidence that such liability has unduly disrupted the actions of government.

Moreover, it is unclear why suits for money damages will be more disruptive of government than suits for injunctive relief against government officers, which already are allowed. The likely answer is that suits for monetary compensation might cost money that could be used for other government activities. This, though, collapses the separation of powers argument into the prior claim concerning the need to protect the government fisc.

Separation of powers never has been understood as insulating the activities of other branches of government from judicial review. Quite the contrary; ever since *Marbury v. Madison*, it has been accepted that separation of powers is judicially enforceable. As Chief Justice John Marshall emphasized, enforcing the limits of the Constitution necessitates judicial review and government accountability.

Also, the effect of recognizing sovereign immunity is to cause lawsuits to be filed against individual government officers. The Supreme Court long has held that sovereign immunity prevents suits against the government entity but not against the officers.[56] Hence, individuals seeking redress from the federal government must sue its officers for money damages to be paid from their own pockets. Many believe that this is undesirable and that it would be preferable to have the government entity sued, rather than its officers.[57] For example, it is argued that the exercise of discretion is more likely to be chilled if officers are personally liable than if the government entity is held responsible.

C. Existence of Adequate Alternatives

Implicit in many defenses of sovereign immunity is the claim that government liability is unnecessary because there are adequate alternatives. Most notably, individual government officers can be sued, particularly for injunctive relief, and this makes suits against government entities unnecessary.

Although such suits are important in ensuring the supremacy of federal law, they are inadequate and do not replace the ability to sue the government entities. Injunctive relief obviously can prevent future violations, but it does nothing to provide redress for past infringements, something that I argued earlier is a constitutional mandate. The probation officers in this case can sue for an injunction to ensure that they are paid overtime in the future, but that does nothing to provide them a remedy for the prior violations of their rights under the federal Fair Labor Standards Act.

Nor are suits against government officers for money damages a substitute for litigation against government entities. Even when a cause of action exists, some officers, such as judges, prosecutors, and legislators, have absolute immunity to suits for money damages. Consider, for example, a claim that state court judges are systematically violating criminal defendants' rights, such as by displaying racism in setting bail or by paying criminal defense attorneys too little to protect defendants' Sixth Amendment rights.[58] Who can be sued in such an instance? The state government cannot be named as a defendant in federal or state law. State judges cannot be sued for damages or for injunctive relief because of a federal law that expressly bars such suits.[59] It seems that no suit could be brought, even though there is an allegation of a serious violation of a basic constitutional right.

Government officials who do not have absolute immunity all have qualified immunity, which often makes recovery for violations of federal law impossible. The Supreme Court has held that government officials can be held liable in damages for constitutional violations, even where a violation has been proven, only if a reasonable official would know that his or her conduct violated a clearly established right.[60] The result is that injured individuals often have no recourse except to sue the government entity. Without such litigation, the supremacy of federal law often cannot be protected. Again, *McCulloch v. Maryland* is instructive: "It is of the very essence of supremacy, to remove all obstacles to its action within its own sphere. . . . This effect need not be stated in terms. It is so involved in the declaration of supremacy, so necessarily implied in it, that the expression of it could not make it more certain."[61]

D. Tradition

The strongest argument for sovereign immunity is tradition: it has existed, in some form, through most of American history and is based on English law. But this begs the central question: is this a tradition that should continue? As Justice Blackmun remarked in another context: "Like Justice Holmes, I believe that '[i]t is revolting to have no better reason for a rule of law than that so it was laid down in the time of Henry IV.'"[62]

Sovereign immunity conflicts with other, more important traditions in American law: enforcing the Constitution and federal laws, ensuring government accountability, and providing due process of law.

Moreover, there is no tradition of finding a constitutional privilege for state governments to not be sued in state court. No decision, prior to today's, ever accorded states this right. As Justice Souter has demonstrated, there was no such clear tradition in the early American states.

But even if there were such a tradition, that is not a reason for following it and making states completely immune from suit. Slavery, enforced racial segregation, and the subjugation of women also were deeply embedded traditions. Sovereign immunity, too, is a repugnant doctrine, at odds with the most basic precepts of the American Constitution, and it should be repudiated.

Conclusion

Criticisms of sovereign immunity are not new. President Abraham Lincoln declared: "It is . . . as much the duty of Government to render prompt justice against itself in favor of citizens as it is to administer the same between private individuals."[63] Unfortunately, the current Supreme Court is unpersuaded by such criticisms and is expanding, not narrowing, the reach of sovereign immunity.

The Court's holding today, that state governments have sovereign immunity and cannot be sued in state courts, is simply wrong. It has no basis in the text of the Constitution, is inconsistent with its most basic values, and serves no desirable objectives. I dissent.

NOTES

1. Alden v. Maine, 527 U.S. 706 (1999).
2. 29 U.S.C. §201, et seq.
3. *Alden*, 527 U.S. at 712.
4. 29 U.S.C. §201, et seq.
5. Marbury v. Madison, 5 U.S. (1 Cranch) 137, 163 (1803).

6. *See* 5 KENNETH DAVIS, ADMINISTRATIVE LAW TREATISE 6–7 (2d ed. 1984) (quoting Blackstone); 2 CHARLES H. KOCH, JR., ADMINISTRATIVE LAW AND PRACTICE 210 (1985).

7. *See, e.g.,* U.S. Const. art. I, §9. ("No Title of Nobility shall be granted by the United States.").

8. *Alden*, 527 U.S. at 728.

9. Hans v. Louisiana, 134 U.S. 1 (1890).

10. *Alden*, 527 U.S. at 713.

11. *See, e.g.,* Antonin Scalia, *Originalism: The Lesser Evil*, 57 U. CINN. L. REV. 849 (1989).

12. *See, e.g.,* Joseph D. Grano, *Judicial Review and a Written Constitution in a Democratic Society*, 28 WAYNE L. REV. 1, 7 (1981) (articulating the originalist philosophy); *see also* ROBERT H. BORK, THE TEMPTING OF AMERICA (1990) (defending originalist constitutional interpretation).

13. Seminole Tribe of Florida v. Florida, 517 U.S. 44, 100 (1996) (Souter, J., dissenting).

14. *See, e.g.,* John J. Gibbons, *The Eleventh Amendment and State Sovereign Immunity: A Reinterpretation*, 83 COLUM. L. REV. 1889, 1902–1914 (1983).

15. THE DEBATES IN THE SEVERAL STATES CONVENTIONS ON THE ADOPTION OF THE FEDERAL CONSTITUTION, (Virginia) 526–527 (Jonathan Elliot ed., J. B. Lippincott Co., 1941).

16. Atascadero State Hospital v. Scanlon, 473 U.S. 234, 265 (1985) (Brennan, J., dissenting) (describing Mason's opposition to Article III).

17. Elliot, *supra* note 15, at 543.

18. *Id.*

19. Gibbons, *supra* note 14, at 1902–1914.

20. Elliot, *supra* note 15, at 575.

21. 14 JOHN P. KAMINSKY & GASPARE J. SALADINO, THE DOCUMENTARY HISTORY OF THE RATIFICATION OF THE CONSTITUTION 204 (1983).

22. THE FEDERALIST NO. 81, at 487–488 (Alexander Hamilton) (C. Rossiter ed. 1961) (emphasis in original).

23. Elliot, *supra* note 15, at 533.

24. *Id.*

25. *Seminole Tribe of Florida*, 517 U.S. at 142–143 (Souter, J., dissenting).

26. Welch v. Texas Dept. of Highways & Pub. Transp., 483 U.S. 468 (1987).

27. *Alden*, 527 U.S. at 764 (Souter, J., dissenting).

28. *Id.*

29. *See* John J. Gibbons, *The Eleventh Amendment and State Sovereign Immunity: A Reinterpretation*, 83 COLUM. L. REV. 1889 (1983); William A. Fletcher, *A Historical Interpretation of the Eleventh Amendment: A Narrow Construction of an Affirmative Grant of Jurisdiction Rather Than a Prohibition Against Jurisdiction*, 35 STAN. L. REV. 1033 (1983).

30. Chisholm v. Georiga, 2 U.S. (Dall.) 419 (1798).

31. *Alden*, 527 U.S. at 741.

32. *Marbury*, 5 U.S. at 180.

33. McCulloch v. Maryland, 17 U.S. (4 Wheat.) 316, 431 (1819).

34. *Id.*

35. *Alden*, 527 U.S. at 754–55.

36. *Marbury*, 5 U.S. at 163.

37. *Id.*

38. Akhil Amar, *Of Sovereignty and Federalism*, 96 YALE L.J. 1425 (1987).

39. *See* Calvin R. Massey, *Sovereign Immunity in America: A Brief History*, 56 U. CHI. L. REV. 61 (1989).

40. James E. Pfander, *Sovereign Immunity and the Right to Petition: Toward a First Amendment Right to Pursue Judicial Claims Against the Government*, 91 Nw. U. L. REV. 899 (1997).

41. *Id.* at 905.

42. *Id.* at 981.

43. *See, e.g.*, Oestereich v. Selective Serv. Local Bd. v. No. 11, 393 U.S. 233, 243 n.6 (1968) (Harlan, J., concurring). *See also* Richard H. Fallon, Jr., *Some Confusions About Due Process, Judicial Review, and Constitutional Remedies*, 93 COLUM. L. REV. 309 (1993) (arguing that the issue of whether there is a constitutional right to judicial review depends on the underlying substantive law).

44. Johnson v. Robison, 415 U.S. 361 (1974); *see also* Webster v. Doe, 486 U.S. 592 (1988) (refusing to find statute to preclude review of a claim by an employee of the CIA who alleged that he was fired because he was a homosexual).

45. *See, e.g.*, United States v. Mendoza-Lopez, 481 U.S. 828 (1987); McNary v. Haitian Refugee Center, Inc., 498 U.S. 479 (1991).

46. Owen v. City of Independence, 445 U.S. 622 (1980).

47. *Id.* at 651.

48. *See, e.g., Ex parte* Young, 209 U.S. 123 (1908).

49. *Alden*, 527 U.S. at 749.

50. *See* The Siren, 74 U.S. (7 Wall.) 152, 154 (1868) ("The public service would be hindered, and the public safety endangered if the supreme authority could be subjected to suit at the instance of every citizen").

51. James S. Sable, Comment, *Sovereign Immunity: A Battleground of Competing Considerations*, 12 Sw. U.L. REV. 457, 465 (1981).

52. Littell v. Morton, 445 F.2d 1207, 1214 (4th Cir. 1971).

53. Larson v. Domestic & Foreign Commerce Corp., 337 U.S. 682, 704 (1949).

54. *See, e.g.*, Mt. Healthy City School Dist. Bd. of Educ. v. Doyle, 429 U.S. 274 (1977); Lincoln County v. Luning, 133 U.S. 529 (1890).

55. Monell v. Department of Social Services, 436 U.S. 656 (1978) (holding that local governments are persons within the meaning of section 1983).

56. *See, e.g.,* Schneider v. Smith, 390 U.S. 17 (1968); Larson v. Domestic & Foreign Commerce Corp., 337 U.S. 682 (1949); Land v. Dollar, 330 U.S. 731 (1947); *Ex parte* Young, 209 U.S. 123 (1908).

57. *See* DAVIS, *supra* note 6, at 22–24; PETER H. SCHUCK, SUING GOVERNMENT 90–91 (Yale University Press, 1983).

58. O'Shea v. Littleton, 414 U.S. 488 (1974) (declaring nonjusticiable a suit contending that the defendants, a magistrate and a judge, discriminated against blacks in setting bail and imposing sentences).

59. Federal Courts Improvement Act of 1996, Pub.L.No. 104–317, (b)–(c), 110 Stat. 3847.

60. Anderson v. Creighton, 483 U.S. 635 (1987); Harlow v. Fitzgerald, 457 U.S. 800 (1982).

61. *McCulloch*, 17 U.S. at 427.

62. Bowers v. Hardwick, 478 U.S. 186, 199 (1986), quoting Oliver Wendell Holmes, *The Path of the Law*, 10 HARV. L. REV. 457, 469 (1897).

63. 7 JAMES D. RICHARDSON, A COMPILATION OF MESSAGES AND PAPERS OF THE PRESIDENTS, 3245, 3252, quoted in Kennecott Copper Corp. v. State Tax Commn., 327 U.S. 573, 580 (1946) (Frankfurter, J., dissenting).

2

Arkansas Educational Television Commission v. Forbes

Betraying Freedom of Political Expression and Undermining Democracy

Jamin Raskin

Introduction

In *Arkansas Educational Television Commission v. Forbes* (1998),[1] the Supreme Court upheld the exclusion of an Independent congressional candidate from a televised debate organized by Arkansas's taxpayer-funded public television network. By a vote of six to three, the majority reversed the Eighth Circuit Court of Appeals and affirmed the state's power to sponsor the general election debate closed to all but the Democratic and Republican candidates. The Supreme Court rejected First Amendment arguments brought by the forsaken Independent, Ralph Forbes, a maverick conservative running for Congress in 1992 in the Third District.

To resolve the case, the Court grappled with two key questions. The first was whether the debate on a state-controlled station constituted a "public forum" for First Amendment purposes and, if so, what type of public forum. In a "traditional" public forum, a place that the people have habitually used for public expression (such as streets, sidewalks, and parks), the government may not discriminate among potential speakers on the basis of the content of their speech unless it shows a compelling interest in doing so. If the government chooses to open new venues for public discourse and create "designated" or "limited" public forums, the same rule of presumed openness to all speakers applies. Thus, the government may not exclude a particular class of potential speakers from a limited public forum unless a compelling government interest requires it.[2] In a "nonpublic forum," which is public property not opened up generally to the public but reserved for special uses and specific speakers, the government may set "reasonable" rules that restrict participation so long as they do not discriminate on the basis of a speaker's "viewpoint."

Given the Court's determination that the candidate debate on the state's public television channel was a "nonpublic forum," the second and conclusive question became whether the exclusion of Ralph Forbes from the debate indeed constituted "viewpoint discrimination." This is the kind of speech suppression forbidden in any public forum.[3]

The majority saw no viewpoint discrimination in Forbes's exclusion from the debate. Justice Kennedy, who authored the majority opinion, was principally moved by the trial jury's finding that Forbes was rejected as a participant by the debate managers not because they disliked his politics but because they correctly deemed his candidacy to be "not viable." Thus, the AETC's exclusion of Forbes was not political viewpoint discrimination but a "reasonable, viewpoint-neutral exercise of its journalistic discretion."[4]

In his dissent, Jamin Raskin concludes that the Court decided both of these questions erroneously and that the Court should have found that Arkansas was required to permit Forbes, a balloted candidate who had nearly become lieutenant governor in the prior election, to participate in the debate.

Dissent by Jamin Raskin

The majority's decision betrays freedom of expression and undermines political democracy. The majority has allowed the state of Arkansas to violate the right of Independent and third-party candidates to equal treatment in opportunities for political speech provided by the government. It has also allowed Arkansas's government to trample the right of all American citizens living in the state to reconstitute their congressional leadership through free debate and unmanipulated choices in the election process.

Both of these rights are protected by the First Amendment free speech clause, which creates a political anti-establishment principle corresponding to the First Amendment's Establishment Clause ban on state endorsement of religion. As Justice Robert Jackson put it so beautifully in *West Virginia State Board of Education v. Barnette*, "Authority [in this country] is to be controlled by public opinion, not public opinion by authority. . . . If there is any fixed star in our constitutional constellation, it is that no official, high or petty, can prescribe what shall be orthodox in politics, nationalism, religion, or other matters of opinion. . . .[5]

The AETC has committed the cardinal First Amendment sin of political viewpoint discrimination. Any third-grader knows that her school cannot set up a debate between two candidates on the ballot for class president but exclude a third. Nor can government justify such naked gerrymandering of debate, either at the elementary school or at the congressional level, by describing the invited candidates as "viable" and "serious" and their excluded opponent as "nonviable" or "frivolous." Indeed, by placing "seriousness" ratings on candidates during a campaign and organizing political debate around its makeshift labels, Arkansas does not excuse its viewpoint discrimination but compounds it.

To confuse the picture, Justice Kennedy drains the meaning out of the doctrine of viewpoint discrimination, discarding his own insightful contributions to it in *Rosenberger v. Rector and Visitors of the University of Virginia.*[6] Today he turns viewpoint discrimination, which has been rightly understood as an objective concept describing any official suppression of dissenting or disfavored political perspectives in a speech context, into a toothless test of subjective personal animus on the part of individual state actors to the censored parties. This approach upsets precedent, turns our attention from what is important to what is trivial, and dangerously weakens First Amendment protection.

The Court's abandonment of freedom of political expression threatens the democratic rights of all Americans, including those who disdain Mr. Forbes's right-wing politics and might be inclined to applaud the majority's cavalier dismissal of his rights. For the Court has begun, in cases like this, to consecrate the establishment of a "two-party system," an institutional arrangement that no doubt commands allegiance from many politicians but has no basis in our Constitution and no proper business legislating and entrenching itself into power. I worry that, if the Court will act in an unprincipled way to legitimize elections based on a closed two-party system, there is nothing to stop us one day from acting in an unprincipled way to prop up a closed one-party system when a party in favor asks a majority of justices on the Court to collaborate in achieving a desired election outcome.

In the case of Ralph Forbes, Arkansas's decision to exclude him from the only televised candidate debate in his congressional campaign sent a negative message about his candidacy to the voters that likely changed the outcome of the election. This is because the eventual Republican winner finished with only a tiny lead over the Democrat. Had Forbes been allowed to debate, he of course might have stolen the show and won the election, the only rule of politics being that anything can happen. But, even more likely, Forbes might have pulled away a bloc of conservative votes, thus allowing the Democrat to win. Whether one considers this desirable or dreadful from a partisan political perspective matters not. As a constitutional matter, we cannot empower states to exclude or include at will—without any formal standards or process at all—Independent and third-party candidates from government-controlled debates. This is the power to manipulate public consensus and shape electoral outcomes.

Excluding a Strong Candidate with a Wholly Arbitrary Process: The Missing Facts of Forbes

The majority carefully obscures both Ralph Forbes's seriousness as a political force in Arkansas and the lawless and arbitrary quality of his exclusion from the government network's televised debate.

Justice Kennedy introduces Forbes as "a perennial candidate who had sought, without success, a number of elected offices in Arkansas."[7] This flippant denigration of a politically active citizen disguises the fact that Forbes was anything but frivolous or irrelevant.

A maverick Christian conservative appealing to moral traditionalists, Forbes throughout the 1980s ran increasingly successful primary campaigns for public office in Arkansas, where he had grown up and spent his entire life. In the 1990 cycle, the election that took place immediately before the events at issue here, Forbes ran for lieutenant governor of the state and captured 46.8 percent of the vote in a three-way race for the Republican Party nomination, trouncing his two rivals. Although he lost in the subsequent runoff election to the candidate hastily backed by the party establishment, Forbes had by all accounts become a political force to be reckoned with in the state. He left the Republican Party because he felt embittered by his treatment at the hands of Republican regulars but remained determined to bring his pro-life, pro-religious, anti-affirmative action, and right-wing politics into government.

In 1992, when the U.S. House seat in the Third District opened up, Forbes declared for Congress as an Independent. Two years before, in his campaign for lieutenant governor, he had swept fifteen of the sixteen counties in the Third District, where he and his family live. He thus had reason to believe that he could win the election, even running as an Independent; certainly his campaign would draw the Republican nominee rightward to avoid losing votes. To comply with state law (which makes it harder for candidates running outside the major parties to secure ballot access), Forbes proceeded to knock on doors throughout the summer, collecting six thousand signatures, four thousand more than necessary, and securing a place on the ballot next to Tim Hutchinson, the Republican candidate, and John Van Winkle, the Democratic candidate.

As the majority acknowledges, television plays a key role in our elections. In the sprawling mountains of the Third District where face-to-face communication is difficult to achieve, it can be decisive. It was therefore significant when the Arkansas Educational Television Commission (AETC) announced plans to sponsor televised debates in all four of Arkansas's U.S. House districts. Statewide in Arkansas, there were only nine candidates for Congress in 1992: four Democrats, four Republicans, and Forbes, the Independent. AETC invited all of the candidates to participate in the debates—except Forbes. As AETC candidly puts it in its petition for certiorari, "AETN made the editorial decision to invite to each debate only the Republican and Democratic candidates."[8]

Indeed, Forbes learned about the Third District debate quite by accident while reading the newspaper. He came across AETC's promotional newspaper ad that featured photographs of his smiling rivals under the headline "Do you know your candidates?" Needless to say, he was shocked and quickly set about to ask to be included in the debate. Without setting forth any policies or factors for considering candidates for invitation and without granting Forbes a hearing or any administrative process on his "viability," AETC's agents simply told Forbes that it was going to "stick with the major candidates." The most concrete answer we can extract from AETC's constantly shifting explanations of how it arrived at that judgment is that a key AETC official judged Forbes unsuitable: "Ms. Oliver concluded that Mr. Forbes was not a 'serious candidate.'"[9] On the evening of the debate, Forbes showed up but was turned away and escorted out after being told by a station manager that the station would "rather show reruns of *St. Elsewhere*" than have a debate with him participating.

Forbes sued *pro se*. He gave his First Amendment case the lively caption *Forbes v. The Arrogant Orwellian Bureaucrats of the AETN; The Crooked Lying Politicians; and The Special Interests*. Although the name of the case was changed, Forbes prevailed in the Eighth Circuit Court of Appeals, where Chief Judge Richard Arnold found that the televised debate was a "limited public forum"—public property opened by the government for specific speech purposes.[10] In such a forum, a particular speaker may not be excluded unless the government shows a compelling reason for doing so. As a balloted candidate, Judge Arnold found, Forbes naturally belonged to the class of speakers invited to the forum, and Arkansas lacked a compelling reason to exclude him. The "government cannot, simply by its own *ipse dixit*, define a class of speakers so as to exclude a person who would naturally be expected to be a member of the class on no basis other than party affiliation."[11] AETC's final putative reason for excluding Forbes—its perception that he was not "viable"—violated the First Amendment because his political viability was a "judgment to be made by the people of the Third Congressional District, not by officials of the government in charge of channels of communication."[12]

AETC appealed, urging this Court to treat its debate not as a public forum of any kind but as an act of private journalistic reportage. On this theory, the First Amendment does not protect Forbes against the government network; it protects the government network against Forbes. By excluding him from its taxpayer-funded debate, AETC invites us to believe, it did nothing more unlawful to Forbes than, say, the *New York Times* did by failing to cover his campaign.

Political Candidate Debates and Viewpoint Discrimination

Let us start with what we agree upon. There is plainly nothing wrong with a public television network sponsoring candidate debates so long as they are impartial and nonpartisan and observe First Amendment standards. Justice Kennedy gets this point. He rejects AETC's extreme claim that its debate is akin to private journalistic reportage that should be shielded from constitutional scrutiny. He agrees that the First Amendment protects political candidates from discrimination by government network program managers rather than program managers from discrimination claims by political candidates. He writes that First Amendment norms must apply to state-sponsored candidate debates because they are designed by the government explicitly as "a forum for political speech by candidates" and "candidate debates are of exceptional significance in the electoral process."[13]

At this point, Forbes's case should be clinched. Once a public network organizes such a debate, as the Eighth Circuit recognized, it has created a limited public forum by "intentionally opening a nontraditional forum for public discourse."[14] Justice Kennedy, however, rejects the Eighth Circuit's conclusion that AETC's debate was a "limited" public forum for all balloted candidates running for the Third District seat. Squinting hard to find a distinction, Justice Kennedy writes that AETC "did not make its debate generally available to candidates for Arkansas' Third Congressional District seat" but rather—one must follow this argument closely—"reserved eligibility for participation in the debate to candidates for the Third Congressional District seat (as opposed to some other seat). At that point . . . [AETC] made candidate-by-candidate determinations as to which of the eligible candidates would participate in the debate. . . . Thus, the debate was a nonpublic forum."[15] As a consequence, he softens the test he applies by treating the debate as a nonpublic forum "subject to constitutional constraints."[16] Although this test also requires viewpoint neutrality, Justice Kennedy's opinion erodes the neutrality doctrine to permit discrimination against Forbes, as we shall see.

In a limited public forum, which the debate clearly was, the government may not restrict the class of speakers without demonstrating a *compelling interest* in doing so.[17] AETC would undoubtedly have had a compelling public interest in confining its debate to the three candidates on the ballot and excluding write-in candidates or interested observers who wanted to participate. The public interest would be in allowing the electorate to witness a dialogue among all *balloted* candidates, those who have been certified as meeting the state's required threshold of public support necessary to establish them as serious. This group comprises those candidates running serious campaigns, as opposed to satirical candidates lampooning the process like Howard Stern running for mayor of New York or Pat Paulsen running for president. This Court has recognized "an important state interest in requiring some preliminary showing of a significant modicum of support before printing"[18] a candidate's name on the ballot, and this is the right place to impose a "seriousness" threshold.

But, here, AETC offers nothing approaching a compelling interest for excluding Forbes from a debate among the other balloted candidates in his district. In its petition for certiorari, it argues that "Mr. Forbes' participation would reduce the time available for debate between the two candidates in whose campaigns, and views, the public was interested."[19] But transferring the debate time of lesser-known or lesser-financed candidates to more established candidates is the antithesis of our First Amendment values and thus not even a legitimate rational interest, much less a compelling one.

As this Court observed in *Buckley v. Valeo*, "[T]he concept that government may restrict the speech of some elements of our society in order to enhance the relative voice of others is wholly foreign to the First Amendment, which was designed to secure 'the widest possible dissemination of information from diverse and antagonistic sources,' and 'to assure unfettered interchange of ideas for the bringing about of political and social changes desired by the people.'"[20]

All of Arkansas's efforts to formulate an interest in excluding Forbes crash upon the same rock: they are forms of viewpoint discrimination, which is unconstitutional in any type of public forum, even the "nonpublic forum" that Justice Kennedy oddly thinks this is. The same is true of the concept that Justice Kennedy and the majority finally settle on as a supposedly neutral justification for Forbes' exclusion: his alleged lack of "viability" as a candidate.

To say that a candidate is not "viable" is only to say that someone thinks he is going to lose. To exclude him from a state-funded speech platform provided to his opponents on this basis is to discriminate against him on the basis of the alleged unpopularity, present and future, of his candidacy.

But the First Amendment protects equally the political speech of popular candidates who have mainstream views and unpopular candidates who have dissenting views. The Court emphasized this axiom of free speech in *Texas v. Johnson*, which upheld the right of political dissenters to burn the American flag: "If there is a bedrock principle underlying the First Amendment, it is that the government may not prohibit the expression of an idea simply because society finds the idea itself offensive or disagreeable."[21] Surely this free speech principle, like others, must have "its fullest and most urgent application precisely to the conduct of campaigns for political office."[22] If not, we are saying that citizens have a First Amendment right to make a spectacle out of themselves by burning the flag but no right to participate on an equal basis in their own elections.

This is the central point: AETC's actions were saturated with viewpoint discrimination, not just on the face of its policy but as the policy was applied, as well. The network excluded Forbes simply because he was neither Democrat nor Republican. There were no formal, much less published, viewpoint-neutral standards used by anyone in making these selections. The AETC did not ask whether the candidates were balloted (Forbes was), or whether they had run for office before (Forbes had), or how well they had performed in prior elections. Had there been a screen imposed on the basis of past performance, Forbes would surely have made the grade, given that he had drawn more than 46 percent of the statewide vote in his run for lieutenant governor in the Republican primaries just two years before. He had received more votes in state elections than either of his two opponents ever had. But Forbes had no opportunity to argue that he was a serious and viable candidate, much less to appeal a contrary judgment made by AETC officials.

This slipshod process vesting decision-making authority with no standards in one unelected official cannot be trusted to protect our most precious political freedoms. As the Court observed in *City of Lakewood v. Plain Dealer Publishing Co.*, the danger of "content and viewpoint censorship" is "at its zenith when the determination of who may speak and who may not is left to the unbridled discretion of a government official."[23] But that was the sum total of due process in this case.

AETC ended up applying its vague, unwritten standards of political viability against Forbes alone. It did not even pretend to apply them to the Democrats or Republicans running for Congress in Arkansas. Thus, it automatically included major-party candidates whose electoral chances were widely considered hopeless.

Consider Arkansas's First Congressional District, one of the most Democratic districts in the country and one that has not sent a Republican to Congress since 1868. In the eight elections prior to 1992, the Democratic candidates took 68.9 percent, 100 percent, 100 percent, 64.8 percent, 97.2 percent. 64.2 percent, 100 percent, and 64.3 percent, respectively, of the general election vote. In 1992, the Democratic nominee, Blanche Lambert, outspent the Republican by eleven to one. Despite being only thirty-one years old, Lambert received 69.8 percent of the vote in this, her first bid for public office, leaving the Republican less than one-third of the vote.[24] Yet the hapless Republican challenger, who, unlike Forbes, had never collected any votes in any public election, was invited by AETC to participate in the debate without being subjected to any of the "seriousness" testing casually applied to Forbes.

In the Second Congressional District debate, AETC invited not only the popular incumbent, Democratic Congressman Ray Thornton, but also the "long-shot Republican challenger Dennis Scott," who "filed at the last minute to run, saying [']no incumbent should get a free ride.[']"[25] A first-time candidate, Scott was able to raise only $5,724—less than was raised by Forbes, who collected $9,754.[26] Congressman Thornton trounced Scott by a three-to-one margin, collecting 74.2 percent of the vote to Scott's 25.8 percent.

To be sure, it might be said that AETC's loose viability test could not have been applied to these sacrificial-lamb Republicans in Arkansas because, without them, there would have been no debate at all in their districts. But this argument proves too much. It suggests, quite properly, that the point of debates is to have an open dialogue among balloted candidates with competing political perspectives, regardless of who has what kind of chances to win. The clear implication is that all ballot-certified candidates—that is, all of those who have passed the state's only formalized test for "seriousness"—should participate in debates.

It is plain that Forbes was kept out of the debate because he was an Independent running outside the two-party system; had he captured either of the major party nominations, as he had done two years before, he would have been invited in with no questions asked. There is no other rational way of understanding what happened to him. Forbes's exclusion was political and partisan viewpoint discrimination.

Justice Kennedy's Redefinition of Viewpoint Discrimination

Justice Kennedy can escape the sweeping evidence of viewpoint discrimination only by completely redefining the concept. He invites us to believe that Forbes's claim about viewpoint discrimination is settled by the trial jury's finding, in answer to the judge's interrogatory, that AETC's managers did not exclude Forbes from the debate "based on 'objections or opposition to his views.'"[27]

But this badly misunderstands what viewpoint discrimination is. The jury's factual finding that Forbes's exclusion was not based on the network managers' "objections or opposition to his views" does not control the constitutional question of whether his exclusion was viewpoint based. The test of First Amendment viewpoint neutrality is an *objective* test focused on the nature of a governmental classification that treats classes of speakers differently according to their particular identity, position, or beliefs in a universe of potential speakers. It is not a *subjective* test focused on the attitudes or motivations of government actors who notify a speaker that he has been excluded from the government's speaking context. Subjective animus may, of course, be *evidence* of the objective viewpoint discrimination taking place, but it is no necessary *element* of it.

Ironically, the objective character of the viewpoint discrimination test was established by Justice Kennedy himself in a lucid majority opinion he wrote in *Rosenberger v. Rector and Visitors of University of Virginia (1995)*.[28] There, the Court struck down the University of Virginia's practice of reimbursing the publishing costs of all student-run periodicals except those religiously identified. Although there was no allegation of *animosity* toward religious students in the case (quite the contrary), the Court found that religiously motivated expression provided a distinctive viewpoint that could not be blocked from public discussion. The university bore no malice toward religion, but when it declined to give the same speech privileges to religious student publications as it did to secular ones, the Court found that it was engaged in unconstitutional viewpoint discrimination.

In the same way, the whole purpose and effect of excluding Forbes's appearance as a candidate was to block presentation of a distinctive political viewpoint deemed unpopular or outside the mainstream and expressed by a candidate deemed unpopular or outside the mainstream. This is political viewpoint censorship pure and simple. The fact that AETC would also have excluded unpopular candidates of left-wing views or centrist views does not rescue the policy. As Justice Kennedy perceptively wrote in *Rosenberger*, "[T]he dissent's declaration that debate is not skewed so long as multiple voices are silenced is simply wrong; the debate is skewed in multiple ways."[29]

Yet, Justice Kennedy remains convinced that Forbes was not discriminated against in Arkansas because he never proved that individual AETC managers disagreed with his politics. Justice Kennedy believes that Forbes was excluded only because he was not "viable" and approvingly quotes AETC's executive director, who

> testified Forbes' views had "absolutely" no role in the decision to exclude him from the debate. She further testified Forbes was excluded because (1) "the Arkansas voters did not consider him a serious candidate"; (2) "the news organizations also did not consider him a serious candidate"; (3) "the Associated Press and a national election result reporting service did not plan to run his name in results on election night"; (4) Forbes "apparently had little, if any, financial support, failing to report campaign finances to the Secretary of State's office or to the Federal Election Commission"; and (5) "there [was] no 'Forbes for Congress' campaign headquarters other than his house."[30]

Justice Kennedy concludes: "It is, in short, beyond dispute that Forbes was excluded not because of his viewpoint but because he had generated no appreciable public interest."[31]

This argument, framed to make Forbes look like a pest and a crank, is a house of cards that cannot withstand the slightest breeze. First of all, the conclusory judgments in the first two points about how the voters and the media did not consider Forbes "a serious candidate" are based on no empirical evidence whatsoever—not even a poll or a survey. They are pure invention and conjecture. Second, they are entirely irrelevant. The constitutional rights of balloted candidates (or other speakers) in public fora do not depend on their political popularity, their estimated favor with reporters, or their fund-raising prowess. In elections, poverty cannot be used to disadvantage citizens, which is why the Court has invalidated, under Equal Protection, practices that reflect plutocratic tendencies, such as poll taxes and high candidate filing fees.[32]

The third point, that "the Associated Press and a national election result reporting service did not plan to run his name in results on election night," is not only irrelevant but comical. The state may not delegate to private media entities the power to define the political rights of citizens running for office. After all, who elected the media and gave them control over free speech rights of the people? Would it change Justice Kennedy's analysis if we were to learn that this decision is the job of a college intern?

As for the final point, that Forbes located his headquarters in his house, the same was true not only of several losing Republican congressional candidates in neighboring districts in Arkansas in 1992 but of numerous winning candidates in history, including John F. Kennedy, who ran his victorious 1960 presidential campaign from his home in Hyannisport, which served as campaign headquarters. The majority's uppity *Better Homes and Gardens* standard obviously cannot be a lawful screen for debate participation under the First Amendment and Equal Protection. It goes to show how much the majority has integrated contempt for less affluent people into its definition of constitutional rights.

It goes without saying that none of these ill-formed standards loosely incorporated into the majority's analysis were imposed on the Democratic or Republican candidates. For example, the modest sums Forbes raised in this election cycle were *more* than the amount collected by two Republican congressional candidates who were invited to participate in AETC's televised 1992 debates. Yet, AETC did not exclude them for the sin of not having raised enough money. Several other candidates ran their campaigns from home but were not disqualified for doing so. The "seriousness" guillotine falls only on those outside the major parties.

If the serious candidate standard were to be applied across the board, there would be precious few debates anywhere in America. In U.S. House races, challengers are rarely considered "viable" against incumbents. Due to partisan political gerrymandering, which this Court has permitted as a practical matter, the member reelection rate is more than 90 percent, and the vast majority of House districts are in either the Democratic or the Republican column on a more or less permanent basis.[33]

What Are Debates and Elections For?

Even if we can usually guess how a campaign is going to come out, this does not mean that we can ever know for sure who the winner will be nor does it mean that a debate is a waste of time. AETC's managers act as if they have a stable of political clairvoyants and psychics on staff whispering oracular secrets into their ears. But no one knows. Remember "Dewey Wins"?

The whole point of campaigns is to *change* public opinion, and, because we have a secret ballot, the history of politics includes great surprises and reversals of fortune, massive shifts of public sentiment at the last minute, late-breaking scandals, and sudden decisions to drop out, not to mention overnight candidate illnesses and deaths. Campaigns are characterized by a fluidity and spontaneity wholly incompatible with the idea of taking a snapshot of the electorate at one moment, superimposing that image on a hypothetical Election Day, and then invoking that distorted image to cut off debate in the present.

The secret of American politics is that third-party and Independent candidates can and do win, especially when given the chance to debate. Vermont gives us the refreshing examples of an Independent House member (perhaps one day a U.S. senator?), Bernie Sanders, and an Independent senator, Jim Jeffords. Minnesota offers the example of Governor Jesse Ventura, a giant, bald-headed all-pro wrestler derided during his maverick 1998 Reform Party campaign as frivolous and unelectable. When the campaign started, he was barely noticeable in the polls and was considered a gadfly and an also-ran. But the League of Women Voters invited him to participate in its gubernatorial debates. On October 18, 1998, after the debates began, he was up to 21 percent in the polls, and by October 30 his numbers had risen to 27 percent.[34] On Election Day, he won. Governor

Ventura has repeatedly said that he would have lost had he been excluded from the debates. No mainstream pollster ever predicted his victory, because polling vastly understates first-time and Independent voters. And, according to the *New York Times*, the vast majority of contacted voters in public opinion polls simply hang up on pollsters or refuse to participate. Response rates have fallen to 20 percent in some cases.

As discussed earlier, a state-controlled "viability" screen constitutes First Amendment viewpoint discrimination, but, in congressional elections, it also offends the spirit of the Qualifications Clause, which specifies the age, citizenship and residency qualifications for congressional candidacy. The Court has found that a state (Arkansas again!) cannot add to these qualifications by requiring balloted candidates not to be incumbents.[35] Similarly, in our representative democracy, state government has no rightful power to predict winners or losers in a federal election and then to publicize its predictions to voters by selectively favoring chosen candidates with free television time. If the state government cannot skew an election by adding the words "(abandoned term limits pledge)" or "(not viable)" or "(likely winner)" next to candidates' names on the ballot, which was the holding in *U.S. Term Limits*, neither can it manipulate public consent by sending such messages, and distributing unequal speech benefits according to them, along the way during the campaign.

The citizenry must decide which candidates are "electable" by electing them. The government's role is to guarantee fair process and secure counting of the ballots. If the people, through their government, decide that a publicly sponsored debate is necessary for enlightenment of the electorate, then the government must find an equal place for *all* ballot-qualified candidates. By picking and choosing "viable" candidates, the government actually usurps the role of the people.

This is not a metaphor. It is likely that, had Forbes been invited to debate by AETC, his participation would have changed the outcome of the race. The Republican victor, Tim Hutchinson, received 125,295 votes, or 50.2 percent of the total, and the Democrat, John Van Winkle, 117,775, or 47.2 percent.[36] Meanwhile, Forbes captured 6,329 votes, or 2.5 percent.[37] If Forbes, a strong conservative with proven vote-getting power, had been allowed to debate and had converted just one out of every fifteen eventual Hutchinson voters, the election would have gone to the Democrat, Van Winkle. Love the result or hate it, it makes no difference: the government's decision to sponsor and close this debate probably elected Congressman Hutchinson.

There are countless contests where candidates behind in the polls surge to win. For example, if AETC had sponsored a debate for candidates in the U.S. Senate Democratic primary in Wisconsin at a comparable time period in 1992, it would have excluded the eventual winner of the election, Russ Feingold, because a major poll showed him at 10 percent of the vote, whereas Congressman Jim Moody was at 42 percent and the businessman Joe Checota at 40 percent.[38] Yet Feingold went on to overcome his rivals less than three weeks after this poll was taken, collecting 69 percent of the vote to 14 percent each for Moody and Checota. Feingold then went on to defeat the incumbent Republican senator, Bob Kasten, in the general election.[39]

Even if "viability" were actually defined and fairly applied to all candidates, and even if the government could achieve political clairvoyance and omniscience, a "viability" test for rejecting balloted candidates would violate the First Amendment. This is because it fundamentally misunderstands what an election is and what a campaign is.

In the continuing public dialogue that is democracy, an election is more than a mechanical contest over who will take office. It is democracy's way of promoting rippling concentric circles of political debate that offer up new priorities and ideas for the public agenda. Losing Socialist Party candidates for president and Congress in the early 1900s ran dynamic campaigns that led to the progressive income tax, women's suffrage, the forty-hour workweek, and many of the progressive reforms of the past century. Ross Perot's dramatic run for president in 1992 placed the budget deficit issue front and center in national politics.

Winning isn't everything. Candidates can run, in part at least, to establish viability for their political ideas and for their own future runs. Defeat can propel political careers. This was the case with Abraham Lincoln, who lost to Stephen Douglas after their famous U.S. Senate campaign debates in Illinois in 1858 but went on to win the presidency two years later on the strength of the political platform he spelled out in that debate. It was the case also with former president Bill Clinton, who (like Ralph Forbes) lost his first race for the House in Arkansas's Third Congressional District (in 1974) but went on to be elected attorney general of Arkansas two years later.

Many politicians have suffered multiple losses before finding success with the voters. For example, Robert Casey "made a second career out of running for Governor" in Pennsylvania, where over the course of twenty years, from 1966 to 1986, he continuously ran for and lost the Democratic nomination before finally winning in 1986. He narrowly won in the general election and was reelected to a second term in 1990 with 68 percent of the vote.[40] Another Pennsylvania politician, Arlen Specter, waged an unsuccessful bid for mayor in 1967, lost his reelection campaign for district attorney of Philadelphia, and piled up back-to-back losses in the 1976 Senate primary and the 1978 gubernatorial primary before succeeding in his bid for a Senate seat in 1980. All of these candidates used their campaigns and the debates within them as building blocks for their political ideas and careers.

When two people debate, it is certain that one of them will lose the election, but this does not nullify the usefulness of debating. It is the same thing with three candidates.

The "Cacophony" Alibi

A final argument advanced by the majority requires refutation. Justice Kennedy argues that if government debate sponsors are not allowed broad discretion to pick and choose participants, they will be "faced with the prospect of cacophony" and "might choose not to air candidates' views at all. . . . In this circumstance, a [g]overnment-enforced right of access inescapably 'dampens the vigor and limits the variety of public debate.'"[41] Justice Kennedy's conclusion parallels AETC's argument before the Court that huge numbers of candidates might flood nonexclusive debates, and "public broadcasters would abandon the effort."

There is no empirical basis for saying that opening up debates to all balloted candidates would produce "cacophony." In the second half of the twentieth century, in twenty-five straight general elections for the U.S. House of Representatives, there was an average of one Independent or minor-party candidate running in each of America's 435 congressional districts. The idea that government debate sponsors could not handle them is preposterous. Most sponsors, such as the League of Women Voters, include them as a matter of course. The 1992 House races in Arkansas nicely capture the national pattern: Ralph Forbes was the only Independent running for Congress in the state.

The claim that multicandidate debates will dissolve into pandemonium is contradicted by our experience with nationally televised debates in the Democratic and Republican presidential primaries, which routinely feature many more than two candidates. For example, in the 1992 presidential primary season, there was a Democratic primary debate in St. Louis with Bob Kerrey, Jerry Brown, Bill Clinton, Tom Harkin, Paul Tsongas, and Douglas Wilder. In the 1988 season, six Republicans met for debate in New Hampshire, including George H. W. Bush, Pete du Pont IV, Alexander Haig, Jr., Bob Dole, Pat Robertson, and Jack Kemp. In recent years, we have been treated to large televised party primary debates that include long shots such as Morry Taylor and Alan Keyes. No one was injured during any of these debates, and no chairs were thrown. The atmosphere remains far more MacNeil-Lehrer than Jerry Springer. Far from experiencing these debates as cacophony, the voters see them as democracy.

In this sense, the people have a far better sense of constitutional values than our self-appointed debate gatekeepers. The whole concept that government can restrict the speech rights of citizens in order to prevent "cacophony" deeply offends the First Amendment norm that all citizens enjoy an equal right to speak. In its 1971 *Cohen v. California*[42] decision, the Supreme Court invoked the necessity in democratic life for multiple voices:

> [The] constitutional right of free expression is powerful medicine in a society as diverse and populous as ours. It is designed and intended to remove governmental restraints from the arena of public discussion, putting the decision as to what views shall be voiced largely into the hands of each of us, in the hope that use of such freedom will ultimately produce a more capable citizenry and more perfect polity and in the belief that no other approach would comport with the premise of individual dignity and choice upon which our political system rests.
>
> To many, the immediate consequence of this freedom may often appear to be only verbal tumult, discord, and even offensive utterance. These are, however, within established limits, in truth necessary side effects of the broader enduring values which the process of open debate permits us to achieve. *That the air at times seem filled with verbal cacophony is, in this sense not a sign of weakness but of strength.* We cannot lose sight of the fact that, in what otherwise might seem a trifling and annoying instance of individual distasteful abuse of a privilege, these fundamental societal values are truly implicated. (Emphasis added)

To argue that major-party candidates will pull out of debates if third-party candidates are invited is an irrelevant distraction from the rights at issue.

To exclude certain candidates because their presence may cause others to choose not to come is, in effect, to impose a prior restraint on their speech that is based on the long-rejected "heckler's veto," or perhaps it is more like a "boycotter's veto." It would be like saying public parks should not be required to desegregate because white parents may choose to stop bringing their kids to the playground. If they were to do so, I suppose that result would be unfortunate, but it would be their choice alone to do that. We cannot deny some citizens their constitutional rights because it might influence others to decline to exercise theirs.

If cacophony were ever to become a *real* problem, government debate sponsors have simple and constitutional alternatives available to them. A sponsor should decide in advance how many candidates the voters can tolerate without losing focus, and it must be a number that cannot be altered for the purpose of major party primary debates. So let us say it is, for example, five candidates. If there are more candidates than places—imagine there are ten—the debate sponsor can add a second debate and randomly divide the candidates up between the two events. If time is so scarce that there is time for only a single debate (although it is hard to imagine this ever being the case), then names should be drawn out of a hat and each candidate given an equal chance to be one of the five included.

Surely this is the solution compelled by the Supreme Court's analysis in *Rosenberger*, where Justice Kennedy stated that "government cannot justify viewpoint discrimination among private speakers on the economic fact of scarcity." He declared it "incumbent on the State, of course, to ration or allocate the scarce resources on some acceptable neutral principle."[43]

To be sure, if the Democratic and Republican candidates in the Third District wanted to meet without Forbes being present, they had every First Amendment right to arrange and pay for an independent and private debate of their own. This was the principle we relied upon in *Hurley v. Irish-American Gay, Lesbian and Bisexual Group of Boston*,[44] which upheld the exclusion of unwanted speakers from a private speech forum, even one taking place on public property. In such an event, everyone would know that the meeting was sponsored by the two major-party candidates and their campaigns.

But, as a state actor using taxpayer monies, including those contributed by Forbes and his supporters, AETC had no right to set up a private two-party debate while excluding Forbes, who met every requirement of candidate seriousness set by Arkansas in order to get on the ballot. He must be treated as an equal in the government's forum. His rights mean something too.

Alas, I must observe that, in cases like this one and *Jenness v. Fortson*,[45] which upheld harsh signature requirements for third-party candidates to get on the ballot, and *Timmons v. Twin Cities Area New Party*,[46] which allowed states to ban the practice of political party "cross-endorsements" that gave life to minor parties in the past, the Court has been suggesting that the Constitution authorizes states to create and prop up a "two-party system" in their elections. This assumption is false and needs to be corrected before we find ourselves in very deep trouble.

In a constitutional sense, we have no two-party system. The Constitution does not mention political parties, much less a two-party system, much less still two specific parties. We no more have a two-party system than a three-party or a one-party system. (Indeed, the more plausible claim is that we have a three-party system, since the Twelfth Amendment specifies that, in the failure of an electoral college majority in a presidential election, the House of Representatives will choose from the top *three* presidential candidates in a contingent election.) The point is that the First Amendment protects the right of all citizens to speak, associate, and participate in politics on an equal basis, without regard to ideology or party affiliation. In our system, we must treat all parties equally.

It is true that, according to "Duverger's Law," the electorate in a single-member-district representative democracy will tend to group and regroup into two main political camps over time, but this pattern is neither legally required nor uniformly true. Nor does it support the constitutional proposition that two leading parties at any one time can confer upon themselves valuable public advantages to entrench their specific rule in time over others. Even those political scientists who believe in "a two-party system" as an empirical matter understand that the system itself must remain fluid and supple so that political and ideological realignments can propel new parties to take the place of old ones, the way the Republican Party replaced the Whigs in the nineteenth century. Democracy must be competitive and maintain low barriers to entry.

By analogy, it is one thing to observe that the United States is a majority-Christian nation but quite another to conclude that the government may therefore establish Christianity as the nation's official religion. Thus, Arkansas cannot record that more of its citizens are registered to the Democratic and Republican Parties than other parties and then establish structural advantages, funding preferences, and selective speech opportunities for those two parties over all others. Everything in our Constitution cries out for viewpoint-neutrality and equal treatment as to contending political parties as well as religious sects.

I dissent.

NOTES

1. Arkansas Educational Television Commission v. Forbes, 523 U.S. 666 (1998).

2. The issues are rather complicated. In order to treat speakers fairly, there must be fair procedures for deciding who gets to speak and at what time. Local ordinances requiring permits to speak or march must be based upon clear criteria for determining when permits will be granted. Those who are denied an opportunity to use a public forum must be given due process of law—a hearing and an opportunity to appeal to a court. Opportunities for speech may be restricted by content-neutral "time, place, and manner" considerations (for example, restrictions against using loud soundtrucks in residential areas at night). For a detailed discussion of these issues, see ERWIN CHEMERINSKY, CONSTITUTIONAL LAW: PRINCIPLES AND POLICIES § 11.4.2.2 (3d ed. 2006).

3. See generally ERWIN CHEMERINSKY, CONSTITUTIONAL LAW: PRINCIPLES AND POLICIES § 11.2.1 (3d ed. 2006).

4. Forbes, 523 U.S.at 676.

5. West Virginia State Board of Education v. Barnette, 319 U.S. 624, 641, 642 (1943). The opinion in Barnette was a ringing endorsement of freedom of speech. Specifically, the Court held that students could not be required to say the Pledge of Allegiance and to salute the flag in public schools.

6. Rosenberger v. Rector and Visitors of the University of Virginia, 515 U.S. 819 (1995). In Rosenberger the Court held that a state university could not pay the costs of all student periodicals except those that were religious in nature.

7. Forbes, 523 U.S. at 670 (1998).

8. AETC Petition For Writ of Certiorari at 2. AETN is the Arkansas Educational Television Network, which is owned by AETC and consists of five non-commercial television stations.

9. AETC Brief at 16.

10. Forbes v. Arkansas Educ. Television Comm'n, 93 F.3d 497 (8th Cir. 1996).

11. Id. at 504 (emphasis in original).

12. Id. at 504–5.

13. Forbes, 523 U.S. 666, 675 (1998).

14. Cornelius v. NAACP Legal Defense and Educ. Fund, Inc., 473 U.S. 788, 802 (1985).

15. *Forbes,* 523 U.S. at 680.

16. *Id.* at 669.

17. *See* Perry Educ. Ass'n. v. Perry Local Educators' Ass'n, 460 U.S. 37, 55 (1983) ("In a public forum, by definition, all parties have a constitutional right of access and the state must demonstrate compelling reasons for restricting access to a single class of speakers, a single viewpoint, or a single subject. . . . When speakers and subjects are similarly situated, the State may not pick and choose.").

18. Jenness v. Fortson, 403 U.S. 431, 442 (1971).

19. AETC Petition for Writ of Certiorari at 15.

20. Buckley v. Valeo, 424 U.S. 1, 48–49 (1976) (citations omitted). In *Buckley,* the Court affirmed certain aspects of the campaign finance laws and held others unconstitutional.

21. Texas v. Johnson, 491 U.S. 397, 414 (1989).

22. *Buckley,* 424 U.S. at 15 (quoting *Monitor Patriot Co. v. Roy,* 401 U.S. 265, 272 (1971)).

23. City of Lakewood v. Plain Dealer Publishing Co., 486 U.S. 750, 763 (1988).

24. *See* Clerk of the U.S. House of Representatives, Statistics of the Presidential and Congressional Elections of Nov. 3, 1992, at 22.

25. "Governor's Run for White House Heads Arkansas' Slate on Nov. 3," Associated Press, Oct. 24, 1992.

26. Federal Election Commission Financial Data for House General Election Campaigns Through Dec. 31, 1992 at 22.

27. *Forbes,* 523 U.S. at 682.

28. Rosenberger v. Rector and Visitors of University of Virginia, 515 U.S. 819 (1995).

29. *Id.* at 831–32.

30. *Forbes,* 523 U.S. at 682.

31. *Id.*

32. Harper v. Virginia State Bd. of Elections, 383 U.S. 663, 666 (1966); Bullock v. Carter, 405 U.S. 134, 143 (1972).

33. *See* Davis v. Bandemer, 478 U.S. 109 (1986).

34. The Appleseed Citizen's Taskforce on Debates, A Blueprint for Fair and Open Presidential Debates in 2000, at 4 (2000).

35. U.S. Term Limits v. Thornton, 514 U.S. 779 (1995).

36. Clerk of the U.S. House of Representatives, Statistics of the Presidential and Congressional Election of November 3, 1992, at 5 (1993).

37. *Id.*

38. *See* "Moody and Checota in Close Race for Senate Nomination," Milwaukee Journal at A1 (August 16, 1992).

39. *See* "Landslide for Feingold," Milwaukee Sentinel at 1A (September 9, 1992).

40. *See* Michael deCourcy Hinds, "A Victory Over Illness Plays Well in Politics," NEW YORK TIMES at A18 (Feb. 20, 1994).

41. *Forbes,* 523 U.S. at 681.

42. Cohen v. California, 403 U.S. 15 (1971).

43. *Rosenberger,* 515 U.S. at 835.

44. Hurley v. Irish-American Gay, Lesbian and Bisexual Group of Boston, 515 U.S. 557 (1995).

45. Jenness v. Fortson, 403 U.S. 431 (1971).

46. Timmons v. Twin Cities Area New Party, 520 U.S. 351 (1997).

3

Cuyahoga Falls v. Buckeye

The Supreme Court's "Intent Doctrine"—
Undermining Viable Discrimination Claims
and Remedies for People of Color

Eva Paterson and Susan K. Serrano

In today's world, racial discrimination
sometimes wears a benign mask.[1]

Introduction

In the United States, the law has been used both as a cudgel and as a shield for African Americans and other people of color. The Fourteenth Amendment was passed after the Civil War to help the descendants of kidnapped Africans whose humanity was finally recognized by the U.S. legal system. Lawyers and activists thought they had a real tool for eradicating barriers to full social and political equality. But that idealism was rewarded with backward rulings from the United States Supreme Court. One of the most egregious decisions was *Plessy v. Ferguson*,[2] which enshrined the doctrine of "separate but equal." This outrageous decision was finally dealt a fatal blow as a result of the brilliant legal strategy devised by Charles Hamilton Houston and his NAACP and Howard University Law School colleagues.[3] Eighty years after *Plessy*, the Supreme Court issued another ruling that attempted to erect one more legal barrier between people of color and true legal equality. The case was *Washington v. Davis*.[4]

In 1970, on the heels of America's massive civil rights and social movements, African American police recruits and officers filed suit against District of Columbia officials. They contended that the Metropolitan Police Department's recruiting procedures, including a written entrance exam, discriminated against them in violation of their right to equal protection of the laws. According to the police department, the exam, which measured verbal ability, vocabulary, reading, and comprehension,[5] was necessary to maintain "standards" and "excellence."[6] But the test excluded African Americans at a rate *more than four times greater* than the rate for whites—a clear disparate impact on African American recruits.[7] The appeals court found it "hard to imagine how disproportionate effect could ever be better demonstrated."[8] It noted that "until . . . the effects of [educational] deprivation [for Blacks] have been completely dissipated, comparable performance on such tests can hardly be expected."[9] The United States Supreme Court disagreed. In *Washington v. Davis*, the Court held that the disproportionate impact of the test was not enough to sustain the African American recruits' claim. The Court held instead that plaintiffs alleging racial discrimination in violation of the Equal Protection Clause must show that the government's challenged acts were motivated by *racially discriminatory intent*.[10] Only a showing that the police department actually *intended* to discriminate against African American recruits would suffice.[11]

In 1996, a full century after *Plessy*, Buckeye Community Hope Foundation, a nonprofit affordable housing developer, filed suit against the city of Cuyahoga Falls, Ohio, and several city officials. Buckeye had purchased land in the predominantly white suburb of Akron to develop a low-income housing complex. At the time, fewer than 2 percent of the city's nearly fifty thousand residents were African American.[12] The public and the mayor immediately expressed strong opposition, arguing that the project was the same type of "social engineering that brought us busing." Some citizens claimed to "know what kind of element is going to move in there."[13] Others voiced concerns about the residents who would be playing loud "boom boxes." Others feared the site would be just like another neighborhood in town—the city's only concentration of minority residents. The mayor even referred to an article entitled "Stuck in the Ghetto," which discussed the problems with Section 8 housing.[14]

Members of the public petitioned for a referendum seeking to overturn the approval of the site plan. The city put the referendum before the voters, which postponed the project pending the outcome. Buckeye brought a civil rights action against the city, alleging, among other things, racial discrimination in violation of the Equal Protection Clause.[15] In *City of Cuyahoga Falls v. Buckeye Community Hope Foundation*,[16] the Supreme Court invoked the restrictive intent standard articulated in *Washington v. Davis* to hold that there was insufficient evidence for Buckeye's equal protection claim to go to trial. According to the Court, Buckeye's equal protection claim foundered because of the alleged lack of intentional discrimination by governmental actors.[17] Noticeably absent from the Court's analysis, however, was any discussion of the history of residential segregation in either the area or nationwide, the present-day validity of the "intent doctrine," or the doctrine's impact on communities of color and their discrimination claims. This lack of reality-based jurisprudence is typical of the analysis (or lack thereof) employed by a conservative judiciary that ignores racial realities that would force it to come to radically different conclusions. The Supreme Court's decision in this case was unanimous, although there was a separate concurring opinion by Justice Scalia, joined by Justice Thomas. Eva Paterson and Susan K. Serrano have authored a dissent.

In both of these cases and in countless others, the Court's "intent" requirement undermines viable discrimination claims and key remedies for people of color.[18] Under this constricted doctrine, plaintiffs must show the near-impossible: a defendant's subjective intent to discriminate. The doctrine views discrimination as an isolated, individual phenomenon resulting from a decision maker's specific and identifiable "intent," rather than as an institutionalized, historically influenced, and often subconscious process. By requiring a specific showing of intent, the Court disregards the social systems that support racism and places the multitude of manifestations of racism beyond legal redress.

Rather than advancing equality, the Court's adherence to the requirement runs counter to the original purpose of the Equal Protection Clause—to ensure meaningful equality for all groups under law.

Eva Paterson and Susan K. Serrano contend that the Court must abandon its flawed and outdated view of racism and the law linked to it. The dissent then briefly sketches alternatives for analyzing equal protection discrimination claims. These alternatives are not based on an outmoded concept of purposeful intent. Instead, more useful alternatives are based on substantial empirical and theoretical research in social cognition theory and organizational sociology. In broad terms, these theories illustrate that discrimination—previously viewed as connected only to blatant or calculated acts—is instead often sustained through institutional structures, implicit categorization and processing, and historical dimensions of racial inequality.[19] This dissent also acknowledges the cold harsh realities of racism in the United States at the present time—a reality the high court and many members of the public chose to ignore.

One positive effect of the civil rights movement is that most Americans do not want to be racists. Activism has changed hearts and minds. If one were to ask most Americans if they harbor negative attitudes about people of color, most would readily affirm their adherence to colorblindness and nondiscriminatory attitudes and behaviors. Yet, a thorough examination of statistics indicates that people of color have higher infant mortality rates, are stopped by the police simply for being the "wrong" color, and die at a younger age than other members of our society.[20] While no one "intends" these tragic and often deadly outcomes, they occur nonetheless.

The alternatives described in this dissent, while varied, all challenge as inadequate the narrow definition of intent articulated by the Court in *Washington v. Davis, Buckeye,* and a growing number of cases.[21] They also focus the inquiry on the dimensions of discrimination that are subconscious, historically rooted, and deeply ingrained in our society's institutions and culture. Finally, at least some of these contextual approaches recognize the purpose of America's antidiscrimination laws to eliminate historical barriers to equality for people of color. Indeed, the American people adopted the Fourteenth Amendment, and specifically the Equal Protection Clause, to eliminate two hundred years of systemic discrimination and blatant racism practiced and indeed perfected against African Americans.

Application of these alternatives reveals the weaknesses in the Court's narrow conception of race and myopic focus on decision makers' elusive "intent." These approaches, attentive to history and context, are reviewed in preliminary fashion and are meant to serve as a starting point from which to examine equal protection "intent" cases. This dissent does not offer one definitive model for analyzing equal protection cases but paints in broad strokes to identify various approaches. Whether the courts adopt a single approach or a combination of many, this dissent urges the Court to abandon the individual intent requirement for a more context-sensitive, empirically and theoretically supported model that better acknowledges modern-day manifestations of racial discrimination.

Dissent by Eva Paterson and Susan K. Serrano

A. The Intent Doctrine in Context

At the time this Court first articulated its "intent doctrine," the United States had emerged from a period of renewed commitment to civil rights for African Americans and other people of color.[22] Substantial African American contributions to the World War II effort, the massive social, legal, and political movements launched by antiracist activists, and the legal reforms of the 1950s and 1960s—highlighted by *Brown v. Board of Education*[23]—culminated in the enactment of the Civil Rights Act of 1964 and the Voting Rights Act of 1965.[24] Along with "the resurrection of the Civil Rights Act of 1870 and the advent of affirmative action, these legal reforms collectively renewed the nation's commitment to civil rights and, even more important, to equality and justice."[25]

Brown breathed new life into the Equal Protection Clause in the face of pervasive segregation and continuing racial violence. In outlawing state-mandated segregation, *Brown* offered the promise of equal treatment for African Americans and compelled national acknowledgment of entrenched forms of racial discrimination. In the years following *Brown*, the Supreme Court nullified Jim Crow policies in streetcars, buses, cafeterias, golf courses, swimming pools, and courtrooms.[26]

In the decade that followed *Brown*, in response to post-*Brown* resistance and continuing discrimination and virulent white supremacy, the civil rights movement pushed Congress to pass the Civil Rights Act of 1964, the Voting Rights Act of 1965, and the Fair Housing Act of 1968. The Court's rulings during this period provided judicial legitimacy to congressional and executive actions protecting the civil rights of racial minorities.[27]

Over time, antidiscrimination laws, executive actions, and court decrees compelled governmental prohibition of racial discrimination, established affirmative action, and generated expanded opportunities and structural improvements for African Americans and other communities of color. These changes included expanded job opportunities, increased access to education, decreased state-sponsored racial violence, immigration reform that offered citizenship to many nonwhites, and a moratorium on the application of the death penalty.[28]

But the victories were short lived. Conservative groups began to wage systematic legal attacks in the courts and legislatures along with a cultural and political crusade through ballot initiatives and the mainstream media.[29] In this setting, this Court severely limited the possibility of legal redress for a significant amount of discrimination by requiring a showing of actual intent in *Washington v. Davis*.[30] By requiring a *prima facie* showing of intent to discriminate, the Court sharply retracted many civil rights gains of the prior decade. In support of its approach, the Court forecast dire consequences for efficient day-to-day governmental operations if black plaintiffs were required only to show the "disparate impact" of a governmental action:

A rule that a statute designed to serve neutral ends is nevertheless invalid, absent compelling justification, if in practice it benefits or burdens one race more than another would be far reaching and would raise serious questions about, and perhaps invalidate, a whole range of tax, welfare, public service, regulatory, and licensing statutes that may be more burdensome to the poor and to the average black than to the more affluent white.[31]

What lies behind this statement is the fact that conservatives do not really want to eliminate the burdens faced by black people. The disparate impact standard, so easily dismissed by the Court, would have compelled society to truly eliminate all vestiges of white supremacy, root and branch.

Later Court decisions further limited the scope of discrimination to be remedied by the courts. In *Personnel Administrator of Massachusetts v. Feeney*,[32] the Court declared that in cases alleging violations of the Equal Protection Clause, it is not enough for a plaintiff to show that the defendant acted with knowledge that its actions would have a discriminatory impact on an identifiable racial group. Instead, plaintiffs must show that the defendant "selected or reaffirmed a particular course of action at least in part "*'because of,'* not merely *'in spite of,'* its adverse effects upon an identifiable group."[33] If a plaintiff cannot overcome these hurdles, the law will not recognize the discrimination he or she has experienced, even though some form of discrimination has come into play.

The intent standard is ineffective to remedy continuing racial inequality and disparity because it *fails to reflect how a large part of discrimination actually occurs.* For this reason, this Court should abandon the intent requirement for a more context-sensitive inquiry that recognizes the modern-day dynamics of how discrimination operates.

The current doctrine views discrimination as an isolated, purposeful phenomenon, detached from history, while overlooking entrenched and systemic disadvantage to racial minorities. By treating discrimination in this fashion, the Court ignores much of what we know about the dynamics of discrimination and denies the sociohistoric reality of race in America.[34] As Professor Charles R. Lawrence III queried: "Does the Black child in a segregated school experience less stigma and humiliation because the local school board did not consciously set out to harm her? Are Blacks less prisoners of the ghetto because the decision that excludes them from an all-white neighborhood was made with property values and not race in mind?"[35] Rather than advancing equality, the Court's continuing adherence to the "intent doctrine" perpetuates stark inequalities and deepens social divisions.

The intent requirement also disregards the historic purpose and original meaning of the Equal Protection Clause and civil rights laws, which took specific account of the social and political significance of race. The Fourteenth Amendment was conceived to rectify the immense burdens on kidnapped Africans and their descendants, who had just emerged from years of slavery and legalized oppression. The Civil Rights Acts and the Thirteenth, Fourteenth, and Fifteenth Amendments to the U.S. Constitution were the centerpieces of a Reconstruction whose clear legislative and popular purpose was to eliminate two hundred years of oppression in the United States. The Equal Protection Clause, in particular, was enacted to remedy the long-standing systemic discrimination against African Americans and later other groups of color. Indeed, the Court long ago recognized that the "the evil to be remedied" by the Equal Protection Clause was the "'gross injustice and hardship' faced by the 'newly emancipated Negroes as a class."[36]

Now, in the face of evidence of continuing group-based social and economic disadvantages, the Court, through its intent requirement, not only ignores relevant history but also disregards the profound impact that race and ethnicity continue to have on the allocation of burdens and benefits in the United States.[37]

B. *Cuyahoga Falls v. Buckeye Community Hope Foundation*

By the time this case reached this Court, America faced a heightened retreat from its commitment to civil rights for all, particularly for those suffering most from historic forms of discrimination. Piece by piece, this Court was dismantling civil rights. The Rehnquist Court gave voice to those who had never embraced the civil rights movement and, indeed, who had chafed at the advances it brought to society. The Court did so under the Fourteenth and Fifteenth Amendments "by invalidating affirmative action programs, limiting federal court powers to monitor school desegregation, rejecting proof of racially discriminatory impact in death penalty sentencing, and countermanding state voter redistricting designed to ensure that votes of minorities count. It also expanded state sovereign immunity under the Eleventh Amendment, restricted Congress's power under the Commerce Clause and drastically undermined the Americans with Disabilities Act."[38] From 1994 to 2004, the Court struck down at least thirty federal statutes.[39]

It is against this backdrop that the majority reiterates its adherence to the "intent doctrine" in this case. Buckeye Community Hope Foundation submitted a site plan for Pleasant Meadows, a seventy-two-unit, multifamily, low-income housing complex, to the city planning commission. Residents of the predominantly white city immediately expressed opposition to the proposal and launched a referendum petition drive to overturn the site plan.

At city council meetings and independent gatherings to discuss the project, citizens voiced concerns in thinly veiled racialized terms: we "know what kind of element is going to move in there"; the project is the same type of "social engineering that brought us busing"; the project would cause crime and drug activity to escalate; and the project "would attract a population similar to the one on Prange Drive," the city's only African American neighborhood. Despite this racialized rhetoric, the planning commission approved the site plan and sent the proposal to the city council for final approval. These statements demonstrate antipathy on the part of some whites toward people of color. The successes of the civil rights movement were a direct threat to people holding these racist viewpoints.

At a city council meeting attended by the city's mayor, many of those in attendance were vocal in their opposition to the project. One citizen claimed that "Cuyahoga Falls [would be] downgrading itself."[40] Another expressed concern about the increased crime and drugs that come with low-income housing. The mayor referred to an article entitled "Stuck in the Ghetto," which discussed the various problems associated with Section 8 housing. He also proclaimed that Cuyahoga Falls had "done [its] part off Graham Road," referring to a city development that housed a substantial number of African Americans.[41] The mayor also declared "that people who spent a lot of money on their condominiums don't want people moving in their neighborhood that are going to be renting for $371."[42] Because the project met all zoning requirements, the city council passed an ordinance authorizing the construction.

News reports at the time also reported that white residents referred to the project as "Pleasant Meadows Ghetto"[43] and that for decades Cuyahoga Falls had been known as "Caucasian Falls."[44] Other citizens voiced racialized fears about those who would move into the housing complex: "I do not see that our school system is correct for these children that would be there" and "[w]hen they get that boom box going, it will be loud."[45]

Subsequently, a group of citizens filed a formal petition with the city requesting that the ordinance be repealed or submitted to a popular vote. "Citizens for the Preservation of Voter Rights" quickly convened with the support of the mayor. Shortly thereafter, a referendum petition was submitted to the city council clerk. The Board of Elections approved the referendum petition and in November of 1996, voters passed the referendum, repealing the site plan ordinance. The city thereafter refused to issue building permits to Buckeye.

Buckeye filed suit in federal court, arguing that the city and its officials had violated, among other things, the Equal Protection Clause by "allowing a site plan approval ordinance to be submitted to the electors of Cuyahoga Falls through a referendum and in rejecting [its] application for building permits."[46] In November 1999, the district court granted the city's motions for summary judgment and dismissed Buckeye's claims.[47]

The Sixth Circuit Court of Appeals reversed. According to the court, Buckeye had produced sufficient evidence to go to trial on the allegation that the city, by allowing the referendum petition to stay the implementation of the site plan, had given effect to the racial bias reflected in the public's opposition to the project.[48] Using the multipronged *Arlington Heights v. Metropolitan Housing Corporation*[49] test to determine whether the city's actions were motivated by "discriminatory intent," the Sixth Circuit noted, first, that the staying of the site plan ordinance had a disproportionate impact on African Americans. The Court next found that the city had departed from the normal procedural sequence, which was also circumstantial evidence of racial discrimination. Testimony had revealed that prior to Buckeye's case, there never had been an apartment complex in the city's history whose site plan had faced a referendum process. For the court, this raised a genuine issue of material fact "as to whether this deviation from the procedural norm was predicated on racial bias, especially in light of the disproportionate impact the decision had on blacks."[50]

The Sixth Circuit also determined that the administrative history of the city's decision provided circumstantial evidence of racial discrimination. According to the court, a jury could reasonably conclude that public statements in opposition to the project, while couched in nonracial terms, had a "decidedly racial component." Those statements, said the court, could be interpreted as opposition to the lower economic status of potential residents, but they could "just as easily be seen as expressions of racial bias against blacks, especially given the fact that racial stereotypes prevalent in our society associate blacks with crime, drugs, and lower class status."[51] The court then cited various scholarly works on the correlation between crime and stereotypes against African Americans.

The court thus held that "plaintiffs have produced sufficient evidence to raise a genuine issue of material fact as to whether (1) the opposition to the low-income housing project reflected racial bias; and (2) whether the defendants gave effect to that racial bias by allowing the referendum to stay the effectiveness of plaintiffs' city council-approved site plan. Accordingly, the district court erred in dismissing plaintiffs' equal protection claim on summary judgment."[52]

This Court reverses the Sixth Circuit Court of Appeals decision. In striking down Buckeye's equal protection claim, this Court also looks to *Arlington Heights v. Metropolitan Housing Corporation*—this time to rule that racially discriminatory intent was *not* present in the case. The majority points out that the city charter's referendum process was racially neutral and that the city's act of placing the referendum on the ballot "cannot be said to have given effect to voters' allegedly discriminatory motives for supporting the petition."[53] In particular, the majority states that Buckeye presented no evidence to show that either of the actions—placing the referendum on the ballot or refusing to issue the building permit—was motivated by racial animus.

According to the majority, because Buckeye claimed "injury from the referendum petitioning *process* and not from the referendum itself," which had not become official,[54] there had never been any "state action" upon which to find the city liable: "Statements made by decisionmakers or referendum sponsors during deliberation over a referendum may constitute relevant evidence of discriminatory intent in a challenge to an ultimately enacted initiative. But respondents do not challenge an enacted referendum."[55] The Court rules that the Sixth Circuit erred in relying on cases in which this Court has subjected "enacted, discretionary measures to equal protection scrutiny and treated decisionmakers' statements as evidence" of discriminatory intent. As such, "[s]tatements made by private individuals in the course of a citizen-driven petition drive, while sometimes relevant to equal protection analysis . . . do not, in and of themselves, constitute state action for the purposes of the Fourteenth Amendment."[56]

According to the majority, Buckeye "point[ed] to no evidence suggesting that these official acts were themselves motivated by racial animus."

Buckeye did not, "for example, offer evidence that the City followed the obligations set forth in its charter *because of* the referendum's discriminatory purpose, or that city officials would have selectively refused to follow standard charter procedures in a different case."[57] Ultimately, according to the Court, neither of the city's official acts reflected the intent required to support equal protection liability. The Court's opinion is not just color-blind; it is totally blind to reality.

The Court focuses its inquiry on the narrow issue of whether individual city actors "intended" to discriminate. Nowhere in its decision does the Court mention historical residential segregation in the city, state, or nation or that the "property values" that the residents sought to protect "had been created through a process of racial exclusion."[58] Nor does the Court make any mention of the efficacy of the "intent doctrine" or its impact on communities of color and their discrimination claims. Most important, the Court makes no effort to rethink its understanding of discrimination or to revisit the underlying bases for the intent requirement in order to bring it in line with the prevailing social psychology and social science research on discrimination and bias. Most Americans do not use ugly racial epithets when expressing their fear or dread of being "forced" to live around black people, particularly poor black people. To force plaintiffs of color to prove an actor's hidden racial animus is to erect an insurmountable hurdle. This hurdle acts as an almost absolute bar to the use of the Fourteenth Amendment as a tool for liberation, justice, and equality for people of color.[59]

C. Redefining How Discrimination Occurs: Implicit and Institutional Racial Processes

Substantial empirical and theoretical research in the fields of social psychology and organizational sociology has concluded that much of society's racism—previously viewed as connected only to blatant or calculated acts—is linked to institutional structures, subconscious categorization, and information processing.[60] This extensive empirical and theoretical work shows that the current law ignores much of what we understand about how both the human mind and societal structures work. The Court's "intentionalist" view of discrimination and the law linked to it thus misunderstand the actual cognitive dynamics of discrimination and the impacts of institutional structures on the daily lives of racial communities.

1. Social Cognition Theory and Implicit Bias

According to social cognition theory, all of us have cognitive biases that influence how we perceive and make decisions about other people.[61] These biases are both automatic and often operate beyond our conscious awareness.[62] Most important, and as discussed later in this chapter, these "implicit biases have real-world consequences—in how we interpret actions, perform on exams, interact with others, and even shoot a gun."[63]

Studies in social cognition show that humans rely on categorization as a basic tool for interpreting perceptions, encoding those perceptions into memory, and making both conscious and subconscious decisions based on those perceptions and memories.[64] "[T]he normal human mind cannot possibly notice, let alone analyze and use, every bit of social information it encounters."[65] Because the amount of potential information is overwhelming, adult minds are remarkably adept at screening, sorting and storing information.[66]

Individuals ordinarily process information quickly and efficiently through shortcuts or "cognitive strategies."[67] "Dividing the social world into categories is an example of a cognitive strategy."[68] Because of this efficiency, individuals are generally unaware of their own mental processes and are often unable to report the reasons for their behavior.[69]

"Stereotyping" is a cognitive strategy that humans employ almost automatically in order to understand their surroundings.[70] It is a *normal* and *ordinary* form of categorizing engaged in by all people as part of the sorting and organization needed to manage large quantities of information.[71] Individuals give substance to a stereotype by creating a "mental prototype, often visual, of the 'typical' category member," based on "a person's accumulated knowledge, beliefs, experiences . . . and expectancies."[72] For example, the mind may create the culturally generated mental prototype of the "midwestern American farmer," "the inner-city Asian American merchant," or the "unwed African American mother." This culturally-generated prototype, or "social schema," operates as a filter that biases "in predictable ways the perception, interpretation, encoding, retention and recall of information about other people."[73] Recent studies show that not only do these cognitive filters and shortcuts distort social perception, "but also what we actually see and remember seeing ('visual perception')."[74]

This process contributes to discrimination in several ways. As a result of this stereotyping process, people perceive members of outgroups to be an "undifferentiated mass"; that is, they all look the same.[75] "Generally, favorable traits are assigned to the individual's own group, and unfavorable traits are assigned to outgroups or 'others.'"[76] In addition, people recall the negative behavior of outgroup members and tend to favor ingroup members in the allocation of rewards. Information that does not correspond with the mental prototype is rearranged or reorganized according to systemic biases, resulting in judgments that tend to favor those seen as ingroup members and disfavor outgroup members *even in the absence of blatant prejudice, ill will, or animus.*[77]

Overwhelming evidence shows that we hold implicit biases, even though we may consciously reject stereotypes about other groups. Indeed, "[t]here is now persuasive evidence that implicit bias against a social category, as measured by instruments such as the [Implicit Association Test], predicts disparate behavior toward individuals mapped to that category. This occurs notwithstanding contrary explicit commitments in favor of racial equality."[78] In other words, one may consciously believe that he or she holds positive attitudes about a particular racial group, but, when beliefs are measured by the implicit bias test,[79] that same person may hold negative attitudes toward that racial group.

These racial stereotypes or "cultural representations" of groups, as both conscious and unconscious forms of bias, affect intergroup judgment and decision making. As Professors Michael Omi and Howard Winant have posited, cultural representation involves the attachment of cultural images to generally recognized racial groups, causing one to interpret events and intergroup dynamics in certain ways and imbuing those events and groups with racial meaning.[80] At one level, cultural representations can be blatantly racialized. These include representations of the black crack dealer, the sinister Chinese, the lazy Mexican, or the white man who can't jump.[81] These widely held racial stereotypes provide people with "common sense" explanations to explain our everyday experiences and perceptions. Organizations and institutions at the same time draw upon "common" racial meanings to support these stereotypes—hiring Asian Americans as midlevel managers, for example, because they follow orders and don't make waves.[82]

On a deeper level, cultural representations involve seemingly neutral cultural depictions that impart nonneutral racial meanings. In this sense, externally neutral debates couched in "neutral" terms can be racially coded.[83] In the context of the Cuyahoga Falls low-income housing debate, racially coded cultural representations included the notions of "protecting property values," "protecting our schools," or comments such as "We know what kind of element is going to move in there."[84] These statements, although outwardly "neutral," are ideologically racial, perpetuating a racial social structure by excluding undesired racialized groups from the city. This is particularly stark in light of the fact that fewer than 2 percent of the city's nearly fifty thousand residents were African American and African American households made up a large percentage of the residents of Buckeye's low-income housing projects in Ohio.[85] Racialized groups can be harmed through these negative cultural images, even while the proponents of those images proclaim, "I'm not racist."

In sum, "people continually use cognitive shortcuts—exaggerations, oversimplifications, generalizations—to allow them to prioritize and, in some gross way, make sense of the overload of incoming information."[86] "Racial stereotyping is one method that people employ almost automatically" in order to make sense of the world.[87] As social cognition studies reveal, even individuals who recognize that racial stereotyping is unsound are still aware of—and still influenced by—those stereotypes. There is little likelihood, therefore, that in a complex institution, such as a university, legislature, or courthouse, all or even most of the various individuals with input into decision-making processes will manage to purge from their perceptions, memory processes, behavior, interpretations, and ultimate evaluations the influence of deep-seated cultural and institutional stereotypes.[88]

2. Organizational Sociology and Institutional Structures

Organizational sociology supports and supplements the conclusion that discrimination can occur independent of any invidious intention. This body of work similarly has concluded that discrimination can be built into institutional structures, practices, and norms—it is in the fabric of how institutions work. Actors within these structures act according to established institutional norms and practices that sometimes reflect discriminatory beliefs. For example, not long ago, the practice of racial and gender exclusion in private clubs was justified by club members who "had nothing against blacks or women" but who were merely upholding traditional club practices. In other words, the discrimination that some groups suffer results not from the tyrannical acts of a dominant ruler but from the daily practices of a generally well-intentioned society—it is "embedded in unquestioned norms, habits, and symbols, in the assumptions underlying institutional rules and the collective consequences of following those rules."[89]

Institutional racism theory stresses how "institutions operate as taken-for-granted understandings of the social context that actors must adopt to make sense of the world."[90] As part of the institutional structure, people "often unintentionally engage in racial discrimination" by relying on "routinized sequences of behavior."[91] At the same time, "persons fail to recognize their reliance on racial notions, and indeed may stridently insist that no such reliance exists, even while acting in a manner that furthers racial status hierarchy."[92] Organizational sociologists thus observe that, to a significant degree, discriminatory human behavior within institutions often does not occur at a high level of consciousness; that is, much of that behavior is not explicitly purposeful. It is, however, subconsciously purposeful in that it stems from the deliberate yet unconsidered repetition of cognitively familiar and *institutionalized routines*.[93] In other words, as Professor Ian Haney Lopez has written, "we often act in definable ways without a consciously formulated purpose," because the institution's practices and norms tell us that this "is the way it is done," and how it is done comports with our subconscious beliefs.

Historical context is also essential to this approach. As Professor Daria Roithmayr has posited, institutional processes that continue over time "can perpetuate racial inequality, even in the absence of intentional discrimination."[94] Early practices—social norms and rules such as residential segregation that gave certain racial groups an early advantage—have in many cases become institutionalized, in that they have "become self-reinforcing and then locked-in over time." These "locked-in" practices serve to reinforce historical disparities in the present day.[95] For example, "neighborhoods and cities, like the stock market, can exhibit patterns of race and income stratification even when individuals are following race-neutral rules. People who follow these rules—'move to a new neighborhood if it is more attractive and you can afford it' or 'protect property values' or 'hire new employees through other employees you already know'—are further reinforcing existing racial inequalities, without necessarily intending to do so."[96] Under this model, as Professor Roithmayr explains, "a municipal decision in an all-white township not to rezone for multifamily housing probably would constitute discrimination, because the decision to rezone would have racially disparate effects and would reinforce racial disparities in residential segregation that have been historically associated with Jim Crow segregation."[97] Thus, even if individual actors believe they harbor no ill will toward others, they may *by their deliberate actions carry out the institution's discriminatory operations,* which are rooted historically in discriminatory stereotypes.

The widely recognized studies discussed here strongly support the Ninth Circuit Court of Appeal's articulation in *Inland Marine* that race-based cognitive stereotyping significantly affects institutional decision making. In *Inland Marine,* the Ninth Circuit affirmed the district court's ruling that an African American employee alleging racial discrimination under Title VII on the basis of a disparate wage structure proved intentional discrimination although "[t]he company did not consciously set out to establish a two-tiered wage structure, and hence did not act maliciously[.]"[98] Recognizing the "benign mask" of racial discrimination, the Ninth Circuit observed that "[c]urrent practices, though harmless in appearance, may hide subconscious attitudes . . . and perpetuate the effects of past discriminatory practices[.]"[99] These studies are also strongly endorsed in the pathbreaking case of *Chin v. Runnels.*[100] There, Federal District Judge Breyer recognized "the natural human tendency to categorize information and engage in generalizations, of which stereotyping is a part, as a means of processing the huge amount of information confronting individuals on a daily basis."[101] In questioning the central assumptions of *Washington v. Davis* and marking a potential shift in how courts view discrimination for purposes of equal protection analysis, Judge Breyer emphasized that "[t]he complete absence of grand jury forepersons of Chinese, Filipino, or Latino descent over a 36-year period begs the question whether unconscious stereotyping or biases may have contributed to the exclusion of these groups notwithstanding the best intentions of those involved."[102]

Social psychology and organizational sociology thus confirm that the intent standard is inadequate to remedy the true conditions of inequality experienced by victims of discrimination because it does not reflect how a large part of discrimination actually occurs in real life. By treating racism as isolated and intentional rather than institutionalized and sociohistorical, the intent requirement denies the reality of race in America. More contextual approaches, discussed later, uncover the weaknesses in the Court's narrow focus on elusive "intent" and refocus the inquiry on the dimensions of discrimination that are subconscious, historically rooted, and deeply ingrained in our society's institutions and culture.

D. Justice Under Law: Alternatives to "Intent"

This Court should abandon its outmoded and discredited individual intent model. As many commentators have persuasively argued, the Court should instead adopt a more context-sensitive, empirically and theoretically supported approach that better acknowledges modern-day manifestations of racial discrimination. In order to do so, the Court must expand the definition of discrimination to include attitudes and biases that are institutionalized, historically influenced, and often implicit.[103]

In this case, the Court is primarily concerned with whether any city actors "intended" to discriminate in violation of the Equal Protection Clause. The case's outcome might have been different if the Court had considered the psychological, historical, and institutional dimensions of the city's acts. Although the referendum at issue never went into effect because of a state court ruling[104] and Buckeye was ultimately able to complete the project,[105] this case provides fertile ground to introduce principles that may be applied in a number of cases in which governmental actions may have racial meaning.

Consistent with extensive and well-recognized psychological and social science understandings, the Court in this case should eliminate the purposeful discrimination requirement first articulated in *Washington v. Davis* and remand this case to the lower courts for further analysis. The alternatives to intent, discussed earlier, would instead require a court to go beyond decision makers' elusive "intent" to examine all of the circumstances giving rise to the framing and adoption of the action. A court would also inquire into the historical context of the governmental act at issue as well as whether implicit stereotyping or biases might have contributed to the government's actions. A court might also inquire into whether state actors, by their deliberate but unconsidered actions, carried out institutional operations that are rooted historically in discriminatory stereotypes. Finally, a court could also examine whether the governmental action was imbued with racial meaning.[106] Such approaches would recast the judicial focus onto the elimination of contemporary forms of discrimination in harmony with the purposes of the Equal Protection Clause.

Here, we consider how the psychological and social science research might be applied and briefly sketch how a court might evaluate the facts. The research suggests that, in addition to examining the disparate impact of the city's actions, which both the district court and the appeals court found clearly present in the case,[107] the court should also look to the racial meaning of the city's acts by reviewing both explicit and implicit stereotypes present in the case, as well as contemporary forms of institutionalized and "locked-in" historical discrimination. We do not offer a single, definitive model for analyzing equal protection intent cases but paint in broad strokes, using the facts in this case to identify various, non-mutually-exclusive approaches. These approaches form a starting point from which courts may develop a new understanding of racism and craft remedies consistent with the requirements of justice.

1. "Racial Meaning" Through Implicit Stereotypes and Cultural Representations

In a pathbreaking work, Professor Charles Lawrence advanced an alternative to the "intent" test that would require the court to instead examine the "cultural meaning" of a governmental act in order to uncover the collective unconscious bias that animated the act.[108] Under this approach, the court would "evaluate governmental conduct to see if it conveys a symbolic message to which the culture attaches racial significance"[109] If the court found that the "population thinks of the governmental action in racial terms, then [the court] would presume that socially shared, unconscious racial attitudes made evident by the action's meaning had influenced the decision makers."[110]

One aspect of this analysis might include an inquiry into both explicit and implicit stereotyping or biases and deeply seated cultural representations that may have affected city officials' judgment and decision making. Using this approach, the court could consider the racial meaning that Cuyahoga Falls residents placed on the city's decision whether or not to approve the low-income housing project. This racial meaning was made clear at a series of meetings where residents forcefully opposed the housing project in carefully coded racial terms. Warning of "loud boom boxes," "crime and drugs," the "ghetto," and "social engineering that brought us busing," the city's residents and mayor thus argued against the project while racializing the issue by rhetorical sleight of hand: "ghetto" refers to inner-city African Americans; "crime and drugs" and "loud boom boxes" are associated with African American stereotypes; and "social engineering that brought us busing" (ironically the architect of *Brown*, Charles Hamilton Houston, famously told his law students at Howard University that they could either become parasites or social engineers) invokes conservative rhetoric used to describe governmental efforts to racially integrate formerly segregated schools. The city's residents also worried about "property values," and they claimed to know "what kind of element was going to move in." As the Sixth Circuit recognized, these comments reflected a "decidedly racial component," even while no one invoked explicit racial labels. Opponents thus argued against the low-income housing complex in externally neutral language while implicitly calling for allocation of resources along racial lines.[111]

In seemingly neutral terms with racialized underpinnings, the city's mayor also revealed the racial nature of the issue. He "linked the project to the same type of 'social engineering that brought us busing,' which the Mayor considered to be an utter failure."[112] As the Sixth Circuit recognized, the mayor "cast the debate over the project in a racial light" by referring to an article, "Stuck in the Ghetto," which discussed the problems with Section 8 housing. The mayor also declared that the city had already "done [its] part" in another African American neighborhood in the city. Finally, he declared that "people who spent a lot of money on their condominiums don't want people moving in their neighborhood that are going to be renting for $371." Thus, according to the mayor, the city council "should not advocate anything that is clearly a step backwards."[113]

The mayor's comments imply what other opponents of housing integration have explicitly declared: in order to preserve a common constellation of white customs and values, we must exclude the racially different. It is unmistakable, for example, that the "people who spend a lot of money on their condominiums" to whom the mayor referred implicitly meant the city's white residents. The mayor's comments were particularly telling in light of the aforementioned context: fewer than 2 percent of the city's residents were black, and African American households made up a large percentage of the residents of Buckeye's low-income housing projects in Ohio.

The Sixth Circuit Court of Appeals recognized the racial nature of the citizens' comments and concluded that Buckeye had raised a genuine issue of material fact as to "whether the opposition to the low-income housing project reflected racial bias" and "whether the defendants gave effect to that racial bias by allowing the referendum to stay the effectiveness" of Buckeye's low-income housing project. This Court, in its quest to find discriminatory intent, however, dismisses this racial stereotyping evidence as wholly separate from the city's motivation for placing the referendum on the ballot. For the Court, the racial meaning Cuyahoga Falls residents placed on the city's decision whether or not to approve the low-income housing project does not merit a finding that racial opposition also motivated the city. If the Court had gone beyond a narrow consideration of "intent" to consider factors such as the racial meaning—conscious or subconscious—of the governmental action, in light of historical context, the Court might have ultimately viewed the governmental action differently. As Professor Lawrence observed in a related context, "[e]ven the court's terse description of the public meetings makes clear that race was prominent in the minds of both opponents and proponents of the project. . . . [I]f the court's inquiry had focused on the meaning this community attached to the decision to exclude the project, this evidence of heated debate on the question of race would necessarily carry a great deal more weight."[114]

This analysis illustrates that there was strong cultural meaning attached to the city's acts, to judge from the residents' and the mayor's "decidedly racial" stereotypes, as well as the historical and institutional context, discussed later. It also suggests that "no one who [was] a part of this culture" could have submitted the referendum petition to the city council clerk "without race on his mind."[115]

2. Contemporary Forms of Institutionalized and Historical Discrimination

This Court's analysis of the Buckeye low-income housing issue is noticeably devoid of social, institutional, and historical context. It simply concludes that the city's act of placing the referendum on the ballot "cannot be said to have given effect to voters' allegedly discriminatory motives for supporting the petition." Alternative analyses, however, may tell another story. Under one approach, the court could consider whether individual actors by their deliberate yet unconsidered actions carried out institutional operations that are rooted historically in discriminatory stereotypes. Relatedly, the court could examine whether the city's actions gave effect to the city's early intentional—and now institutionalized—residential segregation.

First, a court could consider the "historical and contemporaneous meaning of residential segregation" in the city and "in the culture as a whole."[116] This may include an analysis of "the history of statutorily mandated housing segregation as well as the use of restrictive covenants among private parties that aim to prevent blacks from purchasing property in white neighborhoods."[117] It also might entail an examination of the history of the segregated regions of the city, including Graham Road, a city development where the mayor proclaimed that Cuyahoga Falls had already "done [its] part," and Prange Drive, an African American neighborhood in the city. As Professor Lawrence posits, "[o]ur culture attaches racial meaning to residential segregation. When we see an all-white neighborhood in close proximity to an all-black one, we do not imagine that it is white because its inhabitants' forebears settled there generations ago or that blacks have chosen not to live there. Our initial thought is that it is white because nonwhites have been excluded."[118]

It is well established, moreover, that this exclusion of African Americans and other communities of color through residential segregation, restrictive covenants, and other discriminatory measures was a direct result of intentional, invidious discrimination. This historical exclusion of nonwhites has become an established de facto institutional norm and practice. With this in mind, the court may examine whether the city's act "operated in practice to reinforce historical inequalities in property value and residential location associated with intentional discrimination" in the city.[119] As Professor Roithmayr has stated in another context, the Court could have "recognize[d] that the very property values [the residents] sought to protect had been created through a process of [intentional] racial exclusion."[120] Because the city allowed the referendum to stay the implementation of the site plan and thus put the residents' racial bias into effect, a court could conclude that the city's present-day acts gave effect to historical and institutional practices rooted in intentional discrimination.

Put another way, a court might conclude that city actors, by placing the racialized referendum on the ballot (thereby acting according to established and unquestioned institutional norms), may have perpetuated already-existing institutional racial disparities. As Professor Ian Haney Lopez has explained, "institutions operate as taken-for-granted understandings of the social context that actors must adopt to make sense of the world." People within these structures act according to established institutional norms and practices that, sometimes, reflect discriminatory beliefs. Thus, the racialized barriers to residential entry experienced by African Americans in Cuyahoga Falls may not only result from "the immediate intent of the individuals inside the neighborhood, but [reside] in the ostensibly race-neutral institutional practices that prevent mobility."[121]

The federal district court acknowledged that city officials may simply have been carrying out institutional policy when they allowed the referendum to stay the housing project: "the city's policymakers declared the site plan ordinance to be ineffective and refused to issue building permits . . . pursuant to provisions of their City Charter and . . . this city policy was the moving force which gave a staying effect to the citizens' petition and referendum."[122] The court also recognized, however, that although the actions of the government actors were done pursuant to a city policy, the question was whether those actions "authorize[d] the deprivation of federal rights." The Sixth Circuit also recognized that the city actors could not just fall back on their institutionally defined routines: "if there is evidence that residents of Cuyahoga Falls were motivated, in part, by racial bias, the

City can not give effect to that bias simply because its City Charter provides for referendum."[123] The lower courts may have sensed that more was
at play than "neutral" city policy.

Thus, even if individual city officials believed they harbored no ill will
toward others, by their deliberate actions they carried out the institution's
discriminatory operations, which are rooted historically in discriminatory stereotypes. Given the ubiquity of race as an issue in America and
the highly charged racialized debate round the Buckeye low-income housing issue, it is highly unlikely that any city official in that context managed
to purge from his or her perceptions, memory processes, and behavior
the influence of deeply seated cultural and institutional stereotypes. Even
if the city's acts were not overtly or blatantly biased, the evidence may
have shown that their acts, collectively, as part of institutional practices,
were "primarily motivated by subtle, but nevertheless discriminatory attitudes"[124] and resulted in the exclusion of African Americans in Cuyahoga
Falls.

The Court's understanding of discrimination based on this empirical
and theoretical research should focus antidiscrimination law on the elimination of contemporary forms of exclusion, particularly those rooted in
historical group-based discrimination. America's legal history supports
this contextualized operation of antidiscrimination law. As discussed earlier, the purpose of the Equal Protection Clause was to remove the barriers to equality for African Americans, and, later, other people of color,
by taking express account of the social and political significance of race
and remedying pervasive forms of discrimination.[125] Properly viewed, the
Equal Protection Clause should thus be viewed by courts as a vehicle to
promote genuine equality and to fully end forms of historically legalized
group-based discrimination.

E. Conclusion

Not all will embrace the proposed approaches set forth above. Paradigm
shifts occur over time. There is much more refining to be done and serious implications in both the science and the law that need to be explored.
This will involve a long-term, multifaceted, concerted strategy. It is hoped,
however, that the preceding analyses will urge the Court and others to
work beyond traditional legal paradigms to acknowledge race's socially
contingent and value-charged nature and to understand how discrimination actually occurs in contemporary society. If the Supreme Court is to
be true to its duty to ensure equal protection for all of America's people,

then it must rethink its understanding of racism and fashion appropriate alternative remedies to address it.

As the *Buckeye* case and scholarly research reveal, discrimination now often assumes subtle forms, residing in facially neutral institutional practices and policies that are discriminatory in impact. This discrimination often occurs without evil-hearted individual actors but as a result of implicit stereotyping and group-biased decision making at multiple levels of institutional operations. Studies in social psychology and institutional sociology confirm this. The Court must now build legal definitions of discrimination to reflect this reality.[126]

Coming full circle, we end where we began. The law has been used both to advance and to thwart the rights of people of color. A hostile judiciary has often expressed the racist views of the populace. Racism is often covert and unacknowledged but nonetheless exists and powerfully affects all members of society. The intent requirement is one way that discrimination goes unchecked. The elimination of this harmful doctrine will unsheathe a vital tool in the fight against discrimination—namely the Fourteenth Amendment to our Constitution.

NOTES

1. EEOC v. Inland Marine, 729 F.2d 1229, 1236 (9th Cir. 1984) (citing Lynn v. Regents of the University of California, 656 F.2d 1337, 1343 n.5 (9th Cir. 1981)), *cert. denied sub. nom.*, 469 U.S. 855 (1984).

2. Plessy v. Ferguson, 163 U.S. 537 (1896).

3. *See generally* RICHARD KLUGER, SIMPLE JUSTICE: THE HISTORY OF BROWN V. BOARD OF EDUCATION AND BLACK AMERICA'S STRUGGLE FOR EQUALITY (1975); CHARLES J. OGLETREE, JR., ALL DELIBERATE SPEED: REFLECTIONS ON THE FIRST HALF CENTURY OF BROWN V. BOARD OF EDUCATION 2004; Eva Paterson et al., *Breathing Life into Brown at Fifty: Lessons About Equal Justice*, 34 THE BLACK SCHOLAR 2 (2004).

4. Washington v. Davis, 426 U.S. 229, 239 (1976).

5. *Id.* at 235 (citation omitted).

6. *Id.* at 236. The test was implemented in the "immediate context of pressures to desegregate a previously White force[.]" See Ian F. Haney Lopez, *Institutional Racism: Judicial Conduct and a New Theory of Racial Discrimination*, 109 YALE L.J. 1717, 1833 (2000).

7. Davis v. Washington, 512 F.2d 956, 959 (D.C. Cir. 1975) ("Among the applicants tested in the District of Columbia from 1968 through 1971, 57% of the blacks failed the test, as compared to a failure rate of 13% for whites.").

8. *Id.* at 960.

9. *Id.* at 961.

10. *Davis,* 426 U.S. at 229. *See also* Village of Arlington Heights v. Metropolitan Housing Corp., 429 U.S. 252, 265 (1977) ("Proof of racially discriminatory intent or purpose is required to show a violation of the Equal Protection Clause."). According to the United States Supreme Court, "official action will not be held unconstitutional solely because it results in a racially disproportionate impact. 'Disproportionate impact is not irrelevant, but it is not the sole touchstone of an invidious racial discrimination.'" *Id.* at 264–65 (citing *Davis,* 426 U.S. at 242).

11. The District of Columbia Court of Appeals found that the African American recruits had made a sufficient showing of disparate impact:

> The disparity disclosed in this case—more than four to one—is larger than differences held sufficiently disproportionate in other cases. Indeed, absent evidence revealing some other reason for the lopsided failure rates appearing here, it is difficult to imagine how disproportionate effect could ever be better demonstrated. . . . This phenomenon is the result of the long history of educational deprivation, primarily due to segregated schools, for blacks. Until arrival of the day when the effects of that deprivation have been completely dissipated, comparable performance on such tests can hardly be expected.

Davis, 512 F.2d at 960.

12. *See* Anne Gearan, *Justices Back Ohio Town's Housing Fight,* PHILADELPHIA INQUIRER, Mar. 26, 2003, at A3.

13. See Gilbertson Barno, *The Fight over Low-Income Housing: A First-Person Account by the Cuyahoga Falls Nonprofit Developer at the Eye of the Storm,* Shelterforce Online, Issue 131, Sept./Oct. 2003, available at http://www.nhi.org/online/issues/131/cuyahogavbuckeye.html.

14. Buckeye Community Hope Foundation v. City of Cuyahoga Falls, 263 F.3d 627, 631 (6th Cir. 2001).

15. Buckeye also alleged violations of the Fair Housing Act and due process. City of Cuyahoga Falls v. Buckeye Community Hope Foundation, 538 U.S. 188, 193 (2003).

16. *Buckeye,* 538 U.S. at 188.

17. *Id.* at 195–96.

18. In McCleskey v. Kemp, 482 U.S. 920 (1987), for example, the Court denied a defendant's equal protection claim despite overwhelming evidence of racially discriminatory treatment of criminal defendants subject to the death penalty in Georgia. The Court placed a virtually impossible burden on the defendant by requiring proof that the death penalty statute was enacted intentionally to discriminate against African Americans. The Supreme Court's restrictive intent standard also has been employed to limit minority protections against discrimination

in other areas of the law. Eric K. Yamamoto, Susan K. Serrano, et al., *Dismantling Civil Rights: Multiracial Resistance And Reconstruction*, 31 Cumb. L. Rev. 523, 546–47 (2000–2001).

19. Linda Hamilton Krieger, *The Content of Our Categories: A Cognitive Bias Approach to Discrimination and Equal Employment Opportunity*, 47 Stan. L. Rev. 1161, 1187–88 (1995. *See also* Chin v. Runnels, 343 F.Supp.2d 891, 906 (2004) ("There is also increasing recognition of the natural human tendency to categorize information and engage in generalizations, of which stereotyping is a part, as a means of processing the huge amount of information confronting individuals on a daily basis; these unconscious processes can lead to biased perceptions and decision-making even in the absence of conscious animus or prejudice against any particular group.").

20. *See* Rose Cuison Villazor, *Community Lawyering: An Approach to Addressing Inequalities in Access to Health Care for Poor, of Color and Immigrant Communities*, 8 N.Y.U. J. Legis. & Pub. Pol'y 35, 40 (2004–2005); Vernellia R. Randall, *Racial Discrimination in Health Care in the United States as a Violation of the International Convention on the Elimination of All Forms of Racial Discrimination*, 14 U. Fla. J.L. & Pub. Pol'y 45, 51 (2002); Kim Forde-Mazrui, *Taking Conservatives Seriously: A Moral Justification for Affirmative Action and Reparations*, 92 Cal. L. Rev. 683, 696 (2004); Lisa C. Ikemoto, *Racial Disparities in Health Care and Cultural Competency*, 48 St. Louis U. L.J. 75 (2003); William Bradford, *"With a Very Great Blame on Our Hearts": Reparations, Reconciliation, and an American Indian Plea for Peace with Justice*, 27 Am. Indian L. Rev. 1, 14 n.54 (2002–2003); Chris Iijima, *Race over Rice: Binary Analytical Boxes and A Twenty-First Century Endorsement of Nineteenth Century Imperialism in Rice v. Cayetano*, 53 Rutgers L. Rev. 91, 119 n.144 (2000); Marianne Engelman Lado, *Unfinished Agenda: The Need for Civil Rights Litigation to Address Race Discrimination and Inequalities in Health Care Delivery*, 6 Tex. F. on C.L. & C.R. 1 (2001); Angela Onwuachi-Willig, *Volunteer Discrimination*, 40 U.C. Davis L. Rev. 1895 (2007); Kevin R. Johnson, *The Case for African American and Latina/o Cooperation in Challenging Racial Profiling in Law Enforcement*, 55 Fla. L. Rev. 341, 344 (2003).

21. Both courts and legal scholars have advanced a number of approaches based on this impressive body of empirical and theoretical research. One approach, articulated by the federal district court in *Chin v. Runnels*, asks "whether unconscious stereotyping or biases may have contributed to the exclusion of groups notwithstanding the best of intentions of those involved." Chin v. Runnels, 343 F.Supp.2d 891, 906 (N.D. Cal. 2004). Another approach urges taking into account whether governmental actors within organizational structures have unintentionally acted according to established, taken-for-granted institutional norms and practices, as if following "scripts" or "paths." *See* Ian F. Haney Lopez, *Institutional Racism: Judicial Conduct and a New Theory of Racial Discrimination*, 109 Yale L.J. 1717 (2000). Invoking "New Institutionalism," Professor Ian

Haney Lopez describes how he "advances[s] an institutional analysis in which organizational actors follow elaborate scripts, spontaneously triggered complexes of behavior," and also "argue[s] that even when specific scripts do not develop or are not followed, paths come into play, unexamined background understandings that effectively specify the range of legitimate action." *Id.* at 1725. Yet another approach includes an examination into whether a racial group's historical advantage has become "locked in" or "self-reinforcing, even in the absence of intentional discrimination." *See* Daria Roithmayr, *Locked In Segregation*, 12 Va. J. Soc. Pol'y & L. 197, 241 (2004). Finally, an approach entails inquiring into whether the culture attaches racial significance to a particular governmental action in order to uncover unconscious racism deeply ingrained in our culture. *See* Charles R. Lawrence III, *The Id, The Ego, and Equal Protection: Reckoning with Unconscious Racism*, 39 Stan. L. Rev. 317 (1987). There are a number of other approaches suggested by legal scholars that are not discussed here. *See, e.g.,* Rachel D. Godsil, *Expressivism, Empathy and Equality*, 36 U. Mich. J.L. Reform 247 (2003) (articulating an "expressive harm test that requires the court to determine the expressive content of the government action by discerning how a reasonable member of the allegedly affected community would view the action will invite the judge to empathize with the community rather than the allegedly discriminating government actor.").

22. The following four paragraphs are drawn substantially from Yamamoto, Serrano, et al., *supra* note 18.

23. Brown v. Board of Education, 347 U.S. 483 (1954).

24. *See* Angela P. Harris, *Equality Trouble: Sameness and Difference in Twentieth-Century Race Law*, 88 Calif. L. Rev. 1923, 1987–88 (2000) ("The end of the war sparked a new activism in groups considered nonwhite. Returning African American and Mexican American troops found Jim Crow impossible to stomach after having served their country with honor and distinction, and often after having been treated as equals by white Europeans. In the post-war period, anti-racist activists, working both through local, grass roots groups and national organizations like the League of United Latin American Citizens (LULAC) and the National Association for the Advancement of Colored People (NAACP) began to campaign vigorously to end American apartheid."); *Brown v. Board of Education, supra. See also* Richard Kluger, Simple Justice: The History of Brown v. Board of Education and Black America's Struggle for Equality (1975). *See also* Manning Marable, Race, Reform and Rebellion: The Second Reconstruction in America, 1945–1990 (1991) ("The Second Reconstruction was a series of massive confrontations concerning the status of African-American and other national minorities (e.g., Indians, Chicanos, Puerto Ricans, Asians) in the nation's economic, social and political institutions.").

25. Yamamoto, Serrano, et al., *supra* note 18, at 538–39. *See generally* Harris, *supra* note 24, at 1989–96.

26. Yamamoto, Serrano, et al., *supra* note 18, at 539 (citing DERRICK BELL, RACE, RACISM AND AMERICAN LAW 170, 278 (4th ed. 2000)). A year later, however, the Court issued a separate ruling in *Brown II*, 349 U.S. 294 (1955), directing the enforcement of *Brown I's* desegregation decree with "all deliberate speed," essentially permitting Southern whites to resist the requirements of *Brown I. Id.* at 167–70. *See also* Harris, *supra* note 24, at 1991 (describing how the Court during this period also outlawed racially restrictive covenants, restricted the states' ability persecute civil rights organizations and demonstrators, held unconstitutional anti-Asian land laws, and prohibited antimiscegenation statutes)

27. Yamamoto, Serrano, et al., *supra* note 18, at 539–40 (citing Harris, *supra* note 24, at 1994). *See, e.g.,* Griggs v. Duke Power Co., 401 U.S. 424 (1971) (Title VII prohibits neutral employment practices in disparate impact cases if those practices operate to maintain the status quo of prior discrimination); Guardians Assn. v. Civil Service Com'n of City of New York, 463 U.S. 582 (1983)(administrative regulations implementing Title VI of the Civil Rights Act were valid and, accordingly, Title VI reached unintentional, disparate-impact discrimination as well as deliberate racial discrimination).

28. *See* Harris, *supra* note 24, at 1989–96. *See also* Luke Charles Harris & Uma Narayan, *Affirmative Action as Equalizing Opportunity: Challenging the Myth of Preferential Treatment,* 16 NAT'L BLACK L.J. 127, 131–32 (1999–2000) (reporting that "the proportion of employed Blacks who hold middle class jobs rose from 13.4 percent in 1960 to 37.8 percent in 1981 . . . and that [t]he number of Black college students rose from 340,000 in 1966 to more than one million in 1982.") (citing ROBERT BLAUNER, BLACK LIVES, WHITE LIVES: THREE DECADES OF RACE RELATIONS IN AMERICA (1989); Harris, *supra* note 24, at 1995 (2000) (observing that "[t]he creation and operation of affirmative action programs, both voluntary and involuntary, contributed to a surge of people of color into areas of employment and higher education from which they had previously been excluded."); Kevin R. Johnson, *Civil Rights and Immigration: Challenges for the Latino Community in the Twenty-First Century,* 8 LA RAZA L.J. 42, 80–81 (1995) (discussing the impact of the 1965 repeal of national origin quotas in U.S. immigration law on the racial and ethnic communities of the U.S.) (citing, *inter alia,* U.S. Dep't of Justice, *1992 Statistical Yearbook of the Immigration and Naturalization Service* 27-28 (1993)); U.S. Department of Justice, *Introduction, The Federal Death Penalty System: A Statistical Survey* (1988–2000) (stating that "[t]he Supreme Court issued a ruling in 1972 that had the effect of invalidating capital punishment throughout the United States—both in the federal criminal justice system and in all the states that then provided for the death penalty") (referring to Furman v. Georgia, 408 U.S. 238 (1972)).

29. *See* JEAN STEFANCIC & RICHARD DELGADO, NO MERCY: HOW CONSERVATIVE THINK TANKS AND FOUNDATIONS CHANGED AMERICA'S SOCIAL

Agenda 139–154 (1996); Lee Cokorinos, Assault on Diversity: An Organized Challenge to Racial and Gender Justice (2003).

30. *See Davis,* 426 U.S. at 242–44. It is significant that neither party addressed the issue of "intent" in their briefs to the Supreme Court. *See* Brief for Petitioner, in *Washington v. Davis* (No. 74–1492); Brief for Respondent, *Washington v. Davis* (No. 74–1492).

31. *Davis,* 426 U.S. at 248.

32. Personnel Adm'r of Massachusetts v. Feeney, 442 U.S. 256, 279 (1979).

33. *Id.* (emphasis added) ("'Discriminatory purpose' . . . implies more than intent as volition or intent as awareness of consequences. . . . It implies that the decisionmaker . . . selected or reaffirmed a particular course of action at least in part 'because of,' not merely 'in spite of,' its adverse effects upon an identifiable group.'"). "Proof of racially discriminatory intent or purpose is required to show a violation of the Equal Protection Clause." Village of Arlington Heights v. Metropolitan Housing Corp., 429 U.S. 252, 265 (1977). According to this Court, "official action will not be held unconstitutional solely because it results in a racially disproportionate impact. 'Disproportionate impact is not irrelevant, but it is not the sole touchstone of an invidious racial discrimination.'" *Id.* at 264–65 (citing *Washington v. Davis,* 426 U.S. at 242). Determining whether racial discrimination was a motivating factor demands a "sensitive inquiry" into both circumstantial and direct evidence. *See Arlington Heights,* 429 U.S. at 266. As part of its inquiry, a court considers, *inter alia,* (1) disparate impact; (2) the historical background of the decision, particularly if it reveals a series of official actions taken for invidious purposes; (3) the specific sequence of events leading up to the challenged decision; (4) departures from the normal procedural sequence; (5) substantive departures, particularly if the factors usually considered important by the decision maker strongly favor a decision contrary to the one reached; and (6) the legislative or administrative history, especially where there are contemporary statements by members of the decision-making body, minutes of meetings, reports, etc. *See Arlington Heights,* 429 U.S. at 267–68.

34. Bell, *supra* note 26, at 136–144.

35. Lawrence, *supra* note 21, at 319.

36. *See* Brief *Amici Curiae* of the Coalition for Economic Equity, the Santa Clara University School of Law Center for Social Justice and Public Service, the Justice Collective, the Charles Houston Bar Association, and the California Association of Black Lawyers in Support of Respondents, in *Grutter v. Bollinger,* No. 02–241, at 9 (citing Grutter v. Bollinger, 288 F.3d 732, 765 (6th Cir. 2002) (Clay, J., concurring); *Grutter,* 539 U.S. 306 (2003). *See also* Eric Schnapper, *Affirmative Action and the Legislative History of the Fourteenth Amendment,* 71 Va. L. Rev. 753, 754 (1985) (history "strongly suggests that the framers of the [fourteenth] amendment could not have intended it generally to prohibit affirmative action for

blacks or other disadvantaged groups."); Cass R. Sunstein, *The Anticaste Principle*, 92 MICH. L. REV. 2410, 2435 (1994) ("An important purpose of the Civil War Amendments was the attack on racial caste.") (quoting Cong. Globe, 39th Cong., 1st Sess. 2766 (1866)).

37. *See* Expert Report of Eric Foner, Gratz v. Bollinger, No. 97–75321 (E.D. Mich.), Grutter v. Bollinger, No. 97–75928 (E.D. Mich.), *reprinted in* 5 MICH. J. RACE & L. 311, 312 (1999). ("while the nation has made great progress in eradicating the 'color line,' the legacy of slavery and segregation remains alive in numerous aspects of American society."); *Adarand*, 515 U.S. at 273 (Ginsburg, J., dissenting) ("discrimination's lingering effects . . . , reflective of a system of racial caste only recently ended, are evident in our workplaces, markets, and neighborhoods.").

38. Yamamoto, Serrano, et al., *supra* note 18, at 529.

39. *The Rehnquist Court*, STANFORD LAWYER, Spring 2005, at 33, available at http://www.law.stanford.edu/publications/lawyer/issues/72/sl72_TheRehnquistCourt.pdf (quoting Larry Kramer).

40. *Buckeye*, 263 F.3d at 636. According to news reports and editorials, residents of Prescott Commons, an upscale condominium project, were among those who expressed strong opposition to the project. See *Just Follow the Rules: Opponents of Auto Mall Might Recall Another Such Fight*, AKRON BEACON JOURN., June 19, 2000, at A8. *See also* Anne Gearan, *Justices Back Ohio Town's Housing Fight*, PHILADELPHIA INQUIRER, Mar. 26, 2003, at A3.

41. Buckeye Community Hope Foundation v. City of Cuyahoga Falls, 209 F.Supp.2d 719, 728 (N.D. Ohio 1999).

42. *Buckeye*, 263 F.3d at 631.

43. See Craig Webb, *Falls Racism Case Reaches Highest Court—Delay in Construction of Low-Income Housing: Bias Or Due Process?*, AKRON BEACON JOURN., Jan. 20, 2003, at A1.

44. P. Gilbertson Barno, *The Fight over Low-Income Housing: A First-Person Account by the Cuyahoga Falls Nonprofit Developer at the Eye of the Storm*, SHELTERFORCE ONLINE, Issue #131, September/October 2003; *Unpleasant Meadows: A Development Battle Exposes the Racial Divide in Cuyahoga Falls—Where Today's Ally Is Tomorrow's Enemy*," SCENE ENTERTAINMENT WEEKLY, Oct. 30, 2002.

45. *Unpleasant Meadows, supra* note 44.

46. In July 1996, Buckeye filed suit in federal court, alleging violations of the Fair Housing Act, the Equal Protection Clause of the Fourteenth Amendment, and the Due Process Clause of the Fourteenth Amendment. *Buckeye*, 209 F.Supp.2d at 723–24. In June 1997, the federal district court granted in part and denied in part preliminary summary judgment motions in the case. *Buckeye*, 209 F.Supp.2d at 724 (citing *Buckeye*, 970 F.Supp.1289 (1997)). The court ruled that Buckeye had no non-race-based equal protection claim and that the city mayor was entitled to qualified immunity in his individual capacity. 970 F.Supp. at 1322.

The claims that survived the court's first ruling were Buckeye's equal protection, Fair Housing Act, and substantive due process claims. *Buckeye,* 209 F.Supp.2d at 724. Buckeye also filed suit in state court in May 1996 to enjoin the referendum process, arguing that under the Ohio Constitution, the ordinance could not be challenged by referendum because its passage by the city council was an administrative, rather than a legislative, act. The Ohio Supreme Court ultimately declared the referendum invalid on those grounds. Buckeye Community Hope Foundation v. City of Cuyahoga Falls, 697 N.E.2d 181, 186 (Ohio 1998).

47. The district court dismissed Buckeye's equal protection, Fair Housing Act, and substantive due process claims. *Buckeye,* 209 F.Supp.2d at 731. The court did, however, recognize that "The mission of the Buckeye Community Foundation is to provide affordable housing to persons in low-income brackets. Racial minorities and families with small children constitute a significant portion of this bracket." *Id.* at 730.

48. *Buckeye,* 263 F.3d at 639.

49. *Arlington Heights,* 429 U.S. at 265.

50. *Buckeye,* 263 F.3d at 636.

51. *Id.*

52. *Id.* at 639.

53. *Buckeye,* 538 U.S. at 195. The Court also held that "the City Engineer, in refusing to issue the building permits while the referendum was still pending, performed a nondiscretionary, ministerial act." *Id.* For purposes of this chapter, the dissent refers to the Court's opinion as the "majority" opinion, even though the Court's opinion in the case was unanimous.

54. *Id.*

55. *Id.* at 196–97.

56. *Id.* at 196. Buckeye dropped its Fair Housing claim because it was "concerned that the conservative Supreme Court would use the case to declare that a violation of the act could be established only by proof of intentional discrimination, and not merely by evidence of a disproportionate ill effect on minority groups." See Michael Allen, *No Shelter in the Storm: The Supreme Court Hands NIMBY Forces a Powerful Weapon,* Shelterforce Online, Issue #131, September/October 2003, available at http://www.nhi.org/online/issues/131/shelterinstorm.html.

57. *Buckeye,* 538 U.S. at 195.

58. Roithmayr, *supra* note 21, at 241 (2004).

59. The Supreme Court has severely limited the reach of the Equal Protection Clause, except in cases in which whites claim "reverse discrimination." *See* Adarand Constructors, Inc. v. Pena, 515 U.S. 200 (1995); City of Richmond v. J.A. Croson Co., 488 U.S. 469 (1989); Eric K. Yamamoto, Carly Minner & Karen Winter, *Contextual Strict Scrutiny,* 49 How. L.J. 241, 247 (2006). *See also* Sylvia A. Law, *White Privilege and Affirmative Action,* 32 Akron L. Rev. 603 (1999);

Barbara J. Flagg, *"Was Blind, But Now I See"*: *White Race Consciousness and the Requirement of Discriminatory Intent*, 91 MICH. L. REV. 953 (1993).

60. Krieger, *supra* note 19, at 1187–88. *See also* Chin v. Runnels, 343 F.Supp.2d 891, 906 (2004); Anthony Page, *Batson's Blind-Spot: Unconscious Stereotyping and the Peremptory Challenge*, 85 B.U. L. REV. 155, 186 (2005); Linda Hamilton Krieger and Susan T. Fiske, *Behavioral Realism in Employment Discrimination Law: Implicit Bias and Disparate Treatment*, 94 CAL. L. REV. 997, 1004 (2006).

61. Lawrence, *supra* note 21, at 323. Professor Lawrence posits that:

The theory of cognitive psychology states that the culture—including, for example, the media and an individual's parents, peers, and authority figures—transmits certain beliefs and preferences. Because these beliefs are so much a part of the culture, they are not experienced as explicit lessons. Instead, they seem part of the individual's rational ordering of her perceptions of the world. The individual is unaware, for example, that the ubiquitous presence of a cultural stereotype has influenced her perception that blacks are lazy or unintelligent. Because racism is so deeply ingrained in our culture, it is likely to be transmitted by tacit understandings: Even if a child is not told that blacks are inferior, he learns that lesson by observing the behavior of others. These tacit understandings, because they have never been articulated, are less likely to be experienced at a conscious level.

62. Gary Blasi, *Advocacy Against the Stereotype: Lessons from Cognitive Social Psychology*, 49 UCLA L. REV. 1241, 1275 (2002).

63. Jerry Kang, *Trojan Horses of Race*, 118 HARV. L. REV. 1489, 1490 (2005).

64. Krieger, *supra* note 19, at 1187–90 (citing Eleanor Rosch, *Human Categorization*, in STUDIES IN CROSS-CULTURAL PSYCHOLOGY 1, 1–2 (Neil Warren ed., 1977); David E. Rumelhart, *Schemata and the Cognitive System*, in 1 HANDBOOK OF SOCIAL COGNITION 167 (Robert S. Wyer, Jr., & Thomas K. Srull eds., 1984)).

65. J. Brown, S. Subrin, and P. Baumann, *Some Thoughts About Social Perception And Employment Discrimination Law: A Modest Proposal for Reopening the Judicial Dialogue*, 46 EMORY L.J. 1487 (1997).

66. *Id.*

67. *Id.* at 1494 (citing SUSAN T. FISKE & SHELLEY E. TAYLOR, SOCIAL COGNITION 11 (1984)).

68. *Id. See also* Krieger, *supra* note 19, at 1187–88.

69. *Id.* (citing Richard E. Nisbett & Timothy DeCamp Wilson, *Telling More Than We Can Know: Verbal Reports on Mental Processes*, 84 PSYCHOL. REV. 231, 231–59 (1977)). *See also* Anthony G. Greenwald and Linda Hamilton Krieger, *Implicit Bias: Scientific Foundations*, 94 CAL. L. REV. 945, 946 (2006).

70. Krieger, *supra* note 19, at 1188. Applying cognitive psychology, Professor Krieger examines the assumptions about human inference embedded in current disparate treatment theory and questions the premise that discrimination necessarily manifests an intent or motive. She suggests that a large number of biased

employment decisions result not from discriminatory motivation but from a variety of unintentional categorization-related judgment errors characterizing normal human functioning. *See also* John F. Dovidio & Samuel L. Gaertner, *Aversive Racism and Selection Decisions: 1989 and 1999*, 11 PSYCHOL. SCI. 315 (2000); John F. Dovidio et al., *Implicit and Explicit Prejudice and Interracial Interaction*, 82 J. PERSONALITY & SOC. PSYCHOL. 62 (2002); Allen R. McConnell & Jill M. Leibold, *Relations Among the Implicit Association Test, Discriminatory Behavior, and Explicit Measures Of Racial Attitudes*, 37 J. EXPERIMENTAL SOC. PSYCHOL. 435 (2001); Samuel R. Sommers & Phoebe C. Ellsworth, *White Juror Bias: An Investigation Of Prejudice Against Black Defendants in the American Courtroom*, 7 PSYCHOL. PUB. POL'Y & L. 201 (2001); Steven J. Spencer et al., *Automatic Activation of Stereotypes: The Role Of Self-Image Threat*, 24 PERSONALITY & SOC. PSYCHOL. BULL. 1139 (1998); Gary Blasi, *Advocacy Against the Stereotype: Lessons from Cognitive Social Psychology*, 49 UCLA L. Rev. 1241 (2002); Jerry Kang, *supra* note 63, at 1489.

71. Krieger, *supra* note 19, at 1187–88 (citing W. Edgar Vinacke, *Stereotypes as Social Concepts*, 45 J. SOC. PSYCHOL. 229, 241 (1957)).

72. *Id.* at 1199.

73. *Id.* at 1188, 1200 (citing Shelley E. Taylor & Jennifer Crocker, *Schematic Bases of Social Information*, in 1 SOCIAL COGNITION 89 (E. Tory Higgins, C. Peter Herman, & Mark P. Zanna eds., 1981)). "For example, when meeting someone for the first time, individuals rely on categories and distinctions already at their disposal, rather than actively formulating new ones. Once individuals perceive that the person they are meeting belongs to a specific social group, their reactions may be dominated by this single characteristic; and they may fail to notice other important facts about the person." Judith Olans Brown, Stephen N. Subrin, & Phyllis Tropper Baumann, *Some Thoughts About Social Perception and Employment Discrimination Law: A Modest Proposal for Reopening the Judicial Dialogue*, 46 EMORY L.J. 1487, 1495 (1997) (citing ELLEN J. LANGER, THE PSYCHOLOGY OF CONTROL 135–36 (1983). See also Kang, *supra* note 63, at 1499 ("We employ schemas out of necessity. Our senses are constantly bombarded by environmental stimuli, which must be processed, then encoded into memories (short- and/or long-term) in some internal representation.").

74. Kang, *supra* note 63, at 1504. Once an individual is "assigned to a racial category, implicit and explicit racial meanings associated with that category are triggered. These activated racial meanings then influence our interpersonal interaction." *Id.* at 1499.

75. Krieger, *supra* note 19, at 1192 (citing Edward E. Jones, George C. Wood, & George A Quattrone, *Perceived Variability of Personal Characteristics in In-Groups and Out-Groups: The Role of Knowledge and Evaluation*, 7 PERSONALITY & SOC. PSYCHOL. BULL. 523, 523–24 (1981) (other citations omitted)).

76. *See* Brown, Subrin, & Baumann, *supra* note 65, at 1494 (citing John C. Turner, *Towards a Cognitive Redefinition of the Social Group*, in SOCIAL IDENTITY

AND INTERGROUP RELATIONS 17, 30 (Henri Tajfel ed., 1982)). Empirically, however, not all groups show ingroup bias. Studies show that whites show substantial implicit ingroup bias but that "racial minorities show [two] impulses: to favor not only their ingroup . . . but also those on top of the racial hierarchy— Whites." Kang, *supra* note 63 at 1532–34.

77. *See generally* Krieger, *supra* note 19, at 1192; Kang, *supra* note 63, at 1512. "'Illusory correlation,' another cognitive strategy, refers to an individual's tendency to perceive relationships between variables that do not, in fact, exist. . . . For example, cab drivers often refuse to pick up African American riders because of previous bad personal experiences. The driver makes a decision to reject the passenger based on the only information he has other than his past experience: the race of the person flagging the cab. This type of processing facilitates the formation of stereotypes, promotes negative attitudes between groups, generates inappropriate expectations, and leads to dehumanization of outgroup members." Brown, Subrin, and Baumann, *supra* note 65, at 1495–96.

78. Kang, *supra* note 63, at 1514.

79. The IAT "examines how tightly any two concepts are associated with each other." See Kang, *supra* note 63, at 1510.

80. Susan Kiyomi Serrano, *Rethinking Race for Strict Scrutiny Purposes: Yniguez and the Racialization of English Only*, 19 U. HAW. L. REV. 221, 245 (1997) (citing MICHAEL OMI & HOWARD WINANT, RACIAL FORMATION IN THE UNITED STATES: FROM THE 1960S TO THE 1990S 60 (2d. ed. 1994)).

81. *Id. (citing* PATRICIA J. WILLIAMS, THE ALCHEMY OF RACE AND RIGHTS 85–88 (1991); WILLIAM WEI, THE ASIAN AMERICAN MOVEMENT 48 (1993); RONALD TAKAKI, A DIFFERENT MIRROR (1993); MICHAEL OMI & HOWARD WINANT, RACIAL FORMATION IN THE UNITED STATES: FROM THE 1960S TO THE 1990S 59 (2d. ed. 1994)).

82. *Id.* (citing Eric K. Yamamoto, *Critical Race Praxis: Race Theory and Political Lawyering Practice in Post–Civil Rights America*, 95 Mich. L. Rev. 821 (1997)).

83. *Id.*

84. *Buckeye*, 263 F.3d at 630.

85. *See* Anne Gearan, *Justices Back Ohio Town's Housing Fight*, PHILADELPHIA INQUIRER, Mar. 26, 2003, at A3.

86. Brown, Subrin, & Baumann, *supra* note 65, at 1496.

87. *Id.* at 1497.

88. An increasing number of courts have recognized this phenomenon. *See EEOC v. Inland Marine*, 729 F.2d 1229, 1236 (9th Cir. 1984) ("In today's world, racial discrimination sometimes wears a benign mask[, and] "[c]urrent practices, though harmless in appearance, may hide subconscious attitudes . . . and perpetuate the effects of past discriminatory practices[.]") (citation omitted); Lynn v. Regents of the University of California, 656 F.2d 1337, 1343 n.5 (9th Cir. 1981)), *cert. denied sub. nom.*, 469 U.S. 855 (1984); *Chin*, 343 F.Supp.2d at 906

("subjective decision-making allows for subtle biases or unconscious stereotyping to affect selection processes."); Gonzalez-Rivera v. INS, 22 F.3d 1441, 1450 (9th Cir. 1994) ("[a]s we have recognized in prior cases, racial stereotypes often infect our decision-making processes only subconsciously"), *reh'rg denied*, 37 F.3d 1421 (9th Cir. 1994); *United States v. Bishop*, 959 F.2d 820, 826–28 (9th Cir. 1992) (acknowledging that racism often affects decision-making subconsciously); *Regents of the University of California*, 656 F.2d at 1343 n.5 (the subtlety of discriminatory attitudes "does not . . . make the impact less significant or less unlawful. It serves only to make the courts' task of scrutinizing attitudes and motivation, in order to determine the true reason for [the] decision[], more exacting."); Thomas v. Eastman Kodak Co., 183 F.3d 38, 57 (1st Cir. 1999) ("The concept of 'stereotyping' includes not only simple beliefs such as 'women are not aggressive' but also a host of more subtle cognitive phenomena which can skew perceptions and judgments."), *cert. denied*, 120 S. Ct. 1174 (2000); Bush v. Commonwealth Edison Co., 990 F.2d 928, 931–32 (7th Cir. 1993) (considering whether plaintiff produced evidence adequate to show that the employer's subjective determinations "reflected unconscious racial bias"), *cert. denied*, 511 U.S. 1071 (1994); McNeil v. McDonough, 515 F. Supp. 113, 129 (D.N.J. 1980) ("intent . . . is not by any means confined to actual, subjective, individual intent of a purposeful nature. It refers to the legal concept of intent which also embraces *subconscious and institutional intent* as well as an intent inferred from purposeful adherence to some direction or course of action even after an invidious discriminatory effect has been shown to follow from what may have been wholly innocent conduct.") (emphasis added).

89. Iris Marion Young, Justice and the Politics of Difference 41 (1991).

90. Lopez, *supra* note 21, at 1770 (citing Paul J. DiMaggio & Walter W. Powell, Introduction to The New Institutionalism in Organizational Analysis 1, 22–27 (Walter W. Powell & Paul J. DiMaggio eds., 1991)).

91. Lopez, *supra* note 21, at 1827.

92. *Id.*

93. *Id.* at 1723 (citing Peter L. Berger & Thomas Luckmann, The Social Construction of Reality: A Treatise in the Sociology of Knowledge 54 (1966)). Research in "New Institutionalism" theory also demonstrates that "routinized sequences of behavior eventually come to define normalcy, or more broadly, reality. Established constellations of action are seen but not noticed, relied upon but not considered, to such an extent that they become natural— 'the world of daily life known in common with others and with others taken for granted.'" Lopez, *supra* note 21, at 1723. See also Michael Brown et al., Whitewashing Race: The Myth of a Colorblind Society (2003).

94. Roithmayr, *supra* note 21, at 202 (introducing a "lock-in model of racial inequality" that compares "persistent racial disparity to persistent monopoly power

that continues long after the original anti-competitive conduct has ceased."). According to Professor Roithmayr, "the lock-in model better incorporates the latest empirical research in economics and sociology on the racially stratified effects of neighborhood social capital on family assets" as well as "research by education scholars on the links between school funding and family wealth, and research by labor economists on the racial stratification of social networks in referral-based hiring." *Id.* at 250.

95. *Id.*

96. *Id.* at 253.

97. *Id.* at 245–46.

98. *Inland Marine*, 729 F.3d at 1233 (emphasis added).

99. *Id.* at 1234 (emphasis added). See also *Chin*, 343 F.Supp.2d at 891.

100. *Chin, supra.*

101. *Id.* at 906–7 (*citing* Eric K. Yamamoto, Susan K. Serrano, et al., *Dismantling Civil Rights: Multiracial Resistance and Reconstruction*, 31 CUMB. L. REV. 523, 562–65 (2000); Linda Hamilton Krieger, *The Content of Our Categories: A Cognitive Bias Approach to Discrimination and Equal Employment Opportunity*, 47 STAN. L. REV. 1161 (1995); John Barth, *Conditional Automaticity: Varieties of Automatic Influence in Social Perception and Cognition, in* UNINTENDED THOUGHT 3 (James S. Uleman & John A. Bargh eds., 1989)).

102. *Chin*, 343 F. Supp. 2d at 906.

103. *See* Lopez, *supra* note 21 at 1831 ("[t]he question of what racism the law should address, and what it should permit and by implication sanction, requires not just an understanding of racism, but also a vision of law's role in the achievement of social justice.").

104. *See supra* note 46.

105. Pleasant Meadows was completed in 2000. *Supra* note 44.

106. *See* Serrano, *supra* note 80, at 248. *See also* Lawrence, *supra* note 21, at 356.

107. *Buckeye*, 209 F.Supp.2d at 730 (acknowledging that repeal of the Ordinance approving development of the low-income housing site had a disparate effect on racial minorities and families with small children); *Buckeye*, 263 F.3d at 635–36.

108. Lawrence, *supra* note 21, at 358–59.

109. *Id.* at 355–56.

110. *Id.* at 356.

111. *See* Michaell Crews-Yancey, *Should Disparate Impact Claims Be Allowed Against Municipal Corporations in Its Use of Initiative and Referendum Power as to Low or Moderate-Income Housing Projects?*, 4 J. L. SOCIETY 415, 441–42 (2003) ("attempts at proving the discriminatory intent of municipalities in utilizing its initiative and referendum power against low or moderate-income housing are not likely to succeed because if racial exclusion is the "real" reason motivating

its action, this will never be stated directly. Instead, as demonstrated in the Sixth Circuit opinion in Buckeye, code words can be developed and employed in order to cover up any improper motives. Anyone who is a property owner can relate to legitimate concerns regarding safety or property values and declaration of such factors will rarely, if ever, be taken at face value as racially discriminatory.").

112. *Buckeye*, 263 F.3d at 636.

113. *Id.*

114. Lawrence, *supra* note 21.

115. *Id.* at 369.

116. *Id.* at 366–67.

117. *Id.* at 366.

118. *Id.* at 366–67 (In addition, a court could review "[s]tudies of racially segregated housing patterns throughout the United States . . . as well as data and attitudinal surveys on residential segregation and 'white flight' . . . which have indicated that collective and individual tolerances for black neighbors vary from community to community. While they ascribe the intolerance to different causes, they agree substantially on the prominence of race in the minds of both those who flee and those who stay. They also note whites' continuing aversion to housing integration.").

119. Roithmayr, *supra* note 21, at 240.

120. *Id.* at 240–41.

121. *Id.* at 257.

122. 970 F.Supp. at 1311.

123. *Buckeye*, 263 F.3d at 635.

124. *See Inland Marine*, 729 F.2d at 1234.

125. *See* Brief *Amici Curiae* of the Coalition for Economic Equity, the Santa Clara University School of Law Center for Social Justice and Public Service, the Justice Collective, the Charles Houston Bar Association, and the California Association of Black Lawyers in Support of Respondents, in *Grutter v. Bollinger*, No. 02–241, at 4; Yamamoto, Serrano, et al., *supra* note 18, at 540.

126. *Id.* at 566.

4

United States v. Whren

The Fourth Amendment Problem with Pretextual Traffic Stops

Tracey Maclin

The traffic violator is, of course, the easiest offender for the patrolman to apprehend and he can be apprehended in large numbers if departmental policies require it.[1]

Introduction

As late as the mid-1970s, police had unfettered discretion to stop a motorist who was obeying all the traffic laws to determine whether the motorist had a valid driver's license and vehicle registration. This practice was known as a "spot check" or random stop. Not surprisingly, such stops were often motivated by an officer's suspicion or hunch that the driver or an occupant of the vehicle was involved with unrelated criminal conduct.[2] Indeed, some police departments instructed officers that "'[s]pot checks' shall generally be made in connection with some minor violations *or other suspicious circumstance*."[3]

As a matter of legal principle, police no longer have unlimited authority to stop vehicles for license and registration checks. Every police officer (and almost every driver) knows that a car cannot be "pulled over" or stopped, unless there is probable cause to believe that the motorist has committed a traffic offense or reasonable suspicion that the motorist (or someone inside the vehicle) is involved in some other criminal conduct. In this context, "probable cause" means a good reason to believe that the motorist has violated the traffic code.

United States v. Whren[4] addressed a controversial Fourth Amendment question, whether it is legal for the police to use a traffic offense as a pretext to conduct a search for drugs. A unanimous Court ruled that the constitutional validity of a traffic stop does not depend on the actual motivations of the officers. Thus, police can use a minor traffic offense as a pretext to initiate a criminal investigation, even when officers have no intent to enforce the traffic code and lack a legitimate basis for suspecting that the motorist has committed a crime. In criminal procedure circles, this type of police seizure is known as a "pretext stop."[5]

Whren involved issues of racial profiling, traffic enforcement, and how much discretion police officers should have to initiate criminal investigations that intrude upon the liberty and privacy of motorists, even where they have no reasonable suspicion that a crime was committed. Despite these contentious issues, the Court made both the question and the result in *Whren* look easy. In doing so, the Court gave police officers carte blanche to use the traffic code as a means to initiate criminal investigations and to evade otherwise applicable Fourth Amendment safeguards designed to protect motorists from arbitrary police intrusions. As Wayne LaFave, the nation's foremost scholar on the Fourth Amendment, put it, "the Court managed to trivialize what in fact is an exceedingly important issue regarding a pervasive law enforcement practice."[6]

The Fourth Amendment protects against unreasonable searches and seizures by government officials. *Whren* decided whether a seizure of a "motorist who the police have probable cause to believe has committed a civil traffic violation is inconsistent with the Fourth Amendment's prohibition against seizures unless a reasonable officer would have been motivated to stop the car by a desire to enforce the traffic laws."[7] The Court ruled that when the police have probable cause to believe a motorist has violated traffic laws, a stop is always constitutionally reasonable.[8] The Court held that the subjective intent or motivation, including police motives based on racial stereotypes or bias, are irrelevant in this context.

The dissent presented in this chapter argues that the Fourth Amendment requires that when there is a departure from standard police procedure during a traffic stop and the stop becomes a pretext for a narcotics investigation, then the court should determine if the stop was objectively reasonable in the light of the totality of the circumstances that were present. Where the police actions were arbitrary or discriminatory, the court should conclude that the stop violated the motorist's Fourth Amendment rights.

Whren was significant for three reasons. First, the pretext claim raised by the defendants "touched on an issue of persistent ambiguity in constitutional criminal procedure–the relevance of a police officer's motivations."[9] Since 1932, the Court had sent conflicting signals as to the significance of an officer's subjective intent in determining whether a search or seizure was constitutional.[10] Language in some rulings indicated that pretextual searches and seizures were disfavored, if not unconstitutional. In one such case, decided in 1932, the Court commented that "[a]n arrest may not be used as a pretext to search for evidence."[11] For almost sixty years prior to *Whren*, the Court, as well as individual Justices, had intimated that police intrusions conducted with the intent to evade constitutional safeguards violated the Fourth Amendment's prohibition against unreasonable searches and seizures.[12]

More recently, however, the modern Court had questioned the wisdom and practicality of having Fourth Amendment issues turn on the subjective intent of police officers, particularly when trial courts rule on a contested search or seizure at a suppression hearing, inevitably occurring weeks or months after the actual search or seizure. By the late 1960s, some of the Justices believed that "sending state and federal courts on an expedition into the minds of police officers would produce grave and fruitless misallocation of judicial resources."[13] The Court's discomfort with inquiring into the minds of police officers is not unique to Fourth Amendment cases. Questions surrounding the "intent" of governmental actors are notoriously complex in constitutional settings, and the Court has been reluctant to have the results in constitutional cases turn on the subjective intent or motive of governmental actors.[14] This concern is especially pronounced in search-and-seizure scenarios because of the well-known difficulties in ascertaining a police officer's motive and because, in many cases, the Justices believe that bad motives should not invalidate searches or seizures that are objectively reasonable.

At the same time, even the conservative Justices of the Burger and Rehnquist Courts had issued opinions appearing to confine certain types of intrusions—inventory searches of cars and administrative searches of businesses, for example—to situations where there was no police bad faith or pretext.[15] Moreover, the same law-and-order Justices curtailed application of the exclusionary rule, requiring the suppression of criminal evidence obtained in violation of the Fourth Amendment, in cases where the police acted in "good faith" reliance that their conduct complied with constitutional requirements. If "conduct in violation of the Fourth Amendment need not result in suppression because of the 'good faith' of the police,"[16] then a plausible argument could be raised that the "bad faith" of the police should also matter.

In sum, prior to *Whren*, the Court had not definitively resolved when or whether an officer's motive or subjective intent matters in Fourth

Amendment cases. *Whren* gave the Court an opportunity to address one frequently occurring pretext scenario: using a traffic stop as a ruse for conducting a narcotics investigation.

The second important aspect of *Whren* concerned racial profiling. The defendants in *Whren* were African American; in addition, there was no objective evidence that the defendants were involved in narcotics activity. Throughout the proceedings, the defendants contended that police had stopped their car not because there was a legitimate basis for suspecting they were involved with narcotics but because they were black. In their Supreme Court brief, the defendants argued that racially biased traffic enforcement was pervasive on the nation's highways and streets. They contended that if a traffic violation always provides justification for stopping a motorist, police will abuse their power and use traffic offenses to evade otherwise applicable Fourth Amendment safeguards that prevent stopping and questioning motorists unless police have probable cause or reasonable suspicion that the motorist is engaged in criminal conduct.[17]

The defendants' assertions about racially motivated traffic enforcement were hardly novel; their claims had both empirical, as well as anecdotal, support. The targeting of black people for search and seizure predates the founding of the nation.[18] During the late 1700s, blacks, both slave and free, were targeted for searches and seizure solely because of their race, a phenomenon never experienced by white colonists.[19] In modern times, police departments across the country continue to target black motorists for selective traffic enforcement, hoping to discover evidence of criminal conduct. Evidence of this practice is not hard to find. Often, police officers provide the most convincing proof that black motorists are routinely selected for pretextual traffic stops. For example, in 1992, a Maryland State Police intelligence report warned troopers in Allegheny County to be alert for "dealers and couriers (traffickers) [who] are predominately black males and black females . . . utilizing Interstate 68."[20]

The year the Court decided *Whren*, other data and reports indicated that black motorists were targeted for pretextual traffic stops in various jurisdictions. A New Jersey trial court found that New Jersey state troopers had a "*de facto* policy" of targeting black motorists for investigation and arrest on the southern portion of the New Jersey Turnpike.[21] The *News & Observer*, a newspaper in Raleigh, North Carolina, conducted a study of the 1995 patrol records of the Special Emphasis Team of the North Carolina Highway Patrol, whose goal was to interdict narcotics through traffic stops on Interstate 85 and 95. The study found that the Team "charged black male drivers [with traffic offenses] at nearly twice the rate of other troopers working the same roads."[22] The study found that black male drivers received almost 45 percent of the traffic citations issued by the Team, while black male drivers received only 24.2 percent of the traffic citations issued by other North Carolina troopers patrolling the same highways. The report explained that an independent statistical expert believed that it was "'wildly improbable'" that two groups of troopers patrolling the same highways would produce such disparate results by chance.[23]

While the Court was deliberating in *Whren*, these and other statistical data provided *prima facie*, if not persuasive, evidence that police departments and individual officers across the country were targeting black (and sometimes Hispanic) motorists for unwarranted narcotics investigations under the guise of traffic enforcement. The combination of these reports, empirical and anecdotal, demonstrated large-scale, arbitrary, and biased police seizures across the nation. Tellingly, the decision in *Whren* did not question the defendants' claim that racial profiling had occurred in their case or was occurring nationwide.

The third important element of *Whren* concerned the practical aspects of traffic enforcement by the police. Prior to 1979, in many parts of the country, police were permitted to stop vehicles operating on roadways to check the registration of the vehicle and the license of the driver without having observed a traffic infraction.[24] Moreover, many of these so-called spot checks or random stops were far from random. Spot or random stops were frequently used to investigate criminal conduct unrelated to vehicle license and registration laws. As Professor LaFave observed, in 1978, pretextual stops of vehicles occurred "with some frequency."[25] According to LaFave, lower court rulings involving spot checks for license and registration compliance "indicate[ ] that often the selection of the vehicle which was stopped was not a matter of pure chance but rather was because the officer suspected the driver of being engaged in some criminal conduct."[26] Even in cases involving actual traffic offenses, there was ample evidence that police used traffic stops "as a subterfuge" to question motorists about more serious criminal conduct[27] or as a pretext to search the vehicle.[28]

In 1979, the United States Supreme Court ruled, in *Delaware v. Prouse*, that "spot checks" were illegal because they gave police too much discretion to detain motorists. The *Prouse* ruling held that, unless police have "at least articulable and reasonable suspicion that a motorist is unlicensed or that automobile is not registered, or that either the vehicle or an occupant is otherwise subject to seizure for violation of law," stopping a vehicle to check a motorist's license and registration violates the Fourth Amendment.[29] The upshot of *Prouse* is that before police can conduct a vehicle stop, they must have objective evidence that the motorist (or an occupant of the vehicle) has committed a traffic offense or some other crime.

While the result in *Prouse* might have been initially seen as an obstacle for the police, it soon became apparent that *Prouse's* holding would not check the discretion of police to stop and interrogate motorists or to obtain authority to search vehicles for criminal law purposes. The reason is simple enough: every motorist, sooner or later, violates the traffic laws. Professor David Harris has aptly described what every police officer knows: "No driver can go for even a short drive without violating *some* aspect of the traffic code. And since there are no perfect drivers, everyone's a violator."[30] Moreover, discretionary stops are not checked by the requirement that police have probable cause of a traffic offense before pulling over a motorist. Data out of New Jersey, for example, show that 98.1 percent of the vehicles traveling on a section of the New Jersey Turnpike exceeded the speed limit.[31] If nearly every vehicle on the New Jersey Turnpike is violating the law, it is easy for the police to be selective in deciding which motorists to stop. It is similar to shooting fish in a barrel.[32] Interestingly, Justice Scalia's opinion in *Whren* did not dispute the defense claim that traffic violations are ubiquitous and thus it is easy for the police to develop an argument that there is probable cause of a traffic offense in order to justify stopping a motorist.

The incident that gave rise to the *Whren* opinion occurred on June 10, 1993, when two young black men, Michael Whren and James Brown, were riding in Washington, D.C., in a Nissan Pathfinder with temporary tags. The men attracted the attention of two plainclothes vice officers, Efrain Soto, Jr., and Homer Littlejohn, who were patrolling for narcotics activity in an unmarked car in a "high drug area" of the city.[33] The officers claimed that their suspicions were aroused when the Pathfinder paused at a stop sign for what they believed was an inordinate amount of time, more than twenty seconds. The officers observed Brown, the driver, looking into the lap of Whren, the passenger. The officers decided to stop the car, ostensibly because the pause at the stop sign violated a District of Columbia traffic regulation that drivers must pay "full time and attention" to their vehicle while driving.

When the officers made a U-turn in order to stop the Pathfinder, Brown allegedly turned right without signaling and sped off at an "unreasonable" speed.[34] Officer Soto later testified that he had no intention of issuing a citation to the driver but merely wanted to "talk to" him about why he had stopped for so long at the sign.[35] Officer Soto acknowledged that it was not usually the job of vice officers to issue traffic citations, unless a driver was clearly endangering others or engaged in blatantly reckless driving. In fact, plainclothes officers like Soto were prohibited by a Police Department regulation from making traffic stops, unless a motorist committed a violation "so grave as to pose an immediate threat to the safety of others."[36] Nonetheless, the officers stopped the vehicle. When Officer Soto approached the driver's side of the vehicle, he immediately observed Whren holding two plastic bags of what appeared to be crack cocaine. The officers arrested both Brown and Whren and searched the Pathfinder, revealing additional quantities of illegal narcotics.

Whren and Brown were indicted on various federal drug offenses. At a pretrial suppression hearing, they argued that the police seizure of their vehicle violated the Fourth Amendment. The defendants contended that the police lacked probable cause or reasonable suspicion to believe that they were involved with narcotics activity. They argued that Officer Soto's claimed justification for stopping their vehicle, to provide a warning for traffic violations, was pretextual. The federal district court denied their motion, concluding that "[t]here was nothing to really demonstrate that the actions of the officers were contrary to a normal traffic stop."[37]

Whren and Brown were convicted for narcotics offenses, and the Court of Appeals affirmed the convictions. The appellate court rejected the claim that the stop was unconstitutional. The court reasoned that regardless of whether police subjectively believe that a motorist may be involved in criminal activity, "a traffic stop is permissible as long as a reasonable officer in the same circumstances *could have* stopped the car for the suspected traffic violation."[38]

The defendants' argument to the Supreme Court was straightforward. It contended that virtually every motorist commits a traffic violation every time he or she drives a vehicle. Because the typical traffic code contains hundreds of provisions regulating driving, the condition of a vehicle, and the equipment on the vehicle, no driver can go very far without committing some traffic infraction. Thus, they argued, "given the ease with which an officer so inclined can identify technical traffic infractions, merely limiting stops to those circumstances in which the police can say they witnessed such a violation is, as a practical matter, no limitation at all."[39]

Since probable cause of a traffic violation is easy to obtain, the argument continued, officers will use traffic stops as a pretext for investigating other crimes, particularly narcotics offenses, for which they possess no probable cause or even reasonable suspicion. Furthermore, empirical data and other reports show that African Americans and members of other racial or ethnic minorities are disproportionately selected for these pretext stops.

Recognizing the modern Court's general reluctance to have Fourth Amendment issues turn on the subjective motive of the police, the defendants proposed a rule that would not depend upon proof of "bad faith" or improper intent of the officer conducting the challenged stop. Rather, they proposed that a stop be considered unconstitutional when facts showed a deviation from the usual or standard practices of the police. Therefore, where an officer's conduct in making a traffic stop deviated materially from the usual or standard police procedure, so that a reasonable officer in the same circumstances would not have made the stop for the reasons given, then the officer's conduct would be objectively unreasonable under the Fourth Amendment. As Professor LaFave analyzed the theory prior to the *Whren* decision, the concern of judges would be "not with *why* the officer deviated from the usual practice in this case but simply that he *did* deviate."[40] What matters, then, is not the subjective motive of the police but whether the officer *in fact* deviated from the standard practice. If the officer's conduct was a departure from standard practice, then that conduct was arbitrary, "and it is the arbitrariness which in this context constitutes the Fourth Amendment violation."[41]

Under the facts in *Whren*, proving deviation from standard police practices, and thus arbitrariness, was easy. Notwithstanding a police department regulation barring traffic stops by plainclothes officers, Officer Soto stopped the defendants' car for traffic offenses that did not threaten public safety. Under the defendants' theory, no reasonable officer in Officer Soto's shoes would have conducted such a stop because of the departmental prohibition. The Court, however, rejected the defendants' test for determining whether the stop was unconstitutional.

Justice Scalia's opinion for a unanimous Court in *Whren* first explained why the Court's previous precedents undermined the defendants' pretext argument. Justice Scalia acknowledged that a handful of the Court's cases expressed disapproval of pretextual searches. For example, the ruling in *New York v. Burger* upheld the validity of a warrantless administrative search of a vehicle dismantling business.[42] While nevertheless ruling for the government, *Burger* emphasized that the challenged search was not a "pretext" for obtaining evidence of criminal conduct.[43] Similarly, in *Florida v. Wells*[44] and *Colorado v. Bertine*,[45] the Court approved inventory searches, but it specifically noted that such searches "must not be a ruse for a general rummaging in order to discover incriminating evidence"[46] and cautioned that police conducting inventory searches could not act in "bad faith or for the sole purpose of investigat[ing]" criminal conduct.[47] But Justice Scalia chided the defendants for relying on these cases because, as he put it, "only an undiscerning reader would regard these cases as endorsing the principle that ulterior motives can invalidate police conduct that is justifiable on the basis of probable cause to believe that a violation of law has occurred."[48] Cases like *Burger, Wells,* and *Bertine* addressed the validity of searches conducted without probable cause. Passages from those cases that are critical of pretextual motives have no application to situations where police possess probable cause for a search or seizure.

Putting inventory and administrative searches aside, Justice Scalia further explained that the defendants' pretext argument was flawed because the Court had never ruled "that an officer's motive invalidates objectively justifiable behavior under the Fourth Amendment."[49] Indeed, according to Justice Scalia, the Court had "repeatedly held and asserted the contrary."[50] As proof of his point, Justice Scalia cited three cases: *United States v. Villamonte-Marquez*,[51] *United States v. Robinson*,[52] and *Scott v. United States*.[53] In *Villamonte-Marquez* the Court held that an otherwise valid boarding of a ship by customs officers to inspect the vessel's documents was not rendered illegal, either because Louisiana state police officers accompanied the customs officials or because the law enforcement officers were pursuing a tip that the ship might be carrying contraband narcotics. According to Justice Scalia, *Villamonte-Marquez* "flatly dismissed the idea that an ulterior motive might serve to strip the agents of their legal justification."[54]

Similarly, the rulings in *Robinson* and *Scott* did not aid the pretext argument. In Justice Scalia's view, the Court in *Robinson* held that an arrest for a traffic violation was not unconstitutional simply because the arrest was "a mere pretext for a narcotics search"[55] and that a valid search incident to arrest "would not be rendered invalid by the fact that it was not motivated by the officer-safety concern that justifies such searches."[56] *Scott* involved a challenge to the admissibility of wiretap evidence allegedly obtained in violation of a federal statutory requirement that FBI agents undertake reasonable efforts to minimize the calls they intercept. According to Scalia, *Scott* also undercut the *Whren* defendants' argument because it stated that "[s]ubjective intent alone . . . does not make otherwise lawful conduct illegal or unconstitutional."[57]

In sum, Justice Scalia concluded that the Court's precedents "foreclose any argument that the constitutional reasonableness of traffic stops depends on the actual motivations of the individual officers involved."[58] He agreed with the defendants' claim that race-based enforcement of traffic laws offends the Constitution but explained that "the constitutional basis for objecting to intentionally discriminatory application of laws is the Equal Protection Clause, not the Fourth Amendment."[59] According to Scalia, the subjective intentions of the police, including police motives based on racial stereotypes or bias, are irrelevant to ordinary Fourth Amendment analysis.

The next section focused on why the defendants' proposed solution to the pretext issue, that is, asking whether a reasonable officer *would* have made the challenged stop instead of whether an officer *could* have made the stop, was not an objective standard after all. In Justice Scalia's view, the defendants' proposal "is plainly and indisputably driven by subjective considerations."[60] Their solution was designed "to prevent the police from doing under the guise of enforcing the traffic code what they would like to do for different reasons."[61] A proposal to identify pretextual conduct through objective means "might make sense" if the Court's previous cases disavowing reliance on police bad faith were based "upon the evidentiary difficulty of establishing subjective intent."[62] But Justice Scalia explained that the Court's main reason for not inquiring into an officer's subjective intent was "simply that the Fourth Amendment's concern with 'reasonableness' allows certain actions to be taken in certain circumstances, *whatever* the subjective intent" of the police.[63]

Moreover, Justice Scalia doubted the practicality of the defendants' proposal. He thought it "somewhat easier to figure out the intent of an individual officer than to plumb the collective consciousness of law enforcement in order to determine whether a 'reasonable officer' would have been moved to act upon the traffic violation."[64] The latter approach would require judges to speculate "about the hypothetical reaction of a hypothetical constable—an exercise that might be called virtual subjectivity."[65] Justice Scalia also concluded that reliance upon police manuals and other objective standards of police enforcement practices would not promote consistent Fourth Amendment rulings or sound legal analysis. Because police procedures and department regulations "vary from place to place and from time to time," Justice Scalia asserted that Fourth Amendment rules could not turn "upon such trivialities."[66]

To illustrate this concern, he noted that the pretext argument rested on the existence of the District of Columbia Police Department regulation that forbids plainclothes officers in unmarked police cruisers to undertake traffic stops unless there is an immediate threat to the safety of others. Scalia countered that this argument would be unavailable "in jurisdictions that had a different practice"[67] and would not have been successful "even in the District of Columbia, if Officer Soto had been wearing a uniform or patrolling in a marked police cruiser."[68]

Finally, Justice Scalia rejected the argument that the Court should resolve this case by conducting a traditional balancing analysis that weighs the respective governmental and individual interests at stake. Under such a balancing model, the defendants contended, a motorist's interest in not being stopped for arbitrary reasons outweighs the government's interest in advancing traffic safety. Justice Scalia blithely dismissed this argument. Rather, he explained that a balancing analysis is appropriate where police affect a search or seizure without probable cause to believe that an offense has occurred. No balancing is required, however, where a search or seizure is based upon probable cause. Where probable cause exists, the Court employs a balancing analysis only in those few cases involving searches or seizures conducted "in an extraordinary manner, unusually harmful to an individual's privacy or even physical interests."[69] Such intrusions include the use of deadly force, unannounced entries into private homes, entries into private homes without a warrant for minor offenses, or a physical penetration of the body. Officer Soto's stopping of the defendants' vehicle "does not remotely qualify as such an extreme practice."[70] Thus, the stop is controlled by the traditional rule that probable cause that an offense has been committed "outbalances" the individual's interest in avoiding a police intrusion.[71]

Justice Scalia brushed aside the claim that an extraordinary factor existed because it was impossible for a motorist to perfectly comply with the "multitude of applicable traffic and equipment regulations" contained in the typical traffic code.[72] He asserted that no legal principle permitted the Court "to decide at what point a code of law becomes so expansive and so commonly violated that infraction itself can no longer be the ordinary measure of the lawfulness of enforcement."[73] And, even if "such exorbitant codes" could be identified, Justice Scalia continued, no legal standard existed for identifying "which particular provisions are sufficiently important to merit enforcement."[74] Therefore, for the "run-of-the-mill case, which this surely is," probable cause justifies the stop whatever the subjective intent of the police.[75]

Dissent by Tracey Maclin

Since its ratification, in 1791, "a paramount purpose of the [F]ourth [A]mendment is to prohibit arbitrary searches and seizures as well as unjustified searches and seizures."[76] History shows that the Framers believed the best way to guard against arbitrary and unjustified governmental intrusions was to control the discretion of law enforcement officers.[77] "The power asserted by the English messengers and colonial customs officers and condemned by history was 'a discretionary power . . . to search wherever their suspicions may chance to fall,' 'a power that places the liberty of every man in the hands of every petty officer.'"[78] Today's ruling by the Court ignores these fundamental principles. By allowing police officers to use any traffic violation as a subterfuge to conduct an arbitrary and unjustified narcotics investigation, the Court has given police officers across the nation virtually unchecked discretion to interfere with the liberty and privacy of any motorist.

We know, of course, that police officers will not use the discretion granted by today's decision against *every* motorist. Reports from the press, as well as judicial decisions, increasingly indicate that police will utilize this discretionary power selectively. As in this case, African American male motorists will bear the brunt of this arbitrary police power. Astonishingly, the Court's ruling asserts that the Fourth Amendment has nothing to say about this type of arbitrary and race-based traffic enforcement. Disappointingly, the Court implies that the Equal Protection Clause provides constitutional redress for the capricious and selective traffic stop conducted in this case. As I explain later, even a cursory review of our recent equal protection rulings shows that a motorist's chances of succeeding on an equal protection challenge against the conduct at issue here are so remote as to be negligible.

As framed by the Court, the issue addressed in this case may seem technical to the layperson. But the technical quality of the Court's language should not obscure the significance of today's ruling. The Court has permitted police to conduct arbitrary traffic seizures in order to pursue drug investigations unsupported by objective evidence of criminality.

As the nation's foremost scholar on the Fourth Amendment has already noted, such a result "cannot be squared with the fundamental point that arbitrary action is unreasonable under the Fourth Amendment."[79] Because I believe that the Court's reasoning is contrary to these fundamental principles, I must respectfully dissent.

A. Why Pretextual Motive Should Matter
When Resolving Fourth Amendment Issues

The Court forcefully asserts that our prior cases "foreclose any argument that the constitutional reasonableness of traffic stops depends on the actual motivations of the individual officers involved."[80] This is a curious conclusion. Many of our search and seizure cases contain statements from the Court, as well as from individual Justices, suggesting that pretextual police intrusions performed to avoid the warrant or probable cause requirements will not be tolerated; at other times, we have noted that pretextual intrusions raise serious Fourth Amendment issues.[81] Moreover, if our prior cases truly did "foreclose any argument" that the constitutional reasonableness of a traffic stop turns on police motive, one would expect that the lower courts would have understood the import of our cases. In the past few years, however, the lower courts have reached divergent results on the issue we confront today. Furthermore, criminal procedure scholars with differing views on the validity of pretextual searches and seizures agree that our prior precedents have not spoken definitively on the validity of pretextual intrusions generally, nor have cases offered clear guidance on the issue presented in this case.

1. Jones v. United States
The Court insists that our prior cases foreclose inquiry into police motive, but *Jones v. United States*,[82] a case not cited by the Court, is to the contrary. In *Jones*, federal officers entered Jones's home at night, under the authority of a search warrant, searching for an illicit distillery. The search revealed the illegal equipment. This Court explained that the warrant did not authorize a nighttime entry. Therefore, the warrant could not justify the entry and seizure of the evidence. The Court also rejected the government's belated argument that the seizure should be upheld because the officers had probable cause to arrest Jones. Under the government's theory, because the officers had probable cause to arrest Jones, their warrantless entry "was justified and, once in the house, while searching for [Jones], they could properly seize all contraband material in plain sight."[83]

The *Jones* Court succinctly dismissed this claim because the "testimony of the federal officers makes clear beyond dispute that their purpose in entering was to search for distilling equipment, and not to arrest [Jones]."[84] Concededly, the *Jones* Court did not directly address the pretext issue presented here. Nonetheless, *Jones* demonstrates that motive is not an irrelevant factor when assessing the reasonableness of a search or seizure.[85] At a minimum, the result in *Jones* cannot be reconciled with the Court's conclusion that none of our prior precedents justifies judicial examination of an officer's intent when conducting a search or seizure.

2. Missouri v. Blair

Furthermore, if our prior decisions "foreclose any argument" that the constitutional reasonableness of a traffic seizure turns on the motivation of the police, why, *ten years* ago, did we undertake review of *Missouri v. Blair*? The issue in *Blair* was whether the police may use "evidence in a homicide case that has been obtained after an arrest for a traffic violation, where the police lacked probable cause to arrest the defendant for homicide, and the traffic arrest was made at the request of the police homicide unit."[86] As one scholar noted, the facts in *Blair* "posed pretext conundra in a clear-cut fashion" and presented the Court "a golden opportunity . . . to make clear what its position actually is with respect to the constitutionality of pretext[ual]" searches and seizures.[87] Of course, the pretext issue raised in *Blair* was never resolved.[88] But if the Court is correct, that prior cases "foreclose any argument" that the legality of a traffic seizure depends on the motivation of the police, there was no reason to grant review in *Blair* and hear oral arguments. Instead, the Court simply should have summarily reversed the ruling of the Missouri Supreme Court in a *per curiam* opinion and explained that motive is irrelevant when the police have probable cause.

Moreover, if our prior cases did indeed "foreclose any argument" that motive is relevant to the constitutionality of a traffic stop, why did Justice White urge the Court, five years after we dismissed the writ of certiorari in *Blair* in 1991, to review three companion cases where the petitioners alleged that police used a traffic stop as a pretext for conducting a narcotics search?[89] As Justice White noted, the defendants in the three cases raised a "recurring issue" on which the federal courts of appeals had reached divergent results.[90] In sum, the Court misleads when it asserts that our precedents "foreclose any argument" that motive is irrelevant when police have probable cause of an offense. The Court has not spoken clearly on the constitutionality of pretextual searches or seizures. In fact, our prior rulings sent mixed signals on the permissibility of pretextual intrusions. This lack of clarity is reflected in the decisions of the lower courts, and it has been recognized by Fourth Amendment scholars.[91]

3. Inventory & Administrative Search Cases

The Court asserts that statements in our inventory and administrative search cases, which disapprove of pretextual intrusions, have no applicability to police seizures supported by probable cause. According to the Court, "only an undiscerning reader would regard these cases as endorsing the principle that ulterior motives can invalidate police conduct that is justifiable on the basis of probable cause to believe that a violation of law has occurred."[92] The Court opines that this case is distinguishable from the inventory and administrative search cases because those cases addressed the validity of a search "conducted in the *absence* of probable cause."[93]

The Court correctly notes that the inventory and administrative search cases—*Florida v. Wells, Colorado v. Bertine,* and *New York v. Burger*—involved searches performed in the absence of probable cause. In contrast, the traffic stop here was supported by probable cause. But the Court fails to explain why this distinction matters.[94] No one suggests, not even the Court, that perfect compliance with the traffic code is possible. More important, police officers have known for a long time that the traffic code provides a readily available device to stop and question any motorist.[95] "There is no detail of driving too small, no piece of equipment too insignificant, no item of automobile regulation too arcane to be made the subject of a traffic offense. In fact, '[p]olice officers in some jurisdictions have a rule of thumb: the average driver cannot go three blocks without violating some traffic regulation.'"[96] Because the police can easily obtain probable cause of a traffic offense against any motorist, the distinction identified by the Court between this case and inventory and administrative search cases is not compelling. In both contexts, the Fourth Amendment's purpose in preventing arbitrary invasions of privacy and security requires us to focus on the discretion accorded to law enforcement officers in the field by the challenged intrusion.[97]

Indeed, in *Camara v. Municipal Court,* the Court explained that the constitutional evil of warrantless administrative searches of homes is that such a system has the practical effect of leaving the homeowner "subject to the discretion of the official in the field."[98] Similarly, in *South Dakota v. Opperman,* the leading inventory search case, Chief Justice Burger's majority opinion emphasized that the inventory search performed in that case was dictated by standard police procedure, and it was not "a pretext concealing an investigatory police motive."[99] What was implicit in Chief Justice Burger's opinion was explicit in Justice Powell's concurring opinion. Relying on the passage in *Camara*, quoted earlier, Justice Powell explained that the important constitutional factor justifying inventory searches was that "no significant discretion is placed in the hands of the individual officer: he usually has no choice as to the subject of the search or its scope."[100]

In sum, although the Court is correct to note that our inventory and administrative search rulings addressed police intrusions performed "in the *absence* of probable cause,"[101] that fact does not justify dismissing statements from those rulings disapproving pretextual police intrusions. As we recognized in *Camara* and in *Opperman*, administrative and inventory searches present the same constitutional concerns inherent in the police seizure challenged in this case: leaving the individual subject to the arbitrary discretion of the officer in the field.

4. Prior Precedents Do Not Resolve the Question Surrounding Pretextual Traffic Stops

After insisting that we have never held that an officer's motive invalidates objectively justifiable behavior, the Court goes further by declaring, "we have repeatedly held and asserted the contrary."[102] To bolster this claim, the Court cites three cases: *United States v. Robinson, Scott v. United States,* and *United States v. Villamonte-Marquez*. In none of these cases, however, did the Court hold that objectively justifiable police conduct is *per se* reasonable under the Fourth Amendment, regardless of an officer's intent. In fact, not one of these cases dictates the conclusion that police motive is constitutionally irrelevant, let alone compels that same result in a case where the challenged seizure is an obvious and blatant deviation from standard police practice. Although a reader would never know it, each of these cases resolved questions that are fully distinguishable from the issue before us today.

Robinson, decided in 1973, does not support the Court's conclusion that motive is irrelevant under the Fourth Amendment. *Robinson* involved the arrest of a motorist for driving a vehicle after revocation of his operator's permit. A search incident to arrest revealed illegal narcotics. In this Court, Robinson contested the constitutionality of the search. *Robinson* merely held that "in the case of a lawful custodial arrest a full search of the person is not only an exception to the warrant requirement of the Fourth Amendment, but is also a 'reasonable' search under that Amendment."[103]

In fact, *Robinson* expressly stated that it was "leav[ing] for another day" the question whether the Fourth Amendment permits an officer to use a "traffic violation arrest as a mere pretext for a narcotics search." Significantly, *Robinson* explained that "it is sufficient for purposes of our decision that [Robinson] was lawfully arrested for an offense, and that [the officer's] placing him in custody following that arrest was not a *departure from established police department practice.*" Indeed, the arrest in *Robinson* was *required* by departmental regulation, and the search incident to arrest was in accord with departmental instructions. Put simply, *Robinson* not only expressly left open whether an officer's intent to use a traffic violation as mere pretext for a narcotics search might violate the Fourth Amendment. It is also plainly distinguishable from the facts here because, unlike Officer's Soto's actions, the arrest and search in *Robinson* were mandated by police department practices.

Five years later, *Scott* was decided. *Scott* addressed whether FBI agents violated the minimization provision of the federal wiretap statute, which required that agents make reasonable efforts to minimize the telephone conversations they record when conducting electronic surveillance. The agents made no attempt to minimize the calls they intercepted. *Scott* concluded that the agents' subjective intent was irrelevant in determining whether the statute was violated. The Court explained that the statute's minimization provision "made it clear that the focus was to be on the agents' actions not their motives."[104] And the Court ultimately concluded, applying an objective reasonableness standard, that the facts showed that the agents' conduct had not exceeded statutory requirements. Clearly, then, *Scott* did not raise the issue, much less decide, whether officer motive is never relevant when deciding a Fourth Amendment claim.[105]

What the Court's opinion does not acknowledge is that *Scott* was not a "pretext" case for Fourth Amendment purposes.[106] *Scott* simply held that the agents' actions did not violate the statute "under a standard of objective reasonableness without regard to the underlying intent or motivation of the officers involved."[107] When read properly, *Scott* merely held that "improper intent that is not acted upon does not render unconstitutional an otherwise constitutional search."[108]

Villamonte-Marquez is the third case cited by the Court for the proposition that motive never trumps objectively justifiable police behavior. *Villamonte-Marquez* addressed whether customs officials violated the Fourth

Amendment when, without suspicion of wrongdoing, they boarded a vessel under the authority of a federal statute to examine the manifest and other documents. While examining the documents, a customs official smelled marijuana, looked through an open hatch, and discovered burlap-wrapped bales containing marijuana. *Villamonte-Marquez* held that a suspicionless boarding of a vessel to examine documents did not violate the Fourth Amendment. In reaching this conclusion, the Court dismissed, in a footnote, the defendants' argument "that because the customs officers were accompanied by a Louisiana state policeman, and were following an informant's tip that a vessel in the ship channel was thought to be carrying marihuana, [customs officials] may not rely on the statute authorizing boarding for inspection of the vessel's documentation."[109] With no elaboration, the *Villamonte-Marquez* Court asserted that the defendants' pretext argument had already been rejected by *Scott*.

The Court declares that *Villamonte-Marquez* "flatly dismissed the idea that an ulterior motive might serve to strip the agents of their legal justification."[110] This is true enough under the facts in *Villamonte-Marquez*, but the result reached in *Villamonte-Marquez* does not come close to establishing the larger proposition that motive never matters under the Fourth Amendment. For example, customs agents cannot use the authority approved in *Villamonte-Marquez* to conduct a warrantless search of vessel with no intent to check the vessel's manifest and other documents. Indeed, there is nothing in *Villamonte-Marquez* that "suggests that its holding would justify a warrantless search of a vessel where the officers neither make a document inspection nor follow a course of action suggesting that they would have made such an inspection if their plain view observations of incriminating evidence had not intervened."[111]

At most, the footnote in *Villamonte-Marquez*, rejecting the defendants' pretext argument, stands for the limited rule that customs officers may use their authority to board all vessels, including vessels suspected of engaging in narcotics activity, in order to inspect documents. There is no disputing, however, that *Villamonte-Marquez* did not involve a seizure where law enforcement officers deviated from standard procedure and procedures, which makes it a very different case from the facts presented in this case.

Although the Court may think that the cases it cites "foreclose any argument that the constitutional reasonableness of traffic stops depends on the actual motivations of the individual officers involved,"[112] none of these cases establishes the principle that motive never matters in Fourth Amendment cases. More important, none of the cases cited by the Court is a controlling precedent for a pretextual seizure that is a clear departure from standard police procedure. To be sure, these cases contain language disfavoring judicial inquiry into police motive. But only the most unorthodox interpretation of these cases would conclude that they "foreclose any argument" that "pretext" never matters under the Fourth Amendment.

B. The Defendants' Test

The Court's analysis of the defendants' argument is cursory and even somewhat misleading. The Court accurately states that, under defendants' test, the constitutionality of a traffic stop would turn on "whether the officer's conduct deviated materially from usual police practices, so that a reasonable officer in the same circumstances would not have made the stop for the reasons given."[113] Although it is framed in objective terms, the Court insists that this test "is plainly and disputably driven by subjective considerations" and is designed "to prevent the police from doing under the guise of enforcing the traffic code what they would like to do for different reasons."[114]

The Court misleadingly asserts that defendants' test is "driven by subjective considerations." On the contrary, the test is an objective standard, designed to identify arbitrary traffic stops. As Professor LaFave has already explained, this standard is fully consistent with the Court's precedents, including the dicta from *Robinson* and *Scott*, and does not depend upon the subjective intent of the officer:

> [T]he proper basis of concern is not with *why* the officer deviated from the usual practice in this case but simply that he *did* deviate. It is the *fact* of the departure from the accepted way of handling such cases which makes the officer's conduct arbitrary, and it is the arbitrariness which in this context constitutes the Fourth Amendment violation.[115]

The defendants' test is grounded in a concern that dates back to the Framers and continues to govern our Fourth Amendment rulings, preventing arbitrary searches and seizures.[116] The Court does not, and indeed cannot, deny the defendants' claim that police officers are afforded vast discretion to enforce traffic laws. What Professor Kenneth Culp Davis has documented about police discretion generally, certainly applies to traffic enforcement: "The police are among the most important policy-makers of our entire society. . . . [T]hey make far more discretionary determinations in individual cases than any other class of administrators; I know of no close second."[117]

Obviously, the defendants' test does not purport to eliminate all discretionary decisions by officers. Defendants proposed merely to identify traffic stops that a reasonable officer would not conduct because his department has already determined that such stops are unnecessary, improper, or too intrusive on the basis of the totality of the circumstances. Put simply, the test is aimed at identifying traffic stops that are capricious and conducted without standards. If, as this Court has reaffirmed over the years, arbitrary searches and seizures violate the purpose of the Fourth Amendment, then defendants' test promotes Fourth Amendment principles because it identifies and declares illegal traffic stops which are unauthorized by departmental rules. Therefore, it is not only consistent with, but also promotes, one of the fundamental purposes of the amendment:

> Arbitrary searches and seizures are "unreasonable" searches and seizures; ruleless searches and seizures practiced at the varying and unguided discretion of thousands of individual peace officers are arbitrary searches and seizures; therefore, ruleless searches and seizures are "unreasonable" searches and seizures.[118]

Indeed, as one perceptive scholar has written about the issue facing us today, this Court should encourage constitutional analysis that utilizes departmental rules and standard practices of police officers to identify arbitrary intrusions. Otherwise, whether any of us who drive automobiles will be subject to a traffic stop and how that stop will unfold will too often turn on "the state of digestion of any officer who stops us—or, more likely, upon our obsequiousness, the price of our automobiles, the formality of dress, the shortness of our hair or the color of skin."[119]

The Court too quickly dismisses the benefits of the defendants' test. While conceding that departmental rules may help to identify arbitrary police action, the Court believes that, in many cases, judges "would be reduced to speculating about the hypothetical reaction of a hypothetical constable—an exercise that might be called virtual subjectivity."[120] Moreover, because departmental rules and police enforcement practices "vary from place to place and from time to time,"[121] the Court implies that the defendants' test will produce different Fourth Amendment rules depending upon where a search or seizure occurs. Such a result is unacceptable because Fourth Amendment protection should not "turn upon such trivialities."[122]

These objections are weak. The point about "virtual subjectivity" is a red herring. The defendants' test does not purport to control every type of discretionary decision by an officer, even in the traffic enforcement context. Instead, their test is limited to assessing the constitutionality of search or seizure activity that is subject to abuse by the officer in the field and is regulated by departmental rules. Defendants challenge only the initial decision to stop their vehicle for a traffic offense. In this case, there was a departmental rule specifically controlling that discretionary decision. In other cases, where there are no controlling departmental rules or objective enforcement practices for the challenged search or seizure, the defendants' test would not apply. Thus, the Court's stated fear, under the defendants' test, that judges "would be reduced to speculating about the hypothetical action of a hypothetical constable—an exercise that might be called virtual subjectivity," is not even remotely present in this case and does not undermine the workability of defendants' test in future cases.

Another problem with the defendants' test, according to the Court, is that police enforcement differs across the country, and constitutional protection should not "turn upon such trivialities." To illustrate the point, the Court notes that the traffic stop in this case would be permissible in a jurisdiction that had a practice different from that of the District of Columbia, and the stop would be permissible "even in the District of Columbia, if Officer Soto had been wearing a uniform or patrolling in a marked police cruiser."[123]

This is not a serious objection. As the Court well knows, current Fourth Amendment doctrine already permits a considerable amount of variation in police enforcement practices. Often, the result in a Fourth Amendment case depends upon whether police are following departmental rules or standardized procedures. In other contexts, seizures that are exactly similar in scope and operational procedures are distinguished on constitutional grounds depending upon the intent of the police. In still other cases, the legality of the search or stop sometimes turns on the presence or absence of minute factual detail.

For example, an inventory search of a car conducted in Alabama pursuant to standardized policy is permissible under the Fourth Amendment, while the same inventory search conducted in Arizona in the absence of standardized policy is impermissible. Similarly, under our precedents, a roadblock that seizes vehicles is permissible if established with the intent to detect drunk driving or to check the license and registration documents of the motorist.[124] On the other hand, we have not yet decided whether a roadblock that utilizes the same officers and operational procedures, but with the intent to detect narcotic trafficking or gun possession is permissible. Thus, the Court proffers an exaggerated and unconvincing objection when it states that the seizure in this case would be permissible in a jurisdiction that did not have a departmental policy against plainclothes officers making traffic stops and would have been permissible even in the District of Columbia had Officer Soto been in uniform and driving a marked patrol cruiser. The law books are full of Fourth Amendment rulings that turn on fact-bound distinctions. The important point here is that Officer Soto's actions deviated from the usual practice in the District of Columbia. What an officer would have done in New Jersey or Alaska is irrelevant in determining whether *this* stop was arbitrary. Likewise, had Officer Soto been in uniform or driving a marked patrol cruiser is beside the point. Officer Soto was in plainclothes and in an unmarked cruiser, and the traffic offense did not pose an immediate threat to the safety of others. That is all that matters under the applicable departmental regulation.

C. Why Probable Cause Is Not Always Sufficient to Make a Traffic Stop Reasonable Under the Fourth Amendment

The defendants' test provides a workable solution to the pretext issue presented in this case. While I would favor adopting their standard to resolve the Fourth Amendment issue raised by the specific facts here, the Court is right that defendants' test would be useless in a jurisdiction that does not have a similar regulation barring traffic stops by plainclothes officers. In such a jurisdiction, motorists could still be targeted for pretextual traffic stops, and the defendants' test would not be available to resolve whether the stop satisfies the Fourth Amendment. Moreover, the traffic stop executed by Officer Soto is not the only type of pretextual stop subject to abuse. Officers have been known to use traffic infractions as an excuse to stop and search motorists for a variety reasons, including because vehicles had Black Panther, ACLU, or NRA bumper stickers[125] or because the occupants of a vehicle had long hair.[126] For these and other types of pretextual traffic stops, the defendants' test would be ineffectual. But, before outlining the legal framework that should be utilized for handling such cases, I must first address the Court's argument that the existence of probable cause for a traffic offense eliminates the need for additional judicial scrutiny of an officer's conduct.

The Court explains that where probable cause exists, judicial scrutiny of the manner in which a search or seizure is conducted is required only where the challenged intrusion is "conducted in an extraordinary manner, unusually harmful to the individual's privacy or even physical interests."[127] A routine traffic stop by plainclothes officers, the Court says, "does not remotely qualify as such an extreme practice, and so is governed by the usual rule that probable cause to believe the law has been broken 'outbalances' private interest in avoiding police contact."[128] Thus, the Court sees no reason to conduct a traditional balancing analysis to consider the competing interests at stake in this case.

Practically speaking, the rule adopted by the Court means that a routine traffic stop supported by probable cause is *per se* reasonable under the Fourth Amendment. Apparently, there are no limits to this principle. For example, if a municipal trash collector had conducted the traffic stop in this case, the Government concedes that the seizure would still be permissible under the Fourth Amendment.[129] After all, the trash collector *could* have been a police officer. How the city divides the responsibilities of its employees or the fact that a challenged seizure violates state or local law has no bearing on the Fourth Amendment. The trash collector "could have been a cop. He (just) happens not to be."[130]

Similarly, the principle adopted by the Court would not prohibit the enforcement of traffic stops pursuant to the following hypothetical departmental rules: Rule A mandates that all patrol officers are not to waste their time enforcing minor provisions of the traffic code, such as regulations that require motorists always use their turn signals or that prohibit the hanging of fuzzy dice or air fresheners on rear-view mirrors. Rule B mandates that, to assist vice officers, violation of every provision of the traffic code be considered grounds for a traffic stop. Even though the city has put its traffic stop policy in written form, it is obvious that the traffic policy is a sham, designed solely to facilitate suspicionless drug investigations. The Government, however, contends that this hypothetical practice would not violate the Fourth Amendment.[131] Presumably, under the rule adopted by the Court, the Fourth Amendment would not bar the police from enforcing the traffic code only against automobiles with license plates ending with odd numbers or cars painted in rainbow colors.

Evidently, the Court considers evaluating the reasonableness of pretextual traffic stops a waste of judicial time and resources. The Court views the stop in this case—officers brazenly violating departmental rules to stop a vehicle occupied by two black males on pretextual traffic charges in order to pursue a hunch that the occupants were drug dealers—as "the run-of-the-mine case."[132] But many black motorists may find the Court's analysis disturbing, to say the least. Indeed, the defendants contend that a traffic stop based on racial profiling is arbitrary and unreasonable.

The Court's rebuttal to this concern is that the need for probable cause of a traffic offense sufficiently checks police discretion. This reply is illusory. In many contexts, probable cause for a traffic offense not only fails to diminish the discretion possessed by officers but also may actually facilitate arbitrary seizures. A recent empirical study of traffic stops on the New Jersey Turnpike proves the point. Ninety-eight percent of the drivers on a section of the Turnpike were committing traffic offenses. Only 15 percent of those violators were black motorists, but 46 percent of the stops by state troopers on that section of the Turnpike were of black motorists. There was no race-neutral explanation for this disparity.[133] It is evident that the probable cause requirement was not acting as a check on police discretion nor preventing arbitrary seizures. Rather than protecting motorists, under the Court's view of the Fourth Amendment, probable cause acts as a trigger to initiate an arbitrary seizure and then insulates the decision from judicial review.

The Court is untroubled by this reality. It claims that no legal rule permits it "to decide at what point a code of law becomes so expansive and so commonly violated that infraction itself can no longer be the ordinary measure of the lawfulness of enforcement."[134] And the Court adds that, even if it could identify "such exorbitant codes," it does not "know by what standard (or what right) [it] would decide, . . . which particular provisions are sufficiently important to merit enforcement."[135]

As the Court is fully aware, the defendants' complaint concerns not the expansiveness of the District of Columbia traffic code but the arbitrary and selective seizures effectuated pursuant to the code. Nor is there an absence of legal "principle" to handle this symptom of discretionary and arbitrary power. This Court has repeatedly stated that the main purpose of the Fourth Amendment is to protect the liberty and privacy of persons against arbitrary governmental intrusions.[136] Half a century ago,

Justice Robert Jackson explained why the judiciary must remain alert to official abuses under the guise of discretionary authority:

> [N]othing opens the door to arbitrary action so effectively as to allow [government] officials to pick and choose only a few to whom they will apply legislation and thus to escape the political retribution that might be visited upon them if larger numbers were affected. Courts can take no better measure to assure that laws will be just than to require that laws be equal in operation.[137]

Justice Jackson's logic certainly applies to police officers who enforce the traffic laws. The problem in this case is not, as the Court puts it, deciding "at what point a code of law becomes so expansive and so commonly violated that infraction itself can no longer be the ordinary measure of the lawfulness of enforcement." Rather, the problem is deciding whether officers jeopardize Fourth Amendment norms when they conduct seizures under a traffic code in a manner that brazenly deviates from normal procedures or departmental regulations. As Professor Davis has already noted, the police can execute arbitrary seizures even under an otherwise reasonable and neutral law: "If the police enforce a statute against one out of a hundred known violators, and no can know in advance which one will be selected or why, does not the system of enforcement encourage arbitrariness and discrimination, and is it not therefore unconstitutional?"[138]

Finally, the Court will not have to search in vain to determine which provisions of the traffic code are "sufficiently important to merit enforcement." Where police discretion produces arbitrary seizures under a facially valid provision, the remedy is not to invalidate the particular provision of the code but to nullify the official conduct itself.

We did as much in *Batson v. Kentucky*.[139] In *Batson*, when confronted with evidence that individual prosecutors were using their discretionary power via the peremptory challenge to arbitrarily remove black jurors from the trial jury, the Court did not nullify peremptory challenges entirely. Instead, it required prosecutors to provide race-neutral explanations where defendants show a *prima facie* case of discrimination.

Under the legal framework established in *Batson*, a defendant can establish a *prima facie* case by showing that the totality of the circumstances raises an inference of purposeful discrimination—that a prosecutor has used his peremptory strikes in a discriminatory manner. Although "*Batson* itself gave no specific direction as to the measure of a prima facie case,"[140] the Court did explain, as examples, that "a 'pattern' of strikes against black jurors included in the particular venire might give rise to an inference of discrimination," or the "prosecutor's questions and statements during *voir dire* examination and in exercising his challenges may support or refute an inference of discriminatory purpose."[141] Once a *prima facie* case is shown, the state must "come forward with a neutral explanation" for the official action.[142] "The State cannot meet this burden on mere general assertions that its officials did not discriminate or that they properly performed their official duties."[143] Rather, the prosecutor must provide race-neutral explanations for his or her selection criteria.

A *Batson*-like model could be employed to challenge the constitutionality of pretextual traffic stops. Just as *Batson* allows a defendant to make a *prima facie* case by demonstrating a pattern of discriminatory strikes or from the specific conduct of prosecutors during *voir dire*, so too should a motorist, at a pretrial suppression hearing, be permitted to raise an inference of discriminatory or arbitrary enforcement of the traffic code either through statistical data that indicate race-based enforcement or by arguing that the police made an arbitrary stop on the basis of the facts of his case. For example, a motorist could argue that the officer's decision to stop his vehicle for failure to signal a lane change was pretextual considering the totality of the facts, including the officer's past conduct.[144] Alternatively, a *prima facie* case of discriminatory or arbitrary traffic enforcement could be shown by documenting the type of flagrant violation of internal police regulations that occurred in this case.

To be sure, applying a *Batson* framework in this context will not end pretextual traffic stops or eliminate racial profiling by police officers. The protections announced in *Batson* certainly have not prevented prosecutors from exercising their peremptory challenges in a discriminatory manner. "Even a prosecutor who has dismissed jurors for racial reasons can concoct a neutral explanation for his actions that the courts will accept as proof that his strikes were not racially motivated."[145] Thus, if a *Batson* model were applied to pretextual traffic stops, it would not catch every arbitrary traffic stop. But a *Batson*-type framework should identify the worst cases, and is undoubtedly better than the Court's alternative, which endorses a *per se* rule that any traffic stop based on probable cause is always reasonable under the Fourth Amendment.

While *Batson* applied the Equal Protection Clause to a prosecutor's use of peremptory challenges, incorporating the equality norm of our Equal Protection cases into Fourth Amendment analysis certainly promotes the amendment's purpose. Like other provisions of the Bill of Rights that have been interpreted to incorporate equality norms as part of the substantive right accorded by the provision,[146] the Fourth Amendment right against unreasonable searches and seizures is sufficiently important and spacious to include a concern with equality. Furthermore, the history and purpose of the Fourth Amendment provide ample justification for embracing equality norms when deciding the reasonableness of a search or seizure. At its core, the amendment is aimed at discretionary police power. Traffic enforcement obviously affords police officers "a good deal of low visibility discretion. In addition, officers are likely, in such situations, to be sensitive to social station and other factors that should not bear on the decision."[147] Accordingly, Fourth Amendment values would be advanced by asking whether the traffic stop in this case was conducted in an arbitrary and discriminatory manner.

D. Racially Based Pretextual Traffic Stops

What I have said so far is enough to reverse the ruling of the Court of Appeals. Although there is sufficient evidence in the record to support a judgment in favor of the defendants, I would remand the case and instruct the Court of Appeals to decide whether Officer Soto's stop deviated from written police departmental regulations. If it is determined that the stop was a departure from standard practice such that a reasonable officer would not have made the stop, then the seizure was arbitrary and in violation of the Fourth Amendment's bar against unreasonable seizures. Accordingly, the defendants would be entitled to have the evidence revealed by that stop excluded from trial.

While rejecting the defendants' Fourth Amendment claim, the Court suggests defendants' should have raised a Fourteenth Amendment equal protection challenge against the type of race-based pretextual stop conducted in this case. This comment deserves a brief reply.

As the Court well knows, a black motorist who challenges official action under the Equal Protection Clause confronts significant doctrinal hurdles. First, before a black motorist can obtain access to or challenge a police officer's past practices regarding traffic stops under the Equal Protection Clause, he has to overcome a heavy evidentiary burden. Three weeks ago, in *United States v. Armstrong*,[148] the Court addressed "the showing necessary for a defendant to be entitled to discovery on a claim that the prosecuting attorney singled him out for prosecution on the basis of race."[149] *Armstrong* held that the essential elements of a selective prosecution claim must be shown before the prosecution is required to provide access to its files for discovery purposes. Therefore, a defendant must show both a discriminatory effect and a purpose to discriminate by governmental actors before discovery will be allowed. "To establish a discriminatory effect in a race case, the claimant must show that similarly situated individuals of a different race were not prosecuted."[150]

A black motorist might contend that *Armstrong's* holding was grounded in the Court's unwillingness to second-guess executive branch decisions on whom to prosecute. *Armstrong's* holding, the argument would continue, is inapplicable where the enforcement practices of the police are challenged under the Equal Protection Clause because the police are not entitled to the same degree of deference accorded prosecutors. I doubt that most judges will read *Armstrong* in such a narrow fashion. More important, *Armstrong* itself noted that the "requirements for a selective prosecution claim draw on 'ordinary equal protection standards,'"[151] a provision that presumably would also apply to an equal protection challenge brought by a black motorist.

Second, even if a black motorist is able to overcome the obstacles to discovery erected by *Armstrong*, to prevail on the merits of an equal protection claim, he will have to show that (1) he was stopped because of his race, and (2) similarly situated white motorists were not stopped.[152] Put simply, this means that the defendant must prove that the police had a specific intent to stop him because of his race. Unless an officer admits that a driver was stopped for racial reasons, the specific intent standard of our equal protection doctrine will doom the typical pretextual traffic stop case involving a black motorist. In the atypical case involving a defense able to conduct a systematic study of the enforcement practices of a particular police department, there is a slightly better chance of success, if statistics demonstrate that officers are targeting black motorists.

But even where statistics show a strong correlation between race and a particular outcome, the Court has still required the individual criminal defendant to prove that the government officials in *his* case were motivated by a discriminatory intent. For example, in *McCleskey v. Kemp* we ruled that a complex statistical study indicating that racial considerations were affecting capital sentencing decisions during a nine-year period in Georgia were not sufficient to establish an equal protection violation in a single defendant's case.[153] "[T]o prevail under the Equal Protection Clause, [a defendant] must prove that the decisionmaker in *his* case acted with discriminatory purpose."[154]

Finally, even if a black motorist challenging a pretextual traffic stop is able to obtain discovery and to prevail on the merits of an equal protection claim, there is the question of remedy. The Court has shown no signs that it interprets the Equal Protection Clause to embody an exclusionary rule remedy or that the Clause even requires the dismissal of criminal charges in a case involving a race-based prosecution. To illustrate, the *Armstrong* Court observed that whether "dismissal of the indictment, or some other sanction, is the proper remedy if a court determines that a defendant has been the victim of prosecution on the basis of race" was an open question.[155]

To conclude, a successful Equal Protection challenge to a race-based pretextual traffic stop would be extremely difficult to mount. Because of the doctrinal limitations of our Equal Protection cases, black motorists who have been the targets of racial profiling have no incentive to file equal protection claims. Thus, while the Court holds out the possibility that a black defendant could raise a Fourteenth Amendment challenge to the police conduct in this case, a less sentimental and more realistic view of the law indicates that very few such challenges will be raised and even fewer will prevail. Therefore, the Court's sympathetic observation that "We of course agree with defendants that the Constitution prohibits selective enforcement of the law based on considerations such as race"[156] rings hollow. The end result, of course, is that black motorists, like defendants, who are the subjects of racial profiling are left without an effective constitutional remedy. With today's holding, the Fourth Amendment does not proscribe this type of arbitrary and race-based traffic enforcement, and an Equal Protection claim offers no realistic chance of success.

E. Conclusion

Because I believe that the Fourth Amendment's bar against unreasonable seizures forbids the type of arbitrary police seizure involved in this case, I would reverse the ruling of the Court of Appeals.

NOTES

1. James Q. Wilson, Varieties of Police Behavior 51 (1973).
2. 3 Wayne R. LaFave, Search and Seizure: A Treatise on the Fourth Amendment, § 10.8 at 386–87 (1978).
3. United States v. Robinson, 471 F.2d 1082, 1111, n.16 (D.C. Cir. 1973) (Bazelon, C. J., concurring specially), *overruled*, United States v. Robinson, 414 U.S.

218 (1973), quoting Metropolitan Police Department, Memorandum: Subject: Traffic Enforcement (June 9, 1964) (emphasis added by Judge Bazelon).

4. United States v. Whren, 517 U.S. 806 (1996).

5. Police have used pretextual stops for a long time. *See* LAWRENCE P. TIF-FANY ET AL., DETECTION OF CRIME 131 (1967) (reporting statements of police officers on how minor traffic infractions are used as justification to search and question motorists: "You can always get a guy legitimately on a traffic violation if you tail him for a while, and then a search can be made." "You don't have to follow a driver very long before he will move to the other side of the yellow line and then you can arrest and search him for driving on the wrong side of the highway." "In the event that we see a suspicious automobile or occupant and wish to search the person or the car, or both, we will usually follow the vehicle until the driver makes a technical violation of a traffic law. Then we have a means of making a legitimate search."); *cf.* Wilson, *supra* note 1, at 54 ("A traffic 'stop' serves purposes other than enforcing the traffic laws, and these other purposes place the traffic officer in the role of a patrolman deciding whether he has grounds for intervening in a situation that may be more serious than merely speeding or running a red light.").

6. 1 WAYNE R. LaFAVE, SEARCH AND SEIZURE: A TREATISE ON THE FOURTH AMENDMENT § 1.4(f), at 149 (4th ed. 2004).

7. *Whren,* 517 U.S. at 808.

8. When discussing the constitutionality of stopping a motorist, the terms "stop," "seizure," and "detention" are used interchangeably. In 1979, the Court ruled that a random spot check of a motorist to check his license and registration violated the Fourth Amendment. *See* Delaware v. Prouse, 440 U.S. 648 (1979). *See infra* notes 124–25 and accompanying text. Consequently, motorists have a constitutional right to drive unimpeded by the police. In order to stop, seize, or detain a motorist, the police must have probable cause that the motorist has committed a traffic offense or a reasonable suspicion that the motorist is involved with criminal conduct.

9. David Sklansky, *Traffic Stops, Minority Motorists, and the Future of the Fourth Amendment,* 1997 SUP. CT. REV. 271, 285 (1997).

10. *See, e.g.,* Daniel B. Yeager, *The Stubbornness of Pretext,* 40 SAN DIEGO L. REV. 611, 612 (2003) (explaining that the "pretext problem has been percolating in the [Supreme Court] for at least four decades before its putative burial in 1996 by *Whren*"); Ed Aro, Note, *The Pretext Problem Revisited: A Doctrinal Exploration of Bad Faith in Search and Seizure Cases,* 70 B.U. L. REV. 111, 111 (1990) (noting that the Court's "inconsistent and sometimes opaque treatment of the pretext problem, combined with the fourth amendment's general doctrinal complexity and the uncertain role of subjective intent in search and seizure cases, makes resolution of pretext claims a troubling and frustrating task"); John M. Burkoff, *The Pretext Search Doctrine Returns After Never Leaving,* 66 U. DET. L. rev. 363, 364 (1989)

(asserting that there are few Fourth Amendment rulings "more tangled" than the cases and doctrine relating to pretextual Fourth Amendment activity); James B. Haddad, *Pretextual Fourth Amendment Activity: Another View*, 18 U. MICH. J. L. REF. 639, 653–81 (1985) (describing Court's rulings related to pretext issues); John M. Burkoff, *Bad Faith Searches*, 57 N.Y.U. L. REV. 70, 72–84 (1982) (same).

    11. United States v. Lefkowitz, 285 U.S. 452, 467 (1932).

    12. *See, e.g.,* New York v. Class, 475 U.S. 106, 122 (1986) (Powell, J., concurring) (stating that an officer may not use a vehicle identification number inspection "as a pretext for searching a vehicle contraband or weapons"); Brown v. Illinois, 422 U.S. 590, 611 (1975) (Powell, J., concurring) (explaining that if "the evidence clearly suggested that [an] arrest was effectuated as a pretext for collateral objectives, [the provision of *Miranda* warnings to the arrestee would] rarely [be] sufficient to dissipate the taint"); Ker v. California, 374 U.S. 23, 42–43 (1963) (noting that "an arrest may not be used merely as the pretext for a search without a warrant"); Abel v. United States, 362 U.S. 216, 226 (1960) ("The deliberate use by the Government of an administrative warrant for the purpose of gathering evidence in a criminal case must meet stern resistance by the courts"); Jones v. United States, 357 U.S. 493, 500 (1958) (rejecting the government's argument that entry and seizure of evidence inside of a home was valid as search incident to arrest because officials' purpose in entering home was to search and not arrest); United States v. Lefkowitz, 285 U.S. 452, 467 (1932) (stating that an "arrest may not be used as a pretext to search for evidence"); *see also* BERNARD SCHWARTZ, THE UNPUBLISHED OPINIONS OF THE REHNQUIST COURT 48 (1996) (providing the dissenting opinion of Justice Powell in Missouri v. Blair, wherein Powell provides additional citations supporting the conclusion that "police conduct undertaken for the sole purpose of evading the probable cause or warrant requirements could render the police conduct unreasonable and therefore unconstitutional").

    13. Massachusetts v. Painten, 389 U.S. 560, 565 (1968) (*per curiam*) (White, J., dissenting).

    14. *See, e.g.,* Paul Brest, Palmer v. Thompson: *An Approach to the Problem of Unconstitutional Legislative Motive*, 1971 SUP. CT. REV. 95 (1971); John Hart Ely, *Legislative and Administrative Motivation in Constitutional Law*, 79 YALE L.J. 1205 (1970); *see also* JOHN HART ELY, DEMOCRACY AND DISTRUST 125–34 (1980).

    15. *See, e.g.,* Florida v. Wells, 495 U.S. 1, 4 (1990) (noting that "an inventory search must not be a ruse for a general rummaging in order to discover incriminating evidence"); Colorado v. Bertine, 479 U.S. 367, 372 (1987) (while upholding an inventory, acknowledging that there was "no showing that the police, who were following standardized procedures, acted in bad faith or for the sole purpose of [criminal] investigation"); New York v. Burger, 482 U.S. 691, 716–717, n.27 (1987) (approving administrative search of business premises by police officers, in part because the search was not "a 'pretext' for obtaining evidence" of criminal

offenses); South Dakota v. Opperman, 428 U.S. 364, 376 (1976) ("[T]here is no suggestion whatever that this standard [inventory] procedure . . . was a pretext concealing an investigatory police motive.").

16. LaFave, *supra* note 6, §1.4, at 113.

17. Brief for the Petitioners' Brief at 21–29, United States v. Whren, 517 U.S. 806 (1996) (No. 95–5841).

18. *See* A. Leon Higginbotham, Jr., In the Matter of Color 276 (1978).

19. *See generally*, Sally E. Hadden, Slave Patrols: Law and Violence in Virginia and the CArolinas (2001); *see also* William J. Cuddihy, The Fourth Amendment: Origins and Original Meaning 1602–1791, 437–449 (1990) (unpublished Ph.D. dissertation, Claremont Graduate School).

20. David A. Harris, *"Driving While Black" and All Other Traffic Offenses: The Supreme Court and Pretextual Traffic Stops*, 87 J. Crim. L. & Criminology 544, 565 (1997) (*quoting* Maryland State Police, Criminal Intelligence Report (April 27, 1992)). *See also The Color of Suspicion*, N.Y. Times, Magazine, June 20, 1999, at 57 ("'Racial profiling is a tool we use, and don't let anyone say otherwise, [Deputy Bobby] Harris says. 'Like up in the valley,' he continues, referring to the San Fernando Valley, 'I knew who all the crack sellers were—they look like Hispanics who should be cutting your lawn. They were driving cars like this one'—he points to an aging Chevy parked in the [police] station's lot—'and all the cars had DARE stickers on them. That's just the way it is.'"); *id.* ("'Of course we do racial profiling at the train station,' says Gary McLhinney, the president of the Baltimore Fraternal Order of Police. 'If 20 people get off the train and 19 are white guys in suits and one is a black female, guess who gets followed? If racial profiling is intuition and experience, I guess we all racial-profile.'"). *Cf.* Peter Verniero & Paul H. Zoubek, Interim Report of the State Police Review Team Regarding Allegations of Racial Profiling, N.J. Att'y Gen. Rep. at 49–50 (stating that the "phenomena of racial profiling and other forms of disparate treatment of minorities [on New Jersey's highways] are not just a matter of perception; the evidence . . . clearly shows that the problem is real."); Katherine Y. Barnes, *Assessing the Counterfactual: The Efficacy of Drug Interdiction Absent Racial Profiling*, 54 Duke L.J. 1089 (2005) (offering an empirical analysis and model that demonstrates, according to the author, that the Maryland State Police engaged in racial profiling on a section of Interstate 95 between May 1, 1997, and December 31, 2003); *id.* at 1118 ("The category of driver facing the highest overall probability of being searched is a black male motorist from a non–East Coast state, stopped in an older luxury car, traveling southbound."). *See generally*, David A. Harris, Profiles in Injustice: Why Racial Profiling cannot work 48–72 (2002).

21. State v. Pedro Soto, 734 A.2d 350, 360 (N.J. Super. L. 1999) (finding that the defendants "have proven at least a *de facto* policy on the part of the State Police . . . of targeting blacks for investigation and arrest between April 1988 and May 1991 both south of exit 3 and between exits 1 and 7A of the Turnpike.").

22. Joseph Neff & Pat Stith, *Highway Drug Unit Focuses on Blacks*, NEWS & OB-
SERVER (Raleigh, North Carolina), July 28, 1996, at A1.

23. Joseph Neff & Pat Stith, *Could It Happen by Chance?* NEWS & OBSERVER
(Raleigh, North Carolina), July 28, 1996, at A15.

24. *See* 3 LaFAVE, *supra* note 2, § 10.8, at 380 (1978) (explaining that several
lower-court rulings have recognized that a traffic stop "in order to check for a
driver's license or vehicle registration is permissible even in the absence of the
observation of any traffic violation or other prohibited conduct by the driver or
of any facts or circumstances which would give the officer cause to suspect that
the individual stopped is in violation of the driver's license or vehicle registration laws"); Note, *Automobile License Checks and the Fourth Amendment*, 60 VA.
L. REV. 666, 673 (1974) (noting that "the most common view [among the lower
courts] is that the Constitution permits an absolute power in the police to initiate
stops of motorists to check licenses and registrations, a power which the police
may use to serve general crime detection objectives") (footnote omitted).

25. 3 LaFAVE, *supra* note 2, § 10.8, at 386. As one close observer of the Philadelphia police described the practice in 1973:

> A policeman has an unqualified right to stop any car moving on a
> public street to check the operator's license and registration. . . . Most
> stops are made for violations of traffic regulations or to point out some
> fault in the car, and all of them are made under the umbrella of the pa-
> trolman's writ to check licensing, but often these reasons are incidental
> to his real interest. When a patrolman refers to a car stop, he usually
> means a stop he has made for suspicion. While these stops frequently
> reveal infractions of the codes regulating the ownership and use of cars,
> these violations are incidental to the officer's interest in finding stolen
> cars, cars carrying contraband, illegally armed people, and persons
> sought by the police.
> JONATHAN RUBINSTEIN, CITY POLICE 249–50 (1973).

26. 3 LaFAVE, *supra* note 2, § 10.8, at 386.

27. *See, e.g.,* LAWRENCE P. TIFFANY ET AL., DETECTION OF CRIME 30, n.16
(1967) (noting that observation of police conduct "makes it clear that a violation of the traffic code is often used as a subterfuge by officers who desire to
interrogate a person about a more serious offense. Because of this, traffic regulations which normally are unenforced are asserted as justification for field
interrogations.").

28. *Id.* at 15 (stating that "[m]inor traffic infractions are . . . often used by the
police to justify stopping for questioning or searching). *See also id.* at 131–32
(describing that in high-crime areas of large cities, the typical traffic offender is
rarely stopped, and if stopped is typically issued only a verbal warning; however,
"[w]hen motorists are stopped for minor traffic offenses in high-crime areas, the

purpose of the officer is usually to conduct a field interrogation, to search for weapons, or to search for evidence of a suspected crime.").

29. Delaware v. Prouse, 440 U.S. 648, 663 (1979). Only Justice Rehnquist dissented from the majority's judgment.

30. HARRIS, PROFILES, *supra* note 20, at 31. *See also* Harris, *"Driving While Black," supra* note 20, 557–58 ("There is no detail of driving too small, no piece of equipment too insignificant, no item of automobile regulation too arcane to be made the subject of a traffic offense. Police officers in some jurisdictions have a rule of thumb: the average driver cannot go three blocks without violating some traffic regulation."); Sklansky, *supra* note 9, at 298–99 ("Because almost everyone violates traffic rules sometimes, this means that the police, if they are patient, can eventually pull over anyone they are interested in questioning"); Barbara C. Salken, *The General Warrant of the Twentieth Century? A Fourth Amendment Solution to Unchecked Discretion to Arrest for Traffic Offenses*, 62 TEMP. L. REV. 221, 223 (1989) ("The innumerable rules and regulations governing vehicular travel make it difficult not to violate one of them at one time or another. 'Very few drivers can traverse any appreciable distance without violating some traffic regulation.'") (footnote omitted).

31. *Pedro Soto*, 734 A.2d at 352.

32. According to UsingEnglish.com, "[i]f something is like shooting fish in a barrel, it is so easy that success is guaranteed."

33. Officers Soto and Littlejohn were "from the Metropolitan Police Departments' Sixth District station, know locally as 6D. Years later, this precinct's vice squad was the subject of a newspaper expose reporting that the officers, including Littlejohn and Soto, had engaged in excessive use of force, planted evidence, and perjured themselves to secure drug convictions." Kevin R. Johnson, *The Story of Whren v. United States: The Song Remains the Same, in* RACE LAW STORIES (Foundation Press 2008) (footnote omitted).

34. Petitioners' Brief at 6, n.7, United States v. Whren, 517 U.S. 806 (1996) (No. 95–5841) (Another officer in the patrol car, Officer Littlejohn, made no mention of either the failure of the Pathfinder to signal or any speeding violations by the driver of the Pathfinder. Officer Littlejohn testified that there was reasonable suspicion of drug activity to justify the stopping of the vehicle, and it was on that basis that the Pathfinder was stopped.).

35. Brief for the Petitioners at 7, United States v. Whren, 517 U.S. 806 (1996) (No. 95–5841).

36. *See* District of Columbia Metropolitan Police Department General Order 303.1 (effective April 30, 1992), which specifically provided that "[m]embers who are not in uniform or are in unmarked vehicles may take [traffic] enforcement action only in the case of a violation that is so grave as to pose an immediate threat to the safety of others." Gen. Order 303.1(A)(4).

37. *Whren*, 517 U.S. at 809.

38. 53 F.3d 371, 374–75 (D.C.Cir. 1995).

39. Brief for the Petitioners at 7, United States v. Whren, 517 U.S. 806 (1996) (No. 95–5841).

40. 1 LaFave, *supra* note 6, § 1.4 (e), at 130.

41. *Id.* As Professor LaFave explained after the *Whren* ruling, the "petitioners' position is grounded in deviation from usual practice, which of course means that improper motivation unaccompanied by such deviation is not asserted to be 'unreasonable' under the Fourth Amendment." LaFave, *supra* note 6, §1.4 (f), at 139.

42. New York v. Burger, 482 U.S. 691 (1987).

43. *Id.* at 716, n.27.

44. Florida v. Wells, 495 U.S. 1 (1990).

45. Colorado v. Bertine, 479 U.S. 367 (1987).

46. *Wells*, 495 U. S. at 4.

47. *Bertine*, 479 U.S. at 372.

48. *Whren*, 517 U.S. at 811.

49. *Id.* at 812.

50. *Id.*

51. United States v. Villamonte-Marquez, 462 U.S. 579 (1983).

52. United States v. Robinson, 414 U.S. 218 (1973).

53. Scott v. United States, 436 U.S. 128 (1978).

54. *Whren*, 517 U.S. at 812.

55. *Id.* at 813, quoting *Robinson*, 414 U.S. at 221, n.1.

56. *Whren*, 517 U.S. at 813.

57. *Id.*, quoting *Scott*, 436 U.S. at 138.

58. *Whren*, 517 U.S. at 813.

59. *Id.*

60. *Id.* at 814.

61. *Id.*

62. *Id.*

63. *Id.*

64. *Id.* at 815.

65. *Id.*

66. *Id.*

67. *Id.*

68. *Id.*

69. *Id.* at 818.

70. *Id.*

71. *Id.*

72. *Id.*

73. *Id.*

74. *Id.* at 818–19.

75. *Id.* at 819.

76. Anthony Amsterdam, *Perspectives on the Fourth Amendment*, 58 MINN. L. REV. 349, 417 (1974) (footnote omitted); *cf. Camara v. Municipal Court*, 387 U.S.523, 528 (1967) ("The basic purpose of th[e] Amendment, as recognized in countless decisions of this Court, is to safeguard the privacy and security of individuals against arbitrary invasions by governmental officials.").

77. *See generally*, Thomas Y. Davies, *Recovering the Original Fourth Amendment*, 98 MICH. L. REV. 547,556, 736 (1999) (larger purpose for which the Framers adopted the Fourth Amendment was to curb the exercise of discretionary authority of government officers).

78. Amsterdam, *supra* note 76, at 396 (quoting *Wilkes v. Wood*, 19 Howell St. Tr. 1153, 1167 (1763); *Legal Papers of John Adams*, 106–147 (1965)).

79. LaFave, *supra* note 6, § 1.4(e), at 132.

80. *Whren*, 517 U.S. at 813.

81. *See, e.g., Wells*, 495 U.S. at 4 ("an inventory search must not be a ruse for general rummaging in order to discover incriminating evidence"); Arizona v. Hicks, 480 U.S. 321, 334 (1987) ("If an officer could indiscriminately search every item in plain view, a search justified by limited purpose . . . could be used to eviscerate the protections of the Fourth Amendment.").

82. Jones v. United States, 357 U.S. 493 (1958).

83. *Id.* at 499.

84. *Id.* at 500.

85. *See* Amsterdam, *supra* note 76, at 373 (interpreting *Jones* to mean that "if an officer's conduct would be lawful in pursuit of one purpose but unlawful in pursuit of another, it is unlawful when directed to the wrong pursuit") (footnote omitted); Burkoff, *Bad Faith Searches*, *supra* note 10, at 81 (explaining that *Jones* "refused to sanction search and seizure on the basis of a proffered 'objective' legal analysis of the officers' actions, relying instead on the true (improper) intentions of the officers") (footnote omitted).

86. Schwartz, *supra* note 12, at 30.

87. Burkoff, *The Pretext Search Doctrine Returns After Never Leaving*, *supra* note 10, at 365 (1989).

88. The Court ultimately decided that the writ of certiorari granted in *Blair* was "improvidently granted." Missouri v. Blair, 480 U.S. 698 (1987).

89. Cummins v. United States, 502 U.S. 962 (1991).

90. *Id.* at 963 (White, J. dissenting).

91. *See, e.g., Aro*, *supra* note 10, at 152 (noting that the problems related to pretextual searches and seizures "[have] clearly had a long, if somewhat undistinguished and ambiguous history before the Court"); *see also* LaFave, *supra* note 6, § 1.4(e), at 127 (explaining that the ruling in *United States v. Scott* "can hardly be read as a definitive analysis settling that in *all* circumstances Fourth Amendment suppression issues are to be resolved without assaying 'the underlying intent or motivation of the officers involved'").

92. *Whren,* 517 U.S. at 811.

93. *Id.*

94. *Cf.* Sklansky, *supra* note 9, at 285, n.67 (making the same point).

95. Tiffany et al., *supra* note 5, at 131 (1967) (quoting one officer saying, "You can always get a guy legitimately on a traffic violation if you tail him for a while, and then a search can be made.").

96. Harris, *supra* note 20, at 558.

97. *See* LaFave, *supra* note 6, § 1.4(e), at 133. Professor LaFave has explained that while traffic stops differ from administrative searches in that the former are supported by probable cause of a specific offense, while the latter are not, he concludes that that difference is unimportant: "[G]iven the pervasiveness of [minor traffic offenses] and the ease in which law enforcement agents may uncover them in the conduct of virtually everyone, that difference hardly matters, for here as well as there exists 'a power that places the liberty of every man in the hands of every petty officer,' precisely the kind of arbitrary authority which gave rise to the Fourth Amendment." *Id.* (footnote omitted).

98. *Camara,* 387 U.S. at 532; *see also* See v. City of Seattle, 387 U.S. 541, 545 (1967) (applying *Camara*'s reasoning to business premise, noting "the decision to enter and inspect will not be the product of the unreviewed discretion of the enforcement officer in the field").

99. *Opperman,* 428 U.S. at 376 (footnote omitted).

100. *Id.* at 384 (Powell, J., concurring) (footnote omitted).

101. *Whren,* 517 U.S. at 811.

102. *Id.* at 812.

103. U.S. v. Robinson, 414 U.S. 218, 235 (1973).

104. *Scott,* 436 U.S. at 139.

105. *See* LaFave, *supra* note 6, § 1.4 (a), at 115 (explaining that *Scott* "can hardly be read as a definitive analysis settling that in *all* circumstances Fourth Amendment suppression issues are to be resolved without assaying 'the underlying intent or motivation of the officers involved.'").

106. *See* James B. Haddad, *Pretextual Fourth Amendment Activity: Another Viewpoint,* 18 MICH. J. L. REF. 639, 674 (1985) ("Simply put, *Scott* did not involve a pretext claim."); Burkoff, *Bad Faith Searches, supra* note 10, at 83–83 (asserting that *Scott* "merely held that improper intent that is not acted upon does not render unconstitutional an otherwise constitutional search") (footnote omitted). After the quotations just noted, *Scott* explained that the defendants' argument concerning the agents' bad faith were not primarily grounded on Fourth Amendment principles. Indeed, *Scott* itself acknowledged that "[the defendants] do not appear, however, to rest their argument entirely on Fourth Amendment principles. Rather, they argue in effect that regardless of the search-and-seizure analysis conducted under the Fourth Amendment, the statute regulating wiretaps requires the agents to make good-faith efforts at minimization, and the failure to

make such efforts is itself a violation of the statute which requires suppression." *Scott*, 436 U.S. at 138–39.

107. *Scott*, 436 U.S. at 138 (footnote omitted).

108. Burkoff, *Bad Faith Searches*, *supra* note 10, at 83–84.

109. *Villamonte-Marquez*, 462 U.S. at 584, n.3.

110. *Whren*, 517 U.S. at 812.

111. Schwartz, *supra* note 12, at 60, *quoting* the concurring opinion of Justice O'Connor in *Missouri v. Blair*.

112. *Whren*, 517 U.S. at 813.

113. *Id.* at 814.

114. *Id.* at 814.

115. 1 LaFave, *supra* note 6, §1.4 (e), at 130 (footnote omitted).

116. *See* Amsterdam, *supra* note 76, at 411. Professor Amsterdam explained that the Framers of the Fourth Amendment were concerned with "indiscriminate" searches or seizures. Indiscriminate intrusions were problematic partly because they were "conducted at the discretion of executive officials, who may act despotically and capriciously in the exercise of the power to search and seize. This . . . concern runs against *arbitrary* searches and seizures: it condemns the petty tyranny of unregulated rummagers." *Id.*

117. Kenneth Culp Davis, Discretionary Justice 88 (1969).

118. Amsterdam, *supra* note 76 at 417

119. *Id.* at 416. *See also* Wayne R. LaFave, *Controlling Discretion By Administration Regulations: The Use, Misuse, and Nonuse of Police Rules and Policies in Fourth Amendment Adjudication*, 89 Mich. L. Rev. 442, 449 (1990) ("Protection against arbitrary searches and seizures lies in controlling police discretion, which requires a determination that the police action taken against a particular individual corresponds to that which occurs with respect to other persons similarly situated.").

120. *Whren*, 517 U.S. at 815.

121. *Id.*

122. *Id.*

123. *Id.*

124. *See* Michigan Dept. of State Police v. Sitz, 496 U.S. 444 (1990) (upholding a sobriety roadblock); *Prouse*, 440 U.S. at 663 (dicta stating that "[q]uestioning of all oncoming traffic at roadblock-type stops [for license and registration check] is one possible alternative" to the unconstrained exercise of discretion inherent in random or spot check by officers).

125. *See* Appendix A at 9a in Brief for Respondent in *Delaware v. Prouse* (describing 1969 study of fifteen college students representing a cross-section of the population. None of the students had received a traffic ticket in the preceding twelve months, and all had cars in satisfactory condition. Within seventeen days of placing "Black Panther" bumper stickers on their vehicle, the students were given thirty-three traffic citations.) (citing Heusenstamm, *"Bumper Stickers and*

the Cops," TRANSACTION MAGAZINE, February 1971); Esquire Magazine article discussing ACLU bumper stickers; Estep v. Dallas County, Tex., 310 F. 3d 353, 357, n.3 (5th Cir. 2002) (officer searched pickup truck, in part, because he saw NRA bumper sticker on truck).

126. *See* Frank Askin, *When Long Hair Was a Crime,* N.Y. TIMES, March 2, 1994.

127. *Whren,* 517 U.S. at 818.

128. *Id.*

129. Transcript of Oral Argument at 34–35, United States v. Whren, 517 U.S. 806 (1996) (95–5841).

130. *Id.* at 35.

131. *Id.* at 36–38.

132. *Whren,* 517 U.S. at 819.

133. *Pedro Soto,* 734 A.2d at 352–57.

134. *Whren,* 517 U.S. at 818.

135. *Id.* at 818–19.

136. *See* County of Riverside v. McLaughlin, 500 U.S. 44, 66 (1991); Michigan Dept. of State Police v. Sitz, 496 U.S. 444, 459 (1990).

137. Railway Express Agency v. New York, 336 U.S. 106, 112–13 (1949) (Jackson, J., concurring).

138. Kenneth Culp Davis, *An Approach to Legal Control of the Police,* 52 Tex. L. Rev. 703, 714 (1974).

139. Batson v. Kentucky, 476 U.S. 79 (1986).

140. Kenneth J. Melilli, Batson *in Practice: What We Have Learned About* Batson *and Peremptory Challenges,* 71 NOTRE DAME L. REV. 447, 470 (1996).

141. *Batson,* 476 U.S. at 97.

142. *Id.*

143. *Id.* at 94.

144. United States v. Roberson, 6 F. 3d 1088 (5th Cir. 1993) In *Roberson,* shortly after midnight, on a highway, Texas State Trooper Barry Washington passed a minivan that had four black occupants. After climbing a hill, the trooper then pulled over to the shoulder, doused his lights, and waited for the van to pass. When the minivan neared the trooper's cruiser, it was the only moving vehicle on the road. The minivan "changed lanes to distance itself as it passed the [trooper's cruiser] on the right shoulder" but failed to signal the lane change. *Id.* at 1089. Stopping the van for failing to signal a lane change was upheld as reasonable. The court rejected the defendants' claim that the stop was a pretext to search for drugs and thus unreasonable under the Fourth Amendment. The claim was rejected *not* because there wasn't sufficient evidence of pretext. On the contrary, the court observed that Trooper Washington had a "remarkable record" of converting traffic stops into drug arrests in 250 prior incidents, and the court acknowledged its "familiar[ity] with Trooper Washington's propensity for patrolling the fourth

amendment's outer frontier." *Id.* at 1092. In fact, the court quietly admitted that Trooper Washington's seizure in *Roberson* was pretextual but insisted that there was nothing it could do about it. "[W]hile we do not applaud what appears to be a common practice of some law enforcement officers to use technical violations as a cover for exploring for more serious violations, we may look no further than the [trial] court's finding that Trooper Washington had a legitimate basis for stopping the van." *Id.*

145. Michael J. Raphael & Edward J. Ungvarsky, *Excuses: Neutral Explanations Under* Batson v. Kentucky, 27 U. MICH. J. L. REF. 229, 266 (1993). *Cf.* Melilli, *supra* note 140, at 465 (stating that an empirical analysis of lower court rulings "show[s] that, when call upon to do so, *Batson* respondents offer acceptable neutral explanations in almost four out of five situations. This, of course, tends to confirm the hypothesis that the odds are not with the *Batson* complainant ultimately prevailing. On the other hand, the success rates for *Batson* respondents offering explanations is not so high as to suggest that the courts merely rubber stamp virtually all such explanations as satisfactory.").

146. The Court's concern with equal treatment by governmental actors has not been confined to equal protection cases. *See* LAURENCE H. TRIBE, AMERICAN CONSTITUTIONAL LAW § 16–1, at 1437 (2d ed. 1988) ("[N]o single clause or provision [of the Constitution] is the exclusive fount of [equality] doctrine."). Several parts of the Constitution and provisions of the Bill of Rights have been interpreted to incorporate equality norms as part of the substantive right accorded by the provision. For example, the scope of the First Amendment's right of speech is informed by equality norms. *See* Police Dep't of Chicago v. Mosley, 408 U.S. 92, 95–96 (1972). Likewise, the Eighth Amendment's ban on cruel and unusual punishment has been read to incorporate a principle of equality. *See* Furman v. Georgia, 408 U.S. 238, 257 (1972) (Douglas, J., concurring) (noting that the challenged death penalty statutes "are pregnant with discrimination and discrimination is an ingredient not compatible with the idea of equal protection of the laws that is implicit in the ban on 'cruel and unusual' punishments"); *id.* at 310 (Stewart, J., concurring) (concluding that although racial discrimination was not proven, the Eighth Amendment "cannot tolerate the infliction of a sentence of death under legal systems that permit this unique penalty to be so wantonly and so freakishly imposed"); Ely, *supra,* note 14 at 97 (noting that the protection against cruel and unusual punishment "surely had to do with a realization that in the context of imposing penalties . . . there is tremendous potential for the arbitrary or invidious infliction of 'unusually' severe punishments on persons of various classes other than 'our own.'"). In a different context, the modern Court reads the Fifth Amendment's Due Process Clause to impose on federal officials the same equality norms that the Fourteenth Amendment imposes upon the states. *See* Adarand Constructors, Inc. v. Pena, 515 U.S. 200, 213–17 (1995); Bolling v. Sharpe, 347 U.S. 497 (1954). Finally, equality norms were a major component

of the Court's rationale in *Miranda v. Arizona*, 384 U.S. 436 (1966), when the Court read the Fifth Amendment's Self-Incrimination Clause to require that police provide specific warnings to subjects undergoing custodial interrogation. *See Miranda*, 384 U.S. at 472–73. *See also* Yale Kamisar, *Equal Justice in the Gatehouses and Mansions of American Criminal Procedure: From* Powell *to* Gideon, *From* Escobedo *to . . .*, *in* CRIMINAL JUSTICE IN OUR TIME 68–76 (A. E. Dick Howard ed., 1965) (recognizing that equality norms, articulated in the Court's Equal Protection Clause cases, were latent in the constitutional debate concerning police interrogation and confessions).

147. Ely, *supra* note 14, at 97.

148. United States v. Armstrong, 517 U.S. 456 (1996).

149. *Id.* at 458.

150. *Id.* at 465. In *Armstrong*, the Court reserved the question of whether a criminal defendant must satisfy the similarly situated requirement in a case where the prosecutor admits a "discriminatory purpose." *Id.* at 469, n.3. Of course, Officer Soto has never directly admitted that he stopped the petitioners because they were black. *Cf.* Johnson, *supra,* note 33 (explaining that the trial court in *Whren* had been concerned about the "'lengthy pause'" before Officer Soto answered "no" to a "'very straightforward question'" from defense counsel on whether Soto stopped the defendants' vehicle because he believed that two young black men in a Pathfinder with temporary tags were suspicious) (footnote omitted).

151. *Id.* at 465, quoting Wayte v. United States, 470 U.S. 598, 608 (1985).

152. *See id.* at 476 (stating that a selective prosecution claimant must demonstrate that the prosecution policy "'had a discriminatory effect and that it was motivated by a discriminatory purpose'"); Washington v. Davis, 426 U.S. 229 (1976) (finding that disparate racial impact, standing alone, does not constitute equal protection violation and the challenger must show a discriminatory intent or purpose).

153. McCleskey v. Kemp, 481 U.S. 279 (1987).

154. *Id.* at 292.

155. *Armstrong*, 517 U.S. at 461, n.2.

156. *Whren*, 517 U.S. at 813.

5

County of Sacramento v. Lewis

Protecting Life and Liberty Under the Constitution—
Reckless Indifference to Life Does Not Shock the
Conscience of the Supreme Court

Michael Avery

Introduction

In *County of Sacramento v. Lewis*,[1] the Supreme Court decided that an
improper high-speed chase by police officers might violate the constitutional rights of a person injured during the chase. But, at the same time,
the Court set the standard of proof in such cases so high that as a practical matter it could almost never be met. As a result, a roadblock was
erected that precludes civil rights claims based on reckless high-speed
chases.

On May 22, 1990, 16-year-old Philip Lewis was killed when the motorcycle on which he was riding tipped over and the police car that had
been chasing it at speeds up to 100 miles per hour ran into him.[2] The
chase began when two sheriff's deputies, James Everett Smith and Murray
Stapp, who had just finished dealing with an unrelated police call, saw the
motorcycle driven by 18-year-old Brian Willard approaching them at high
speed. Stapp turned on the rotating overhead lights on his cruiser, yelled
for the motorcycle to stop, and pulled his cruiser closer to Smith's vehicle
in order to pen the motorcycle in.

Unfortunately, Brian did not stop but maneuvered his motorcycle between the two police cars and drove off. Deputy Smith gave chase. The
two teenagers were not wanted for any criminal violation other than Brian's violation of the speed limit and his failure to stop when ordered to
do so. Deputy Smith activated his lights and siren and pursued the motorcycle for 1.3 miles through a residential neighborhood at speeds that
reached 100 miles per hour. He followed the boys at a distance as short as
100 feet, although at 100 miles per hour it would have taken 650 feet to

stop his car. The officer reported that the motorcycle wove in and out of traffic, forcing two cars and a bicycle to swerve off the road.

After 75 seconds the chase came to a tragic end, described by the Supreme Court as follows:

> The chase ended after the motorcycle tipped over as Willard tried a sharp left turn. By the time Smith slammed on his brakes, Willard was out of the way, but Lewis was not. The patrol car skidded into him at 40 miles an hour, propelling him some 70 feet down the road and inflicting massive injuries. Lewis was pronounced dead at the scene.[3]

Phillip's parents, Teri and Thomas Lewis, filed suit against Sacramento County and Deputy Smith in state court under the federal Civil Rights Act.[4] They claimed that Smith had deprived Phillip of his life "without due process of law." The doctrine of "substantive due process" on which they relied is one of the most complex and controversial doctrines in all of constitutional law. In its simplest terms, the claim was that the government's law enforcement goals were insufficient to justify Smith's actions that led to the loss of Phillip's life.

The district court ruled for the defendants, entering a summary judgment in their favor. The summary judgment procedure allows a court to decide for the defendants without a trial if it determines that even if all the plaintiffs' factual claims were true, the law would provide them no relief. Here the district court found that Deputy Smith was entitled to immunity from suit because it concluded that there was no precedent at the time of the chase that the doctrine of substantive due process protected persons injured in a high-speed police chase.[5] The district court also ruled in favor of the County, because it concluded that the plaintiffs had not demonstrated that it provided insufficient training on high-speed chases.

The Lewises appealed to the Ninth Circuit Court of Appeals, which reversed the decision of the district court and held that they were entitled to a trial in the case.[6] The Ninth Circuit concluded the law regarding high-speed chases had been clearly established by the time of this incident. The Court of Appeals also based its decision on the fact that the General Orders of the Sheriff's Department required officers in a high-speed chase to determine whether a chase presents unreasonable hazards to life and property and to discontinue such pursuits when the hazards outweigh the benefits of the immediate capture of the persons they are chasing.[7] The

Court of Appeals found there was enough evidence to justify a trial on the question of whether Deputy Smith had followed the General Orders in this case.

The Supreme Court took the case because there was a conflict among the Courts of Appeals about the standard that should be applied to decide whether a law enforcement officer has violated the substantive due process rights of a person injured in a police chase.[8] The Supreme Court had never before ruled on this question.

The Court's opinion, written by Justice David Souter, established that the Due Process Clause of the Constitution guarantees more than merely a fair procedure before life, liberty, and property can be taken by the government. It also provides substantive protection to life, liberty, and property by "barring certain government actions regardless of the fairness of the procedures used to implement them."[9] Justice Souter recognized that the Lewises' claim fell within this category, because they claimed that "Smith's actions in causing Lewis's death were an abuse of executive power so clearly unjustified by any legitimate objective of law enforcement as to be barred by the Fourteenth Amendment."[10]

The Court decided an important threshold issue in the Lewises' favor. The defendants had argued that the Court should not apply substantive due process in high-speed police chases because a more specific provision of the Constitution should control the case—the Fourth Amendment's command against unreasonable searches and seizures. The defendants argued that because the Fourth Amendment generally governs the circumstances under which police may take someone into custody and how much force they may use in doing so, it should be applied here. They also argued that on the basis of the facts of this case the Fourth Amendment would provide no remedy to the Lewises and that the Court should not fill that void with the substantive due process doctrine.

Justice Souter acknowledged that the Court's general rule was "[w]here a particular Amendment provides an explicit textual source of constitutional protection against a particular sort of government behavior, that Amendment, not the general notion of substantive due process, must be the guide for analyzing these claims."[11] The rule is meant to limit the circumstances under which the Court might expand the concept of substantive due process, which doctrine is generally not favored by the Supreme Court.[12] Justice Souter, however, concluded that the defendants were reading the rule requiring reliance on specific Amendments other than the due process clause too narrowly.

The Court's previous cases had made clear that a high-speed chase, even where the vehicle chased is eventually stopped, does not result in a "seizure" as the term is used in the Fourth Amendment unless the vehicle is stopped by means intentionally applied by the police to do so.[13] For example, if the pursued vehicle were to crash into a roadblock set up to stop it, there might be a Fourth Amendment seizure. But if the suspect vehicle chased by the police accidentally crashes into another vehicle or the driver loses control and the car runs off the road, there is no seizure covered by the Fourth Amendment.[14]

The Court rejected the argument of the defendants in *Lewis* that the Fourth Amendment governs an attempted seizure and concluded instead that a high-speed police chase ending in a crash that was not intended by the officers is simply not covered by the Fourth Amendment.[15] The Court also concluded that the plaintiffs should not be left without any claim and that substantive due process could be applied to allegations of government misconduct that was physically abusive.[16]

The Court then came to the crucial question of what standard must be met to prove a violation of the substantive due process clause in the case of a high-speed police chase. The Court applied language that had been used in a number of cases over the previous fifty years and held that to prove a violation of substantive due process, it is necessary to show that an official's conduct was "shocking to the conscience."[17]

The Court, relying on its previous cases, rejected any argument that simple negligence by government officials could be described as conscience shocking.[18] Justice Souter suggested that liability for a substantive due process violation would probably be found where an official intended to injure someone in a way unjustified by any legitimate government interest. But he found that government misconduct that fell between those two extremes, more than negligent but less than intentional misconduct, presented "closer calls."[19]

The Court concluded that there is no single definition for what is conscience shocking in all circumstances. The Court decided that in high-speed police chases it is necessary to prove that the officers improperly intended to cause harm to the injured party unrelated to the legitimate object of arrest for the judicial conscience to be shocked.[20] Such proof, of course, will rarely be available. On the assumption that high-speed pursuits involve "instant judgment" by officers, the Court held that even recklessness was not enough to shock the conscience.[21] The Court specifically decided that police who exhibit only a "reckless indifference to life" or a "reckless disregard for life" do not violate the Constitution's guarantee of substantive due process.[22] As a result, the Court reversed the Ninth Circuit Court of Appeals and concluded that the Lewises were not entitled to a trial on their claims. None of the Justices dissented from the decision.

Following the decision in *Lewis*, federal constitutional law provided no meaningful guidelines for when the police might conduct high-speed pursuits. At present the Court continues to ignore the dangers posed by police pursuits at high speeds and to fail to hold officers accountable for the fatalities and serious injuries that they cause. In *Scott v. Harris*,[23] in 2007, the Court held that an officer was not liable for a constitutional violation under the Fourth Amendment where he intentionally rammed the suspect vehicle at a high rate of speed, causing it to leave the road and rendering the driver a quadriplegic.

As the dissent here points out, the thinking of police administrators has been substantially more concerned about the dangers of high-speed pursuits than the Supreme Court. Within months after *Lewis* was decided, the International Association of Chiefs of Police published a Training Key on Vehicular Pursuits that cautioned officers that the decision "must not be thought to be a license to engage in high-speed chases without thought of the consequences."[24] The IACP then expanded on the cautions contained in the 1989 Model Policy cited in the dissent.[25] The 1998 Training Key provides:

> The first and most important requirement in the decision to initiate a pursuit is . . . the officer must not pursue unless the officer determines that immediate danger to the public created by the pursuit is less than the immediate or potential danger to the public if the suspect remains at large. This is not an easy decision, but it must be made in every case, and it must be made objectively and rationally. Virtually every police officer has an instinctive desire to pursue a suspected perpetrator; indeed, perhaps it might be said that every good police officer has this instinctive desire. But the dangers involved in pursuit make it absolutely necessary that this instinct be subordinated to rational evaluation of the risk versus the potential advantages of it.

In *Scott* the Supreme Court had before it an amicus brief describing a canvass of police departments across the country conducted by Prof. Karen Blum and students at Suffolk University Law School that documented that the majority had restrictive policies with respect to high-speed pursuits.[26] The information was ignored by the Court in *Scott*, as it had been in *Lewis*.

Professor Michael Avery argues that the Court in *Lewis* should have protected the lives of innocent civilians against high-speed pursuits by police officers conducted with reckless disregard for the safety of the public.

Dissent by Michael Avery

The opinion of the Court makes a series of errors in constitutional analysis and in judgment that lead it to the conclusion that a police officer who chases teenagers on a motorcycle at high speeds for a mere traffic violation does not violate the constitutional rights of a youth killed during the chase, even where the officer acts with reckless disregard for the lives of those on the motorcycle driver and the public at large. I suspect this conclusion is disturbing to the average American. Because the doctrine of substantive due process should protect the rights of those injured by police actions that demonstrate a reckless disregard for human life, I dissent.

The opinion for the Court properly recognizes that the "core of the concept" and the "touchstone" of substantive due process is "protection of the individual against arbitrary action of government."[27] One might think that it would be relatively straightforward to decide that endangering lives in order to arrest someone for a traffic violation is sufficiently irrational to be considered arbitrary. Justice Souter, however, immediately gets off the track with his next assumption that the "criteria to identify what is fatally arbitrary differ depending on whether it is legislation or a specific act of a governmental officer that is at issue."[28] The use of two different standards to decide when a legislature and a government officer violate substantive due process rights is not justified by constitutional doctrine.[29] It results in an artificially high burden that citizens injured by arbitrary conduct by government officials have to meet in order to vindicate their constitutional rights.

We have repeatedly recognized that when state action infringes upon fundamental rights the courts must apply strict scrutiny to determine whether the constitution has been violated. We have defined that to mean that the state action must be in the service of a "compelling governmental interest" and that the action must be "narrowly tailored" to avoid significant interference with individual rights and interests beyond the extent necessary to achieve the compelling goals.[30] We have applied this test both when the state action resulted from legislative action and when it was the result of decisions by executive agencies or individual government officials.[31]

The opinion for the Court, however, asserts that, with respect to decisions made by individual government officials, it is only "the most egregious official conduct" that can be said to be "arbitrary in the constitutional sense."[32] Justice Souter cites only our decision in *Collins v. Harker Heights*[33] to support this assumption, but, as I discuss later, that case arose in a very specific context and stands for a much narrower proposition than the Court implies.[34]

Reflection suggests that, from a doctrinal point of view, it should not be more difficult for the judiciary to characterize the actions of an individual government official as a violation of substantive due process than it is to reject the collective judgment of a democratically elected legislature on the same constitutional grounds. If anything, the decisions of the legislature should come to this Court protected by a greater presumption of constitutionality than the actions of a single, perhaps rogue, patrol officer. There is even less reason to afford deference to the officer when his conduct violated the General Orders of his police department.

The Court insists upon egregiousness as an element of a constitutional violation by an individual official not because it makes sense from the standpoint of the constitutional doctrine of separation of powers but simply because it is a method for limiting the number and scope of constitutional claims that can be made against government officials. Justice Souter argues that "executive action challenges raise a particular need to preserve the constitutional proportions of constitutional claims, lest the Constitution be demoted to what we have called a font of tort law."[35] In other words, constitutional claims have to be hard to prove, or we might have too many of them. That is hardly a principled analysis.

This Court has cautioned against allowing the Constitution to become a "font of tort law" on several previous occasions[36] but has never once demonstrated that there is any significant danger of that happening. Although it is true that the number of civil rights suits filed each year has grown, those who resist recognition of substantive due process claims have never shown that this growth is the result of the existence of newly defined claims. Indeed, in the past several decades, the Court has so seldom recognized a new substantive due process right likely to result in individual damages claims that it would be astonishing if suits based on those grounds were anything more than a trivial percentage of suits filed on more traditional grounds. Justice Brennan understood that the "font of tort law" argument was "disingenuous" in 1976, the first time it was made.[37] It is time to recognize that this defense against the recognition of substantive due process rights is merely a rhetorical shield erected against claims some Justices find undesirable for other reasons.

If we were to use the accepted strict scrutiny analysis in this case, we would readily conclude that Deputy Smith violated Philip Lewis's constitutional rights. Philip Lewis had a recognized fundamental liberty interest in his bodily integrity.[38] Crashing into his body with a speeding police cruiser violates that liberty interest unless it is justified by a compelling governmental interest. Apprehension of a motorcyclist for traffic violations does not, without more, constitute a governmental interest sufficiently compelling to race on public roads at speeds approaching 100 miles per hour.[39] Moreover, attempting the apprehension by means of a dangerous high-speed chase is not a "narrowly tailored" approach with no safer options available, such as noting down the license plate and making the arrest at a later time. The government interest and the method of achieving it would not remotely justify the risk to the life of the person pursued, his passenger, or those of innocent bystanders.

It is, however, not necessary in this case to reach the question of whether strict scrutiny, with the requirements of a compelling governmental interest and narrow tailoring, should be used as the standard to determine whether official defendants are liable in damage actions for substantive due process violations. If the Court had recognized that high-speed pursuits conducted with reckless disregard for the risks to human life constitute substantive due process violations, it would have been apparent that this case should have been sent back to the district court for trial.

The Court's second major error is the use of the "shocks the conscience" language to define the level of culpability it insists upon to establish a substantive due process violation. This phrase has no inherent objective content and is an invitation for judges to determine whether constitutional violations have occurred according to their subjective response to the facts of a case. A calloused or cynical judge may embrace law enforcement tactics that would be "shocking" to the conscience of a judge with more developed sensibilities.

This was illustrated in the case of *Temkin v. Frederick County Commissioners*.[40] There, the Fourth Circuit Court of Appeals affirmed summary judgment in favor of a police officer who had chased a vehicle at speeds up to 105 miles per hour in connection with an alleged theft of $17 worth of gasoline. The officer chased the suspect's vehicle into a congested area near a carnival. The pursued vehicle failed to navigate a curve, crossed the centerline, and struck an oncoming car, which was then struck by the police car, causing serious injuries to the driver of the third vehicle.

The most striking aspect of *Temkin* is that the court made no effort to justify the high-speed pursuit of an alleged misdemeanant. The court simply asserted that the facts were similar to or less egregious than those in other reported decisions. It concluded that the officer's conduct did not "shock the conscience," although it was "disturbing and lacking in judgment."[41] The case is a prime example of a failure to conduct a reasoned analysis. This was made possible through the invocation of the "shocks the conscience" standard.

Although we come at this problem from different perspectives, I agree with Justice Scalia that the "shocks the conscience" test is entirely subjective. Borrowing his terminology from Cole Porter, he writes, "today's opinion resuscitates the *ne plus ultra*, the Napoleon Brandy, the Mahatma Gandhi, the Cellophane of subjectivity, th' ol' 'shocks-the-conscience' test."[42]

This troublesome phrase originated in *Rochin v. California*,[43] where the Court found that the involuntary forcible pumping of the defendant's stomach to obtain evidence "did more than offend some fastidious squeamishness or sentimentalism about combating crime too energetically" and "shocks the conscience."[44] The Court did not hold that this was the standard required for a constitutional violation but at most stated that conduct that shocks the conscience would suffice to state a claim of constitutional deprivation.[45] Indeed it was not the only language the Court employed to justify its conclusion. The Court also stated, "Due process of law, as a historic and generative principle, precludes defining, and thereby confining, these standards of conduct more precisely than to say that convictions cannot be brought about by methods that offend 'a sense of justice.'"[46] The *Rochin* Court simply did not attempt to define a firm standard or test for establishing a substantive due process violation.

Indeed, this Court has never held that "shocks the conscience" is the standard by which substantive due process claims are to be judged. In *Daniels v. Williams* the Court held that proof of negligence is not sufficient to establish a constitutional violation but expressly reserved the question of "whether something less than intentional conduct, such as recklessness or 'gross negligence,' is enough to trigger the protections of the Due Process Clause."[47] There would have been no need to treat this as an open question if "shocks the conscience" had been recognized as the definitive test in *Rochin* or later cases.[48]

The Court's opinion in this case grounds its invocation of the "shocks the conscience" language upon *Collins v. Harker Heights*, where we rejected a claim that a municipality has a constitutional obligation to provide safe working conditions for its employees. The Court cites *Collins* as authority for the notion that "shocks the conscience" is the test for a substantive due process violation. But *Collins* established no such thing. The Court in *Collins* used the phrase "shocks the conscience" only once, as a characterization of the plaintiff's contention,[49] and only once used the phrase "conscience shocking." On that occasion, the phrase was used not exclusively but in the disjunctive with "arbitrary."[50] "Arbitrary" was the predominant term used to assess the due process violation in *Collins*. The Court stated that its "refusal to characterize the city's alleged omission in this case as arbitrary in a constitutional sense rests on the presumption that the administration of government programs is based on a rational decisionmaking process . . .";[51] concluded that the petitioner "has not alleged that the deprivation of this liberty interest was arbitrary in the constitutional sense"; and maintained that "the city's alleged failure to train and warn did not constitute a constitutionally arbitrary deprivation."[52] The last substantive sentence of the opinion concludes that "the city's alleged failure to train or warn its sanitation department employees was not arbitrary in a constitutional sense."[53] No reference to any "shocks the conscience" test was made in any of these portions of the opinion. If the language used by the Court could be read to establish implicitly the standard for proving a substantive due process violation, that standard would be arbitrariness.[54]

The Court's opinion here insists upon using "shocks the conscience" as a standard even though Justice Souter himself acknowledges that "the measure of what is conscience shocking is no calibrated yard stick" but merely "points the way."[55] In fact, the Court limits the circumstances under which conscience shocking "points the way" to those "only at the ends of the tort law's spectrum of culpability."[56] In other words, where conduct is merely negligent, it is "categorically beneath the threshold of constitutional due process," and where it is intended to injure in some way unjustified by any government interest, it is "most likely to rise to the conscience shocking level."[57] But, as the Court's opinion tells us, when injuries are produced with culpability in a middle range, more than negligence but less than intentional conduct, such as recklessness or gross negligence, whether they are conscience shocking "is a matter for closer calls."[58]

One might ask why the Court retains a standard that can do no more than suggest that cases are "close calls" when they do not fall at the extreme ends of the culpability spectrum. What is the value of making any inquiry into whether behavior is "conscience shocking" if some other measure is required to decide the close calls? I can only conclude that a majority of the Court perceives the value of the "conscience shocking" standard to lie in its rhetorical implication that the standard is difficult to meet. In other words, we are back to the notion that constitutional claims have to be hard to prove or we might have too many of them.

The opinion of the Court does recognize that at least in one circumstance, the "conscience shocking" standard permits the conclusion that "deliberate indifference" to the risk of constitutional injury is a sufficient basis for a substantive due process claim. Where jail officials are deliberately indifferent to the serious medical needs of their prisoners and more serious injuries result, the officials may be held liable for due process violations.[59] That is not adopted as the standard of what would be "conscience shocking" in the present case, however. The Court notes, "Deliberate indifference that shocks in one environment may not be so patently egregious in another, and our concern with preserving the constitutional proportions of substantive due process demands an exact analysis of circumstances before any abuse of power is condemned as conscience shocking."[60] In other words, if the "deliberate indifference" standard does not set the bar high enough in a given situation to "preserve the constitutional proportions of substantive due process,"that is, make the case difficult enough to prove, the "conscience shocking" standard allows us to raise it.

In line with that analysis, Justice Souter then turns his attention to the circumstances in high-speed police pursuits and concludes that the "deliberate indifference" standard is inappropriate because in a rapidly developing pursuit actual deliberation is not practical. The Court's analysis falls far short of the "exact analysis of circumstances" that it promises, however. It makes the assumption that decisions about police pursuits must be made "in haste, under pressure, and frequently without the luxury of a second chance" and constitute "split-second judgments—in circumstances that are tense, uncertain, and rapidly evolving."[61] Thus, the Court concludes that, "when unforeseen circumstances demand an officer's instant judgment, even precipitate recklessness fails to inch close enough to harmful purpose to spark the shock that implicates 'the large concerns of the governors and the governed.'"[62]

This simplistic analysis of the decision-making process in initiating or continuing a high-speed pursuit ignores most of what researchers have learned about police pursuits and what police agencies have determined constitute appropriate guidelines for them. A realistic appraisal of the problem would lead to very different conclusions.

When this Court issues its opinion in this case, there is a virtual statistical certainty that sometime that day, someone in the United States will die in a high-speed vehicular police pursuit.[63] The experience of the law enforcement community demonstrates that high-speed pursuits are inherently dangerous, likely to end in a collision, and more often than not initiated for trivial reasons. A review of the studies cited in the STOPP amicus brief in this case indicates that it is not uncommon for 40 percent of pursuits to end in a collision and for 20 percent to result in injuries.[64] Analyzing National Safety Council estimates for injury and fatal accidents, James Auten concluded that the most common terminating event for high-speed pursuits was a wreck.[65]

Moreover, Auten calculated that 31 percent of pursuit accidents involved innocent bystanders.[66] In eight of nine studies cited in the STOPP brief, more than half the vehicular pursuits were initiated for traffic offenses. In the ninth study, 45 percent were initiated for that reason.[67] In the largest study described in the brief, the Minnesota Highway Patrol found that of 5,903 pursuits, 70 percent were initiated for traffic offenses.[68]

The data also show that police officers rarely voluntarily terminate pursuits. In three of the four studies cited by STOPP that included data on this issue, only 4 percent of pursuits were voluntarily terminated.[69] Given that 40 percent of pursuits end in collisions, the available data suggest that in many departments a pursuit is 10 times more likely to end in a crash than to have an officer abandon it. What should be shocking to the conscience is that so many chases are conducted despite this vast body of experience.

Police administrators and experts have been less confused than the federal courts about the standards by which high-speed pursuits should be judged. There is little dispute among law enforcement professionals that the propriety of a high-speed pursuit must be determined by balancing the law enforcement objectives to be served against the risks to lives and safety that it might engender. Many U.S. police agencies, in written rules or guidelines, recognize this standard for determining when to initiate a pursuit and when to abandon it. Indeed, the defendant in this case, the Sacramento County Police Department, like many other police agencies, incorporated its pursuit policy in its General Orders. These orders, internally generated, serve as the procedural guidelines that govern the actions of all sworn personnel.

The Sacramento County General Orders prescribed that with respect to operating department vehicles, an officer has a duty "to exercise that amount of care which, under all circumstances, would not impose an unreasonable risk of harm upon others."[70] The Sacramento orders mandate consideration of whether "the seriousness of the offense warrants a chase at speeds in excess of the posted limit," whether "the need for, and possibility of, apprehension justify a pursuit under the existing conditions," and whether "the pursuit presents unreasonable hazards to life and property."[71]

Police practices experts agree that these are national norms. The Model Policy on vehicular pursuit promulgated by the International Association of Chiefs of Police (IACP) on December 1, 1989, provided in part:

> 1. The decision to initiate pursuit must be based on the pursuing officer's conclusion that the immediate danger to the public created by the pursuit is less than the immediate or potential danger to the public should the suspect remain at large.
> 2. Any law enforcement officer in an authorized emergency vehicle may initiate a vehicular pursuit when ALL of the following criteria are met:
>   a. The suspect exhibits the intention to avoid arrest by using a vehicle to flee apprehension for an alleged felony or misdemeanor that would normally require a full custody arrest;
>   b. The suspect operating the vehicle refuses to stop at the direction of the officer; and
>   c. The suspect, if allowed to flee, would present a danger to human life or cause serious injury.[72]

The IACP Model Policy also requires that once a chase is begun, the decision to continue should be made by a superior officer or police dispatcher—not by the officer behind the wheel whose adrenaline is pumping.[73]

It is evident from the studies that have been done that the stakes in high-speed police pursuits are considerably higher than the opinion of Justice Souter reflects. The likelihood that innocent bystanders will be seriously injured or killed is unacceptably high when pursuits have as their only goal the apprehension of traffic offenders. Moreover, for our purposes it is significant that police supervisors expect that patrol officers will be able to appreciate the risk of pursuits and balance them against their law enforcement goals, before commencing dangerous high-speed chases. The authors of the Sacramento County General Orders obviously do not agree with the Court that the mantra of "split-second decision making" excuses an officer's failure to recognize that his first obligation is to protect public safety.

Police officers do not go out into the streets unprepared to perform their duties with an eye toward public safety. When officers follow what they have been taught in training and proceed according to the rules and regulations of their department, the need for split-second decision making can be substantially reduced. It is the very purpose of training to prepare officers to confront emergency situations in the field in line with the best practices of their profession.

This is not to say that a constitutional violation may be established merely by proof of a failure to follow police rules and regulations. But it does suggest that proof of a reckless disregard for human life that leads to a death is sufficient to constitute a deprivation of life and liberty without due process of law. The Court's conclusion that establishing a due process violation requires proof of an officer's intent to harm suspects physically is not warranted given the demonstrated risks of high-speed chases and the existence of police regulations that require officers to take those risks into account.

The Court adopts the intent to harm requirement in part because it chooses to treat high-speed police pursuits as equivalent to prison riots. I cannot agree with Justice Souter's assertion that the analogy "would be hard to avoid."[74] Establishing liability against prison guards for excessive force in quelling a prison riot requires proof of an Eighth Amendment violation, namely the imposition of cruel and unusual punishment. Hence the Court adopted the test of "whether force was applied in a good-faith effort to maintain or restore discipline or maliciously and sadistically for the very purpose of causing harm."[75] Police officers chasing teenagers for traffic violations are not dealing with convicted prisoners in an institutional setting with extraordinary security issues. Nor is the question of whether an officer's conduct has violated the liberty interests of a free citizen equivalent to the issue of whether the Eighth Amendment's ban against cruel and unusual punishments has been violated.

The opinion of the Court creates an anomaly between the high standard that must be met to justify the use of deadly force against people at liberty through firearms, under our decision in *Tennessee v. Garner*,[76] and the lack of meaningful judicial review of police chases. In *Garner* we recognized that the police had probable cause to attempt to arrest a fleeing 15-year old burglary suspect but held that it was a violation of the Fourth Amendment to use deadly force to do so in the absence of probable cause to believe that the suspect had committed a crime involving serious physical harm or posed a risk of serious physical harm to the officer or others. We said plainly that, "notwithstanding probable cause to seize a suspect, an officer may not always do so by killing him."[77]

The STOPP brief advises that the data collection efforts on firearms and pursuit deaths are incomplete but that "many criminologists believe that more people are killed each year during the course of high-speed pursuits than any other police activity, including firearms."[78] Given these data, our unwillingness to insist upon police accountability for injuries caused by high-speed pursuits is not justifiable. This case provides an appropriate opportunity to fashion a standard for high-speed police pursuits that recognizes that deadly force is involved and requires the police to use appropriate discretion in deciding whether to conduct vehicular pursuits.

The appropriate test for whether an officer has committed a substantive due process violation in connection with a high-speed police pursuit is whether he has caused an injury by proceeding with reckless disregard for public safety. "Reckless disregard" exists when someone "does an act . . . knowing or having reason to know of facts which would lead a reasonable man to realize, not only that his conduct creates an unreasonable risk of physical harm to another, but also that such risk is substantially greater than that which is necessary to make his conduct negligent."[79] The Model Penal Code defines recklessness as conscious disregard of "a substantial and unjustifiable risk."[80]

In the context of high-speed police pursuits, this standard would impose liability against a police officer for a substantive due process violation when the circumstances under which he begins or continues the pursuit indicate a risk to public safety or human life that is unreasonable or not justified by the law enforcement goal of the pursuit. The standard embodies the basic guarantee of the substantive due process clause, that a person should not be deprived of his life or his liberty interests without a sufficient justification in terms of the governmental interests at issue.

Today's opinion by the Court is all the more unfortunate because it creates a sharp contrast between our recent efforts to protect property from arbitrary state action and our failure to provide a meaningful remedy for the loss of life resulting from police pursuits. In *B.M.W. v. Gore*,[81] the Court held that a punitive damages award in a civil case that is "grossly excessive" in relation to the state's interests in punishment and deterrence enters the zone of arbitrariness that violates substantive due process. The Court made no mention of a "shocks the conscience" standard. Instead, it employed a balancing test, to weigh whether the amount of punitive damages awarded were justified by the state's interests that such damages served. In Justice Breyer's concurring opinion, he notes that the "constitutional concern . . . arises out of the basic unfairness of depriving citizens of life, liberty, or property, through the application, not of law and legal processes, but of arbitrary coercion."[82] When a high-speed police pursuit is conducted with reckless disregard for the safety of innocent civilians, lives that are lost are taken arbitrarily, by force, without sufficient legal justification. But the opinion of the Court has eschewed a balancing test in this case, permitting the lower courts to find a substantive due process violation only where the government officials improperly intend to cause harm. The opinion of the Court provides no principled reason why the method of analysis is so radically different in the present case than it was in the punitive damages arena. It goes without saying that the B.M.W. Corporation deserves no greater protection for its property than Philip Lewis deserved for his life.

For the reasons stated, I dissent from the Court's failure to hold that where an officer conducts a high-speed chase with reckless disregard for public safety and human life, a person killed during the chase has suffered a violation of his substantive due process rights to life and liberty. I would remand this case for trial.

NOTES

1. County of Sacramento v. Lewis, 523 U.S. 833 (1998).

2. The facts recited here are taken from the Supreme Court's opinion, *Lewis*, 523 U.S. at 836–37.

3. *Id.* at 837.

4. 42 U.S.C. § 1983. The defendants moved the case to federal district court under a Reconstruction Era civil rights statute that allows cases that involve rights under a federal statute to be transferred from state court to federal court. The statute was originally passed to allow former slaves who could not get a fair trial from state court judges to take their cases to federal court. Ironically, this statute is now frequently used by police officers to move civil rights cases to

federal court, where the officers believe they will get a more favorable hearing from juries that have fewer minority members and from conservative federal judges appointed by Republican presidents.

5. The doctrine of qualified immunity, which the district court applied in this case, requires that in order for police officers to be liable for civil rights violations, the constitutional principles have to have been clearly established in previous cases and a reasonable officer would have to know that his conduct in this case would violate these principles. The doctrine of qualified immunity is the subject of David Rudovsky's chapter in this book.

6. Lewis v. Sacramento County, 98 F.3d 434 (9th Cir. 1996).

7. *Id.* at 441–42.

8. The Court noted the conflict between the Ninth Circuit in this case, which found that liability could be based on "deliberate indifference" to or "reckless disregard" for life, *Lewis,* 98 F.3d at 441, n.3, and other circuits that required the police actions to "shock the conscience" of the court as a basis for liability: *Evans v. Avery,* 100 F.3d 1033, 1038 (1st Cir. 1996), *cert. denied,* 520 U.S. 1210 (1997); *Williams* v. *Denver City,* 99 F.3d 1009, 1014–1015 (10th Cir. 1996); *Fagan v. Vineland,* 22 F.3d 1296, 1306–1307 (3d Cir. 1994) (*en banc*); *Temkin v. Frederick County Commissioners,* 945 F.2d 716, 720 (4th Cir. 1991), *cert. denied,* 502 U.S. 1095 (1992); and *Checki v. Webb,* 785 F.2d 534, 538 (5th Cir. 1986).

9. *Lewis,* 523 U.S. at 840, quoting from *Daniels,* 474 U.S. 327, 331 (1986).

10. *Id.*

11. *Lewis,* 523 U.S. at 842, quoting from Albright v. Oliver, 510 U.S. 266, 273 (1994). *Albright* was a very significant case, in which the plaintiff had attempted to make a claim under the substantive due process doctrine for malicious prosecution. The Court held that because the question of whether an arrest without probable cause violated the Constitution could be analyzed under the Fourth Amendment, there was no substantive due process right to be free from a malicious prosecution. In *Albright* the plaintiff had not made an argument that his arrest and prosecution violated the Fourth Amendment, and so the Court did not decide whether or under what circumstances the Fourth Amendment provides a remedy for a malicious prosecution claim. As a result, the law has been hotly contested in the lower federal courts ever since *Albright,* resulting in a confusing morass of decisions. For a discussion of these cases, *see* MICHAEL AVERY, DAVID RUDOVSKY AND KAREN BLUM, POLICE MISCONDUCT: LAW AND LITIGATION, §️ 2:14 (Thompson, West 2007–2008).

12. Justice Souter noted that the Court has "always been reluctant to expand the concept of substantive due process." *Lewis,* 523 U.S. at 842, citing Collins v. Harker Heights, 503 U.S. 115, 125 (1992). In the early part of the twentieth century, the Supreme Court used the doctrine of substantive due process to hold that much progressive legislation enacted to protect workers, women and children was unconstitutional. In a famous case, the Court struck down as

unconstitutional a law that would have limited the number of hours that workers in bakeries could be forced to work in a week. Lochner v. New York, 198 U.S. 45 (1905). Ignoring the realities of the differences in bargaining power between workers and employers, the Court held that the law interfered with the "freedom of contract" rights of the workers to agree to work long hours. During Franklin Roosevelt's second term, in 1937, the Court changed course and began to sustain progressive legislation, including wages and hours laws. *See, e.g,* West Coast Hotel Co. v. Parrish, 300 U.S. 379 (1937). The Court's dislike for substantive due process stems in part from the historical disrepute in which the "Lochner era" has been held since that time. In part, it also reflects the unwillingness of justices to employ a doctrine that is as open-ended as substantive due process, on the ground that it gives too much power to judges to make law.

13. In *Brower v. County of Inyo,* the Supreme Court held that "a Fourth Amendment seizure does not occur whenever there is a governmentally caused termination of an individual's freedom of movement (the innocent passerby), nor even whenever there is a governmentally caused and governmentally *desired* termination of an individual's freedom of movement (the fleeing felon), but only when there is a governmental termination of freedom of movement *through means intentionally applied.*" 489 U.S. 593, 596–97 (1989).

14. The Court made this clear by citing to cases involving such accidental crashes as examples of where no seizure had taken place. *Lewis,* 523 U.S. at 844.

15. *Id.* at 843–44.

16. The precedent cited by Justice Souter for this conclusion was that, in the previous year, the Court had reviewed the criminal conviction, under a federal criminal civil rights statute, 18 U.S.C. § 242, of a state judge who had sexually assaulted several women in his chambers. United States v. Lanier, 520 U.S. 259 (1997). The Court recognized that the judge had violated the women's constitutional rights by depriving them of their liberty, in this case their personal bodily integrity, in violation of the substantive due process doctrine.

17. *Lewis,* 523 U.S. at 836, 846.

18. *Id.* at 848–49, citing *Daniels, supra* (finding no constitutional violation where a deputy sheriff negligently left a pillow on the stairs in the jail and an inmate slipped and was injured) and Davidson v. Cannon, 474 U.S. 344 (1996) (finding no constitutional violation where a prison official negligently failed to protect a prisoner from physical assault by another inmate).

19. *Lewis,* 523 U.S. at 849.

20. *Id.* at 836, 854.

21. Substituting rhetoric for reasoning, the Court concluded, "But when unforeseen circumstances demand an officer's instant judgment, even precipitate recklessness fails to inch close enough to harmful purpose to spark the shock that implicates 'the large concerns of the governors and the governed.'" *Lewis,* 523 U.S. at 853, citing *Daniels,* 474 U.S. at 332.

22. *Lewis,* 523 U.S. at 836, 854.

23. Scott v. Harris, 127 S.Ct. 1769 (2007).

24. Training Key #499 (IACP, 1998).

25. See text at n. 72, *infra.*

26. Amicus Curiae Brief of the National Police Accountability Project in Support of Respondent, 2007 WL 128585.

27. *Id.* at 845.

28. *Id.* at 846.

29. I find Justice Scalia's conclusion that the "shocks the conscience" test makes it easier to fault executive action on constitutional grounds than legislative action to be unsupported in the case law and highly disingenuous. Nonetheless, I agree with Justice Scalia that there is no precedent for Justice Souter's conclusion that there should be a different test for substantive due process depending on whether the action was taken by a legislature or an executive official. *Lewis,* 523 U.S. at 861, n.2 (concurring op.). Justice Scalia and I do not agree on what that single test should be, however.

30. ERWIN CHEMERINSKY, CONSTITUTIONAL LAW, PRINCIPLES AND POLICIES (3d ed., 2006, Aspen) §10.1, 797.

31. *See, e.g.,* Adarand Constructors, Inc. v. Pena, 515 U.S. 200, 227 (1995) ("all racial classifications, imposed by whatever federal, state, or local governmental actor, must be analyzed by a reviewing court under strict scrutiny"); Reno v. Flores, 507 U.S. 292 (1993) (assuming that if detention of juveniles pursuant to administrative regulations promulgated by the Attorney General involved fundamental liberty interests that a compelling governmental interest and narrow tailoring would be required); Skinner v. Railway Labor Executives' Ass'n., 489 U.S. 602 (1989) (reviewing regulations promulgated by the Federal Railroad Administration under the authority of the Secretary of Transportation and finding that a compelling state interest in safety justified warrantless, suspicionless urine tests of railroad employees and that procedures employed were no more intrusive than necessary).

32. *Lewis,* 523 U.S. at 846.

33. *Collins v. Harker Heights, supra.*

34. In *Collins,* this Court decided that a governmental employer's duty to provide its employees with a safe working environment is not a substantive component of the due process clause. The Court indicated that it was reluctant to expand the concept of substantive due process into new areas, and noted that the plaintiff's claim was unprecedented. The Court concluded that the plaintiff's claim was analogous to a "fairly typical state law tort claim" and involved omissions by the city that could not "properly be characterized as arbitrary, or conscience shocking, in a constitutional sense." 503 U.S. at 128. By contrast, the Court in the present case recognizes that substantive due process does protect life in the context of a high-speed police chase. The issue here is only what the standard for finding a violation should be.

35. *Lewis,* 523 U.S. at 847, n.8.

36. *Albright, supra;* Zinermon v. Burch, 494 U.S. 113 (1990); *Daniels, supra;* Parratt v. Taylor, 451 U.S. 527 (1981); Paul v. Davis, 424 U.S. 693 (1976).

37. *Paul v. Davis,* 424 U.S. at 717 (dissenting op.).

38. Graham v. Connor, 490 U.S. 386 (1986).

39. Where the driver violating the law has already placed the lives of other motorists and pedestrians at significant risk, the safety of others on the road may constitute a compelling governmental interest. Where the suspect driver has not done so, however, initiating a high-speed chase merely creates a dangerous risk where none existed before.

40. Temkin v. Frederick County Commissioners, 945 F.2d 716 (4th Cir. 1991).

41. *Id.* at 723.

42. *Lewis,* 523 U.S. at 861 (concurring op.).

43. Rochin v. California, 342 U.S. 165 (1952).

44. *Id.* at 172.

45. The Court said that the stomach pumping was "too close to the rack and the screw to permit of constitutional differentiation." *Id.*

46. *Id.* at 173.

47. *Daniels,* 474 U.S. at 334, n.3.

48. This argument is persuasively made by Judge Cowen in his thorough and scholarly critique of the "shocks the conscience" language in his dissenting opinion in *Fagan v. City of Vineland,* 22 F.3d 1296, 1309, 1311 (3d Cir., *en banc,* 1994), a police pursuit case. Judge Cowen's detailed history of the employment of the "shocks the conscience" language conclusively establishes that this Court has never previously held that it was the standard or test for determining substantive due process violations. *Id.* at 1316–21. The discussion of these issues in the Court's opinion in this case is shallow by comparison, consisting of little more than a series of string cites without analysis, and thus reaches an incorrect conclusion. *Lewis,* 523 U.S. at 846–47.

49. *Collins,* 503 U.S. at 126.

50. *Id.* at 128.

51. *Id.*

52. *Id.* at 129–30.

53. *Id.* at 130.

54. See Judge Cowen's analysis of *Collins* in *Fagan,* 22 F.3d at 1311–13.

55. *Lewis,* 523 U.S. at 847.

56. *Id.* at 848.

57. *Id.* at 849.

58. *Id.*

59. *Id.* at 850, citing City of Revere v. Massachusetts Gen. Hospital, 463 U.S. 239 (1983).

60. *Lewis,* at 850.

61. *Id.* at 853.

62. *Id.,* citing *Daniels,* 474 U.S. at 332.

63. The National Highway Traffic Safety Administration reported 2,104 deaths in police pursuits between 1991 and 1996, or an average of 350 each year. Amicus Brief Of STOPP (Solutions To The Tragedies Of Police Pursuits) In Support Of Respondents, 1997 WL 907568, filed in this case, 9, data attached to brief as Appendix B.

64. STOPP brief, *supra* at 12–22. *See also* Geoffrey P. Alpert et al., *The Constitutional Implications of High-Speed Police Pursuits Under a Substantive Due Process Analysis: Homeward Through the Haze,* 27 U.MEM.L.REV. 599 (1997); GEOFFREY P. ALPERT & LORIE A. FRIDELL, POLICE VEHICLES AND FIREARMS: INSTRUMENTS OF DEADLY FORCE (1992).

65. STOPP brief, *supra* at 20, citing JAMES AUTEN, AN ANALYSIS OF POLICE PURSUIT DRIVING OPERATIONS, Champaign, Illinois Police Training Institute (1994), 867.

66. *Id.*

67. *Id.* at 12–22.

68. *Id.* at 18.

69. *Id.* at 13, 14, 17, 19.

70. *Lewis,* 98 F.3d at 442, n.6.

71. *Id.*

72. MICHAEL T. CHARLES ET AL., POLICE PURSUIT IN PURSUIT OF POLICY: THE PURSUIT ISSUE, LEGAL AND LITERATURE REVIEW, AND AN EMPIRICAL STUDY (AAA Foundation for Traffic Safety, April, 1992), Appendix A (IACP Model Policy for Vehicular Pursuits).

73. *Id.*

74. *Lewis,* 523 U.S. at 853.

75. Whitley v. Albers, 475 U.S. 312, 320–321 (1986).

76. Tennessee v. Garner, 471 U.S. 1 (1985).

77. *Id.* at 9.

78. STOPP brief, *supra* at 2 and *see* materials cited at n.2 therein: WILLIAM A. GELLER & HANS TOCH, AND JUSTICE FOR ALL, Police Executive Research Forum: Washington, D.C. (1992); GEOFFREY P. ALPERT & LORIE A. FRIDELL, POLICE VEHICLES AND FIREARMS: INSTRUMENTS OF DEADLY FORCE, Waveland Press (1992); Charles, *supra;* and in n.4 therein: Geoffrey P. Alpert & Patrick Anderson, *The Most Deadly Force: Police Pursuits,* 3 JUSTICE QUARTERLY 1 (1986).

79. RESTATEMENT (SECOND) OF TORTS, § 500.

80. MODEL PENAL CODE, §2.02(2)(c).

81. B.M.W. v. Gore, 517 U.S. 559 (1996)

82. *Id.* at 587 (concurring op.).

6

Chavez v. Martinez

The Court Fails to Hold That Police Interrogation by Means of Torture Is Unconstitutional

Marjorie Cohn

Introduction

In *Chavez v. Martinez*,[1] the United States Supreme Court was confronted with the question of whether the coercive interrogation by a police sergeant of a critically wounded man, in a hospital emergency room, violated the Constitution.[2] Oliverio Martinez claimed that such questioning by Sergeant Ben Chavez violated his right to remain silent and to avoid self-incrimination under the Fifth Amendment and his right to due process of law under the Fourteenth Amendment. Despite the fact that Martinez was not given his *Miranda*[3] warnings before or during the questioning, and although he was screaming in pain while lapsing in and out of consciousness during the interrogation, the Court held that Martinez's Fifth Amendment rights had not been violated. The Court determined the Fifth Amendment comes into play only when a statement obtained in violation of *Miranda* is introduced in evidence at a criminal proceeding. It concluded that coercive interrogation itself does not violate any Fifth Amendment rights. The Court sent the case back to the Ninth Circuit Court of Appeals to determine whether there had been a violation of Martinez's due process rights under the Fourteenth Amendment.[4]

Chavez v. Martinez was an extremely important case for a number of reasons. To appreciate its significance, we must consider the earlier development of the *Miranda* rule, which required the police to advise suspects in custody of their constitutional rights before interrogation begins. The landmark 1966 *Miranda* decision held that the prosecution could not use a criminal defendant's statement made to the police while in custodial interrogation against him unless he had been advised of his constitutional rights. As is well known, the decision has long been criticized by conservative commentators and judges, and the Supreme Court has cut back on

Miranda protections in a number of cases. One of the most significant limitations on *Miranda* was the Supreme Court's decision in 1971 in *Harris v. New York*,[5] in which the Court held even if the police did not give *Miranda* warnings, the prosecution could introduce a defendant's statement as rebuttal evidence if the defendant testified at the trial and contradicted the statement. Under those circumstances the Court decided the prosecutor could impeach the defendant's testimony by contradicting him with his earlier statement to the police.

Some police departments, and even some academic commentators, had concluded the police might rationally ignore *Miranda* in many cases and question suspects without warning them. They argued that even though the prosecution could not initially introduce evidence of a statement from such questioning, the existence of an incriminating statement would discourage a defendant from testifying on his own behalf.[6] One of the key elements of this argument was that the Fifth Amendment is not violated by the interrogation itself but only when an incriminating statement is introduced into evidence at a criminal trial. Whether Fifth Amendment rights are violated by a custodial interrogation without warnings was the precise question before the Court in *Chavez*.

Chavez was also important because it would have given the Court an opportunity to demonstrate that the Constitution requires that treaties to which the United States is a party be enforced in our domestic courts. For several years, interest in international law principles, particularly in the area of human rights, has been increasing. Recently, some Supreme Court Justices have referred to international law in their opinions,[7] although that has provoked some controversy in conservative quarters.[8] The Supreme Court could have seized the opportunity *Chavez* presented to make a clear ruling enforcing the treaties that would have been applicable to the case. Unfortunately, the Court failed to address this question in its decision. This omission was particularly grievous given the significance of torture issues in connection with the so-called War on Terror.

The Dissent by Professor Cohn concludes that Sgt. Chavez did violate Martinez's Fifth Amendment privilege against compelled self-incrimination and his Fourteenth Amendment right to due process. Her analysis is informed by the government's obligations under the Convention Against Torture and Other Cruel, Inhuman or Degrading Treatment or Punishment[9] and by the International Covenant on Civil and Political Rights,[10] two treaties ratified by the United States and therefore the supreme law of the land under Article VI of the Constitution.[11]

Dissent by Marjorie Cohn

The Ninth U.S. Circuit Court of Appeals initially affirmed the district court's decision that Chavez was not entitled to summary judgment and would have sent the case back for trial. The appellate court said:

> The record before us reveals that Sergeant Chavez doggedly pursued a statement by Martinez despite being asked to leave the emergency room several times. He ignored Martinez's pleas to withhold questioning until he had received medical treatment. A reasonable officer, questioning a suspect who had been shot five times by the police and then arrested, who had not received Miranda warnings, and who was receiving medical treatment for excruciating, life-threatening injuries that sporadically caused him to lose consciousness, would have known that persistent interrogation of the suspect despite repeated requests to stop violated the suspect's Fifth and Fourteenth Amendment right to be free from coercive interrogation.[12]

For the reasons stated in this dissent, I agree with the Ninth Circuit's conclusion that Martinez's allegations, if accepted by a jury, would establish that Chavez violated his constitutional rights.

While riding his bicycle home from his girlfriend's house, Oliverio Martinez found himself in the wrong place at the wrong time. Although he was innocent of any criminal activity, two officers stopped Martinez, an altercation ensued, and one officer shot Martinez five times. Martinez was left blind and paralyzed. While Martinez was receiving medical treatment at the hospital, Sergeant Ben Chavez interrogated him.

Two Oxnard, California, police officers, Maria Pena and Andrew Salinas, had been investigating suspected narcotics activity in the area where Martinez was riding his bicycle. The officers ordered Martinez to dismount, spread his legs, and place his hands behind his head. Martinez complied. Salinas conducted a pat-down frisk and discovered a knife in Martinez's waistband. An altercation ensued. There is a disagreement about what happened next.

Given the procedural posture of this case, the court below was required to assume that Martinez's version of the facts was true. This is a suit under the Civil Rights Act, 42 U.S.C. § 1983, in federal district court. The portion of the case that we are concerned with here involves Martinez's claim that Chavez interrogated him in violation of his constitutional rights. Sgt. Chavez filed a motion for summary judgment in his favor in advance of trial, which the district court denied. Chavez appealed from that ruling. In ruling on a motion for summary judgment, trial courts are required to assume that the plaintiff's version of the facts is true, even though if the case were to go to trial a jury might reject his testimony.

The officers maintained that Martinez ran away from them and that they pursued and tackled him. Martinez asserted that he never attempted to flee and that Salinas tackled him without warning. The officers claimed that Martinez drew Salinas's gun from its holster and pointed it at them; Martinez said Salinas began to draw his gun and Martinez grabbed Salinas's hand to prevent him from doing so. Both sides agreed that Salinas yelled, "He's got my gun!"

Pena then drew her gun and shot Martinez five times. One bullet struck Martinez in the face, damaging his optic nerve and rendering him blind. Another bullet fractured a vertebra, paralyzing his legs. Three more bullets tore through his leg around the knee joint. The officers then handcuffed Martinez.

Sgt. Ben Chavez arrived minutes later and accompanied Martinez to the emergency room in the ambulance with the paramedics. He then questioned Martinez while he was receiving treatment from medical personnel in the emergency room. At no time during the interrogation did Chavez give Martinez *Miranda* warnings. The interrogation spanned a 45-minute period. The medical staff asked Chavez to leave the trauma room several times, but he repeatedly returned and resumed questioning Martinez. The transcript of the recorded conversation totals 10 minutes. During the interrogation, Martinez was screaming in pain and lapsing in and out of consciousness. Martinez was never charged with a crime.

This is an English translation of portions of the tape-recorded Spanish language questioning of the blinded and paralyzed Martinez in the emergency room. As is evident from the text, both parties believed that Martinez was about to die:

Chavez: What happened? Olivero, tell me what happened.
O[liverio] M[artinez]: I don't know.
Chavez: I don't know what happened [*sic*]?
O. M.: Ay! I am dying. Ay! What are you doing to me?
No, . . . ! (unintelligible scream).
Chavez: What happened, sir?

O. M.: My foot hurts. . . .

Chavez: Olivera. Sir, what happened?

O. M.: I am choking.

Chavez: Tell me what happened.

O. M.: I don't know.

Chavez: "I don't know."

O. M.: My leg hurts.

Chavez: I don't know what happened [*sic*]?

O. M.: It hurts. . . .

Chavez: Hey, hey look.

O. M.: I am choking.

Chavez: Can you hear? Look listen, I am Benjamin Chavez with the police here in Oxnard, look.

O. M.: I am dying, please.

Chavez: OK, yes, tell me what happened. If you are going to die, tell me what happened. Look I need to tell [*sic*] what happened.

O. M.: I don't know.

Chavez: You don't know, I don't know what happened [*sic*]? Did you talk to the police?

O. M.: Yes.

Chavez: What happened with the police?

O. M.: We fought.

Chavez: Huh? What happened with the police?

O. M.: The police shot me.

Chavez: Why?

O. M.: Because I was fighting with him.

Chavez: Oh, why were you fighting with the police?

O. M.: I am dying. . . .

Chavez: OK, yes you are dying, but tell me why you are fighting, were you fighting with the police?

. . . . .

O. M.: Doctor, please I want air, I am dying.

Chavez: OK, OK. I want to know if you pointed the gun [to yourself] at the police.

O. M.: Yes.

Chavez: Yes, and you pointed it [to yourself]? [*sic*] at the police pointed the gun? [*sic*] Huh?

O. M.: I am dying, please. . . .

. . . . .

Chavez: OK, listen, listen I want to know what happened, OK?

O. M.: I want them to treat me.

Chavez: OK, they are do it [*sic*], look when you took out the gun from the tape [*sic*] of the police . . .

. . . . .

O. M.: I am dying. . . .

Chavez: Ok, look, what I want to know if you took out [*sic*] the gun of the police?

O. M.: I am not telling you anything until they treat me.

Chavez: Look, tell me what happened, I want to know, look well don't you want the police know [*sic*] what happened with you?

O. M.: Uuuggghhh! my belly hurts. . . .

. . . . .

Chavez: Nothing, why did you run [*sic*] from the police?

O. M.: I don't want to say anything anymore.

Chavez: No?

O. M.: I want them to treat me, it hurts a lot, please.

Chavez: You don't want to tell [*sic*] what happened with you over there?

O. M.: I don't want to die, I don't want to die.

Chavez: Well, if you are going to die tell me what happened, and right now you think you are going to die?

O. M.: No.

Chavez: No, do you think you are going to die?

O. M.: Aren't you going to treat me or what?

Chavez: Look, think you are going to die, [*sic*] that's all I want to know, if you think you are going to die? Right now, do you think you are going to die?

O. M.: My belly hurts, please treat me.

Chavez: Sir?

O. M.: If you treat me I tell you everything, if not, no.

Chavez: Sir, I want to know if you think you are going to die right now?

O. M.: I think so.

Chavez: You think [*sic*] so? OK. Look, the doctors are going to help you with all they can do, OK? That they can do.

O. M.: Get moving, I am dying, can't you see me? come on.

Chavez: Ah, huh, right now they are giving you medication.

The sound recording of this interrogation vividly demonstrates that Martinez was suffering severe pain and mental anguish throughout Chavez's persistent questioning. It is clear from Martinez's statements to Chavez— "Aren't you going to treat me or what?, " My belly hurts, please treat me," and "If you treat me I tell you everything, if not, no"—that Martinez thought Chavez was exercising his power to approve or withhold medical treatment. I agree with Justice Kennedy's conclusion in his opinion that Martinez "thought his treatment would be delayed, and thus his pain and condition worsened, by refusal to answer questions."[13] Justice Kennedy also pointed out that Martinez's "blinding facial wounds made it impossible for him visually to distinguish the interrogating officer from the attending medical personnel. The officer made no effort to dispel the perception that medical treatment was being withheld until Martinez answered the questions put to him. There was no attempt through *Miranda* warnings or other assurances to advise the suspect that his cooperation should be voluntary. Martinez begged the officer to desist and provide treatment for his wounds, but the questioning persisted despite these pleas and despite Martinez's unequivocal refusal to answer questions."[14]

1. Chavez's Interrogation of Martinez Violated His Privilege Against Self-Incrimination

The Fifth Amendment to the Constitution provides, "No person . . . shall be compelled in any criminal case to be a witness against himself."[15] A plurality of this Court now determines that a violation of the Self-Incrimination Clause does not take place unless and until a privileged statement is introduced at a criminal proceeding. Since Martinez was not charged with a crime, this Court holds that his Fifth Amendment rights were not violated. Justice Thomas, citing an 1872 case,[16] writes for the plurality that a "criminal case" requires the initiation of legal proceedings. I agree with Justices Kennedy and Ginsburg that the Self-Incrimination Clause is violated at the moment police use compulsion to extract a statement from a suspect. I would affirm the Ninth Circuit's decision that Chavez violated Martinez's Fifth Amendment privilege against self-incrimination.

Martinez was never given his *Miranda* warnings. *Miranda v. Arizona* was a watershed in the Court's jurisprudence governing confessions. Before *Miranda* was decided, the Fifth Amendment protected defendants only from compelled self-incrimination in the courtroom. *Miranda* extended the privilege to the interrogation room. "It is obvious," the Court reasoned, "that such an interrogation environment is created for no purpose other than to subjugate the individual to the will of his examiner. This atmosphere carries its own badge of intimidation. To be sure, it is not physical intimidation, but it is equally destructive of human dignity."[17] The Court continued, "The current practice of incommunicado interrogation is at odds with one of our Nation's most cherished principles—that the individual may not be compelled to incriminate himself. Unless adequate protective devices are employed to dispel the compulsion inherent in custodial surroundings, no statement obtained from the defendant can truly be the product of his free choice."[18]

Thus, when a law enforcement officer interrogates a suspect in a custodial setting, the officer must advise him of his right to remain silent, that anything he says can and will be used against him, that he has the right to an attorney, and that one will be appointed for him if he cannot afford one. The suspect must also be told that if he begins answering questions, he may stop at any time. After the suspect is advised of his rights, the police cannot question him unless he waives his rights, even though he has not yet been charged with a crime. Statements obtained in violation of *Miranda* are inadmissible in the prosecution's case-in-chief. "The failure to administer *Miranda* warnings creates a presumption of coercion," the Court said in *Oregon v. Elstad.*[19]

As Justice Kennedy observes in his opinion, "[o]ur cases and our legal tradition establish that the Self-Incrimination Clause is a substantive constraint on the conduct of the government, not merely an evidentiary rule governing the work of the courts. The Clause must provide more than mere assurance that a compelled statement will not be introduced against its declarant in a criminal trial. Otherwise there will be too little protection against the compulsion the Clause prohibits."[20] The transcript of the taped interrogation of Martinez confirms that he felt compelled to answer Chavez's questions or risk being denied medical treatment.

Justice Thomas and the plurality draw a semantic distinction between a Fifth Amendment *privilege* and a Fifth Amendment *right.* They admit that "our cases have permitted the Fifth Amendment's self-incrimination privilege to be asserted in non-criminal cases . . . [it] *can be asserted in any* proceeding, civil or criminal, administrative or judicial, investigatory or adjudicatory."[21] However, they maintain, "that does not alter our conclusion that a violation of the constitutional *right* against self-incrimination occurs only if one has been compelled to be a witness against himself in a criminal case."[22]

This argument is fundamentally inconsistent with our conclusion in *Miranda* that a person undergoing custodial interrogation by the police has a *right* to remain silent. We did not instruct the police to tell suspects that they have an evidentiary privilege they might exercise at a trial. We required that the police notify suspects they wish to interrogate that they have a right to remain silent—to avoid the interrogation altogether. Indeed, we specifically required the police to tell suspects that even if they begin to answer questions, they have a right to stop the interrogation at any time.

The rights protected by the *Miranda* decision are constitutional rights, as we recently held in *Dickerson v. United States*.[23] Chief Justice Rehnquist wrote for the majority in *Dickerson* that "Miranda has become embedded in routine police practice to the point where the warnings have become part of our national culture."[24] When a law enforcement officer fails to comply with the dictates of *Miranda*, he violates the suspect's constitutional right to remain silent.

In *Mincey v. Arizona*,[25] we found a Fifth Amendment violation as the result of an interrogation very similar to Martinez's. The officer ceased the interrogation of Mincey only during intervals when he lost consciousness or received medical treatment. After each interruption, the officer returned relentlessly to his task. The statements at issue were thus the result of virtually continuous questioning of a seriously and painfully wounded man on the edge of consciousness. Like the interrogator in *Mincey*, Chavez persisted in questioning Martinez except when he was being treated by the medical personnel, as he lapsed in and out of consciousness.

By its terms, the Fifth Amendment to the U.S. Constitution protects defendants in federal proceedings. The Court, however, applied the Fifth Amendment's protections—which, it said are "implicit in the concept of ordered liberty"[26]—to state proceedings via the Fourteenth Amendment's Due Process Clause.[27] As Justice Stevens pointed out in his dissent in *Oregon v. Elstad*, the Fifth Amendment is the most specific provision in the Bill of Rights "that protects all citizens from the kind of custodial interrogation that was once employed by the Star Chamber, by 'the Germans of the 1930's and early 1940's' and by some of our own police departments only a few decades ago."[28] Chavez's interrogation of Martinez resembled those interrogations. I agree with Justice Stevens's conclusion in his opinion in this case: "[O]fficial interrogation of that character is a classic example of a violation of a constitutional right 'implicit in the concept of ordered liberty.'"[29]

Justice Kennedy aptly quotes former Harvard Law School Dean Griswold on the critical role the Self-Incrimination Clause plays in our legal heritage: "The Fifth Amendment has been very nearly a lone sure rock in a time of storm. It has been one thing which has held quite firm, although something like a juggernaut has pushed upon it. It has, thus, through all its vicissitudes, been a symbol of the ultimate moral sense of the community, upholding the best in us, when otherwise there was a good deal of wavering under the pressures of the times."[30]

Notably, Justices Stevens, Kennedy, and Ginsburg discuss the interrogation of Martinez with reference to *torture*. In determining that the police can violate the Fifth Amendment whether or not criminal charges are ever brought against a suspect, Justice Kennedy writes, "A constitutional right is traduced the moment torture or its close equivalents are brought to bear. Constitutional protection for a tortured suspect is not held in abeyance until some later criminal proceeding takes place."[31] Justice Stevens aptly characterizes Martinez's interrogation as "the functional equivalent of an attempt to obtain an involuntary confession from a prisoner by torturous methods. As a matter of law, that type of brutal police conduct constitutes an immediate deprivation of the prisoner's constitutionally protected interest in liberty."[32]

By denying Martinez's self-incrimination claim, we hereby send a message to law enforcement officers that they are free to use torture during interrogations without running afoul of the Fifth Amendment. As Justice Kennedy writes, "[t]o tell our whole legal system that when conducting a criminal investigation police officials can use severe compulsion or even torture with no present violation of the right against compelled self-incrimination can only diminish a celebrated provision in the Bill of Rights."[33]

None of the Justices, however, discusses the Convention Against Torture and Other Cruel, Inhuman or Degrading Treatment or Punishment or the International Covenant on Civil and Political Rights. These treaties forbid the use of torture and other cruel, inhuman, or degrading treatment or punishment. Both were ratified by the United States and are therefore part of the supreme law of the land under the Supremacy Clause of the Constitution. The government's obligations under these treaties should inform the analysis of whether Chavez violated Martinez's Fifth Amendment and Fourteenth Amendment rights, as I discuss below.

2. Chavez's Interrogation of Martinez Violated His Due Process Rights

A majority of the justices cannot agree that Chavez violated Martinez's due process rights. The Fourteenth Amendment to the Constitution provides that no person shall be deprived "of life, liberty, or property, without due process of law."[34] Although Justices Stevens, Kennedy, and Ginsburg find a due process violation, they agree to remand the case to the district court in order to achieve a majority for such determination. I also find that Chavez violated the Due Process Clause and believe the Court should have held that he did.

Justice Thomas admits in his opinion, with Chief Justice Rehnquist and Justices O'Connor and Scalia concurring, that his refusal to find a Fifth Amendment violation does "not mean that police torture or other abuse that results in a confession is constitutionally permissible so long as the statements are not used at trial; it simply means that the Fourteenth Amendment's Due Process Clause, rather than the Fifth Amendment's Self-Incrimination Clause, would govern the inquiry in those cases and provide relief in appropriate circumstances."[35] I believe that both the Self-Incrimination and Due Process Clauses are grounds for civil relief whether or not the statements that the violations produce are offered at trial.

In *County of Sacramento v. Lewis*,[36] this Court stated that substantive due process prevents the government from engaging in conduct that "shocks the contemporary conscience" or interferes with rights "implicit in the concept of ordered liberty." The substantive due process guarantee protects against government power arbitrarily and oppressively exercised, and it was intended to prevent government officials "from abusing [their] power, or employing it as an instrument of oppression [citations omitted]."[37] We concluded in *Lewis* that conduct intended to injure in a way "unjustifiable by any government interest is the sort of official action most likely to rise to the conscience-shocking level."[38]

Chavez's intent to injure Martinez can be inferred from his unrelenting cross-examination of this severely injured man. I disagree with Justice Thomas that "there is no evidence that Chavez acted with a purpose to harm Martinez by intentionally interfering with his medical treatment" because medical personnel "were able to treat Martinez throughout the interview."[39] In fact, the emergency room staff had to repeatedly ask Chavez to leave the room so they could administer life-saving aid to Martinez.

We reiterated in *Lewis* our earlier ruling that when the government takes a person into custody, the Constitution imposes upon it a corresponding responsibility to provide for his safety and well-being, including the provision of medical care. No "substantial countervailing interest" will excuse the State from providing decent care and protection to those it locks up. "[T]he State's responsibility to attend to the medical needs of prisoners [or detainees] does not ordinarily clash with other equally important governmental responsibilities."[40] Justice Thomas elevates "the need to investigate whether there had been police misconduct" in the shooting of Martinez to "a justifiable government interest."[41] And, in Justice Thomas's opinion, the governmental need is sufficient to justify Chavez's unconscionable badgering because "evidence would have been lost if Martinez had died"[42] without telling his side of the story. Justice Thomas's tortured reasoning would permit a police officer to torture a severely wounded man in order to bring another police officer to justice.

The Due Process Clause also prohibits the government from violating "fundamental liberty interests" unless the infringement is narrowly tailored to serve a compelling state interest.[43] Our firmly established due process jurisprudence requires that once we have determined a liberty interest is fundamental, only the most significant interests of the government, those that are truly compelling, can justify invading that liberty. And, even then, the invasion must be limited to the narrowest means that are necessary to serve the government's ends so that liberty is not unjustifiably forfeited. First, the right to be free from excruciating interrogation while undergoing lifesaving medical treatment is surely a fundamental liberty interest, "deeply rooted in this Nation's history and tradition" and "implicit in the concept of ordered liberty."[44] Unlike Justice Thomas, I do not find the claim that Chavez was interested in the preservation of evidence demonstrating that there was police misconduct to be a compelling governmental interest under the circumstances of this case sufficient to excuse Chavez's grilling of Martinez, who was writhing in pain.

"[I]t seems to me a simple enough matter to say that use of torture or its equivalent in an attempt to induce a statement violates an individual's fundamental right to liberty of the person," Justice Kennedy writes.[45] As we held in *Brown v. Mississippi*, our first due process confession case, "[t]he rack and torture chamber may not be substituted for the witness stand."[46] Chavez's persistent questioning of Martinez, who was screaming in pain from the wounds that had just blinded and paralyzed him, shocks the conscience and thus violated his due process rights. Under the totality of circumstances, the test for determining voluntariness under the Due Process Clause,[47] Chavez's interrogation of Martinez violated the Fourteenth Amendment.

A. Applying International Treaties to the Due Process Analysis

i. Human Rights Treaties Inform the Analysis of U.S. Constitutional Rights

Justice Thomas decries the lack of any "guideposts for responsible decisionmaking" in interpreting the doctrine of substantive due process.[48] In contrast, I would look to our treaty obligations to inform that analysis.

Taking our treaty obligations into account is particularly appropriate in cases filed under the civil rights act, as this case was.

Title 42 U.S.C. § 1983 was passed originally as the 1871 Civil Rights Act. It provides:

> Every person who, under color of any statute, ordinance, regulation, custom, or usage, of any State or Territory or the District of Columbia, subjects, or causes to be subjected, any citizen of the United States or other person within the jurisdiction thereof to the deprivation of any rights, privileges, or immunities secured by the Constitution and laws, shall be liable to the party injured in an action at law, suit in equity, or other proper proceeding for redress. . . .

The 1871 Civil Rights Act was enacted to be "remedial and in aid of the preservation of human liberty and human rights."[49] That purpose has been repeatedly cited by justices of this Court.[50] Indeed, "our Founding Fathers conceived a Constitution and Bill of Rights replete with provisions indicating their determination to protect human rights," Justice Douglas wrote in *Laird v. Tatum*,[51] quoting Chief Justice Earl Warren.

> Once ratified, human rights treaties become U.S. law, under Article VI, the Supremacy Clause of the Constitution:
> This Constitution, and the Laws of the United States which shall be made in Pursuance thereof; and all Treaties made, or which shall be made, under the Authority of the United States, shall be the supreme Law of the Land; and the Judges in every State shall be bound thereby, any Thing in the Constitution or Laws of and State to the Contrary notwithstanding.

The Supremacy Clause makes these treaties binding on states as well as the federal government. It is the duty of all relevant government officials to uphold the treaties' obligations.

International law is increasingly used as an aid to interpret the U.S. Constitution. According to Professor Jordan J. Paust, "In view of the actual trends in use of human rights standards, it is fairly clear that most of the Supreme Court Justices have recognized that human rights can provide useful content for identification, clarification and supplementation of constitutional or statutory norms."[52] For example, in *Thompson v. Oklahoma*, a plurality of the Court cited the International Covenant on

Civil and Political Rights as support for its conclusion that it would offend civilized standards of decency to execute a person who was under 16 years old at the time of the offense.[53]

ii. The Convention Against Torture
and Other Cruel, Inhuman or Degrading Treatment or Punishment
Article 1 of this treaty defines *torture* as:

> any act by which severe pain or suffering, whether physical or mental, is intentionally inflicted on a person for such purposes as obtaining from him or a third person information or a confession . . . when such pain or suffering is inflicted by or at the instigation of or with the consent or acquiescence of a public official or other person acting in an official capacity.

When the U.S. Senate gave its advice and consent to ratification of the Torture Convention, it specified that "in order to constitute torture, an act must be specifically intended to inflict severe physical or mental pain or suffering and that mental pain or suffering refers to prolonged mental harm caused by or resulting from: (1) the intentional infliction or threatened infliction of severe physical pain or suffering; . . . (3) the threat of immediate death. . . ."[54]

Chavez interrogated Martinez, an apparently mortally wounded man lapsing in and out of consciousness, leading Martinez to believe he would be denied medical care if he failed to answer Chavez's questions. Under these circumstances, it is reasonable to conclude that Chavez specifically intended to inflict on Martinez severe mental suffering, including the threat of immediate death. Although Chavez argues here that his purpose was to gather evidence of potential police misconduct, it defies credulity that he had no interest in obtaining a confession from Martinez that he had violated the law, if that were the case. Chavez's conduct, taking the facts in the light most favorable to Martinez, constituted torture.

Even if Chavez's questioning did not rise to the level of torture, it certainly amounted to cruel, inhuman, or degrading treatment, which is also proscribed by the Convention against Torture. In its ratification, the United States limited the analysis of "cruel, inhuman or degrading treatment or punishment" in the Torture Convention to U.S. jurisprudence interpreting "the cruel, unusual and inhumane treatment or punishment prohibited by the Fifth, Eighth, and/or Fourteenth Amendments to the Constitution of the United States."[55]

iii. Constitutional Proscriptions Against Torture

The Eighth Amendment to the Constitution prohibits the infliction of "cruel and unusual punishments." Although we have never applied the Eighth Amendment to interrogations, it is significant that the Framers enacted the Amendment to outlaw torture, including the use of torture for the purpose of eliciting confessions. Justice Burger, dissenting in *Furman v. Georgia*, wrote, "The records of the debates in several of the state conventions called to ratify the 1789 draft Constitution submitted prior to the addition of the Bill of Rights show that the Framers' exclusive concern was the absence of *any* ban on tortures. The later inclusion of the 'cruel and unusual punishment' clause was in response to these objections."[56]

In the Eighth Amendment case of *Estelle v. Gamble*,[57] we concluded:

> deliberate indifference to serious medical needs of prisoners constitutes the 'unnecessary and wanton infliction of pain' [citation omitted], proscribed by the Eighth Amendment. This is true whether the indifference is manifested by prison doctors in their response to the prisoner's needs or by prison guards in intentionally denying or delaying access to medical care or intentionally interfering with the treatment once prescribed. Regardless of how evidenced, deliberate indifference to a prisoner's serious illness or injury states a cause of action under § 1983.

Chavez exhibited deliberate indifference to Martinez's life-threatening injuries when he relentlessly badgered the seriously wounded man.

It is well established that Eighth Amendment analysis involves an examination of the evolving standards of decency that mark the progress of a maturing society. In determining that the execution of a mentally retarded person constitutes cruel and unusual punishment, Justice Stevens wrote for the six-member majority in *Atkins v. Virginia*:[58] "A claim that punishment is excessive is judged not by the standards that prevailed in 1685 when Lord Jeffreys presided over the 'Bloody Assizes' or when the Bill of Rights was adopted, but rather by those that currently prevail. As Chief Justice Warren explained in his opinion in Trop v. Dulles: 'The basic concept underlying the Eighth Amendment is nothing less than the dignity of man. . . . The Amendment must draw its meaning from the evolving standards of decency that mark the progress of a maturing society."[59] The reason the government gives for Chavez's interrogation of Martinez was to secure information about the police shooting, which might implicate the officer who had shot Chavez. As I have noted, however, it is just as likely that the sergeant was seeking information that would incriminate Martinez. And continually plaguing an apparently dying man is indecent, and cruel and unusual. Moreover, by intentionally leading Martinez to believe he would be denied life-saving medical care if he remained unresponsive to the officer's questions, Chavez tortured Martinez.

iv. The International Covenant on Civil and Political Rights (ICCPR)
Countries that ratify the ICCPR agree that "[a]ll persons deprived of their liberty should be treated with humanity and with respect for the inherent dignity of the human person."[60] Chavez's treatment of Martinez manifestly failed to comply with this mandate.

Article 7 provides, "No one shall be subjected to torture or to cruel, inhuman or degrading treatment or punishment." Article 4(2) prohibits any derogation from the prohibitions in Article 7. When the Senate ratified this treaty, it specified "that the United States considers itself bound by Article 7 to the extent that 'cruel, inhuman or degrading treatment or punishment' means the cruel and unusual treatment or punishment prohibited by the Fifth, Eighth and/or Fourteenth Amendments to the Constitution of the United States."[61]

The Human Rights Committee is the international body charged with monitoring compliance with the ICCPR by the United States and other parties to the treaty. Countries that ratify the ICCPR agree to submit to the Human Rights Committee periodic reports on their progress in complying with the treaty. The United States submitted its initial report in 1994. It barely mentioned the issue of police brutality. Instead, the report merely cited federal criminal civil rights statutes that could be used to prosecute police officers who commit serious abuses. The Human Rights Committee expressed concern about police abuse in its response to the U.S. report: "The Committee is concerned at the reportedly large number of persons killed, wounded or subjected to ill-treatment by members of the police force in the purported discharge of their duties."[62]

By granting Chavez immunity for his torture and cruel, inhuman and degrading treatment of Martinez, this Court would sanction impunity for the most serious concerns raised by the Human Rights Committee. For the reasons outlined in the discussion of the Torture Convention above,

Chavez's interrogation of Martinez also violated the International Covenant on Civil and Political Rights.

Conclusion

The central purpose of § 1983 is "to provide protection to those persons wronged by the misuse of power."[63] As Michael Avery wrote in an article in the Fordham Urban Law Journal, "Coercive interrogation, even in the absence of physical violence, and even when it does not elicit statements later used in criminal proceedings, subjects suspects to inquisitorial methods, fear of inhumane treatment, degradation of individual personality, invasion of privacy, humiliation, and mental and emotional stress and suffering."[64]

After being shot five times and left blinded and paralyzed, Oliverio Martinez was charged with no crime. While he was screaming in severe pain and lapsing in and out of consciousness, Sergeant Ben Chavez persisted in interrogating him, stopping only when requested to do so by the medical personnel treating the critically wounded man. The record confirms that Martinez thought Chavez would cause medical treatment to be withheld from him if he refused to answer Chavez's questions. Martinez now seeks relief for the violations of his Fifth Amendment right to be free from compelled self-incrimination and his Fourteenth Amendment right to due process occasioned by Chavez's torturous interrogation of him. The government's obligations under the Convention Against Torture and the International Covenant on Civil and Political Rights confirm Chavez's violations of Martinez's constitutional rights.

I agree with the Ninth Circuit Court of Appeals that "[i]n light of the extreme circumstances in this case, a reasonable police officer in Sergeant Chavez's position could not have believed that the interrogation of suspect Martinez comported with the Fifth and Fourteenth Amendments."[65] Chavez cannot be excused from liability under the doctrine of qualified immunity in this case. The appellate court properly denied Chavez summary judgment. I would affirm the rulings of the Court of Appeals and allow Martinez's lawsuit against Chavez to proceed to trial on the merits.

NOTES

1. Chavez v. Martinez, 538 U.S. 760 (2003).

2. The defendant Sgt. Chavez made a motion for summary judgment based on a claim for qualified immunity. The qualified immunity doctrine is explained in detail in David Rudovsky's chapter. For our purposes in this chapter, we treat the issue in the case as directly involving the question of the constitutionality of Sgt. Chavez's conduct.

3. Miranda v. Arizona, 384 U.S. 436 (1966) (requiring police officers to warn a suspect in custody before questioning him that he has a right to remain silent, that any statement he does make can and will be used as evidence against him, that he has the right to an attorney, and that if he cannot afford one, one will be appointed for him).

4. Chief Justice Rehnquist and Justices Thomas, O'Connor, Scalia, Souter, and Breyer decided there was no Fifth Amendment violation. Justices Souter, Stevens, Kennedy, Breyer, and Ginsburg agreed to remand the case to the district court to determine whether Martinez may pursue a claim of liability for violation of his substantive due process rights under the Fourteenth Amendment. (For a discussion of substantive due process rights, see Michael Avery's chapter.) On remand from the Supreme Court, the Ninth Circuit held that the plaintiff's allegations were sufficient to state a claim that his due process rights had been violated. *Martinez v. City of Oxnard*, 337 F.3d 1091 (9th Cir. 2003). Before the case had gone to the Supreme Court, both the district court and the Ninth Circuit had held that Chavez's conduct as alleged by Martinez had violated both his Fifth Amendment and his due process rights.

5. Harris v. New York, 401 U.S. 222 (1971).

6. Several police departments in California decided, as a matter of policy, to *train* their officers to question suspects "outside *Miranda*," in other words, without the required warnings. The Ninth Circuit Court of Appeals held this unconstitutional in *CACJ v. Butts*, 195 F.3d 1039 (9th Cir. 2000). The practice and training materials are described in detail in a law review article by one of the lawyers in that case, Prof. Charles D. Weisselberg, *Saving Miranda*, 84 Cornell L. Rev. 109 (1998). Prof. Steven Clymer concluded that the practice of taking statements without giving warnings was rational in his article, *Are Police Free to Disregard Miranda?*, 112 Yale L.J. 447 (2002).

7. Justice Kennedy, for example, referred to international law and the law of other countries in *Lawrence v. Texas*, 539 U.S. 558, 560 (2003) (holding unconstitutional the Texas sodomy law that applied only to homosexuals) and *Roper v. Simmons*, 543 U.S. 551 (2005) (holding unconstitutional the application of the death penalty to juveniles).

8. A number of conservative senators introduced a bill to proscribe the use of foreign sources in U.S. judicial opinions and providing for the impeachment of

judges who do cite such law. The Constitution Restoration Act of 2005, introduced as S. 520 on March 3, 2005, by Sens. Shelby, Brownback, and Burr.

9. Convention Against Torture and Other Cruel, Inhuman or Degrading Treatment or Punishment, Apr. 18, 1988, 1465 U.N.T.S. 85, S. Treaty Doc. No. 100–20.

10. International Covenant on Civil and Political Rights, opened for signature Dec. 19, 1966, 999 U.N.T.S. 171 (entered into force Mar. 23, 1976) (hereinafter ICCPR).

11. U.S. Const. art. VI, cl. 2.

12. Martinez v. Oxnard, 270 F.3d 852, 858 (9th Cir. 2001).

13. *Chavez,* 538 U.S. at 797.

14. *Id.* at 798.

15. U.S. CONST. Amend. V.

16. Blyew v. United States, 80 U.S. 581, 595 (1872).

17. *Miranda,* 384 U.S. at 457.

18. *Id.* at 457–58.

19. Oregon v. Elstad, 470 U.S. 298, 307 (1985).

20. *Chavez,* 538 U.S. at 791.

21. *Id.* at 770, emphasis in original.

22. *Id.*

23. Dickerson v. United States, 530 U.S. 428 (2000).

24. *Id.* at 443.

25. Mincey v. Arizona, 437 U.S. 385 (1978).

26. *See* Poe v. Ullman, 367 U.S. 497, 517, n. 9 (1961).

27. *See* Malloy v. Hogan, 378 U.S. 1, 6, 8 (1964) (a person has a right "to remain silent unless he chooses to speak in the unfettered exercise of his own will, and to suffer no penalty . . . for such silence.").

28. *Elstad,* 470 U.S. at 371 (Stevens, J., dissenting).

29. *Chavez,* 538 U.S. at 788.

30. *Id.* at 794 (Kennedy, J., dissenting), citing E. GRISWOLD, THE FIFTH AMENDMENT TODAY 73 (Harvard University Press, 1955).

31. *Id.* At 789–90 (Kennedy, J., dissenting).

32. *Id.* at 783–84 (Stevens, J., concurring in part and dissenting in part).

33. *Id.* at 794 (Kennedy, J., dissenting).

34. U.S. CONST. Amend. XIV.

35. *Chavez,* 538 U.S. at 773.

36. County of Sacramento v. Lewis, 523 U.S. 833 (1998).

37. *Id. at* 840.

38. *Id.* at 834.

39. *Chavez,* 538 U.S. at 775.

40. *Lewis,* 523 U.S. at 851–52, quoting Whitley v. Albers, 475 U.S. 312, 320 (1986).

41. *Chavez*, 538 U.S. at 775.

42. *Id.*

43. *See* Washington v. Glucksberg, 521 U.S. 702, 721 (1997).

44. *See id.*

45. *Chavez*, 538 U.S. at 796.

46. Brown v. Mississippi, 297 U.S. 278, 285–286 (1936).

47. *See* Schneckloth v. Bustamonte, 412 U.S. 218, 226 (1973).

48. *Chavez*, 538 U.S. at 776.

49. Cong.Globe, 42d Cong., 1st Sess. App. 68 (1871).

50. *See, e.g.,* Briscoe v. Lahue, 460 U.S. 325, 348 (1983) (Marshall, J.); Allen v. McCurry, 449 U.S. 90, 109–10 n.8 (1980) (Blackmun, J.); Owen v. City of Independence, 445 U.S. 622, 636 (1980) (Brennan, J.); Lake Country Estates, Inc. v. Tahoe Regional Planning Agency, 440 U.S. 391, 400 (1979) (Stevens, J.).

51. Laird v. Tatum, 403 U.S. 1, 20 (1972).

52. *See* JORDAN J. PAUST, INTERNATIONAL LAW AS LAW OF THE UNITED STATES 12, 217 (2003).

53. Thompson v. Oklahoma, 487 U.S. 815, n. 34 (1988).

54. CONG. REC. S17486–01 (daily ed., Oct. 27, 1990).

55. *Id.*

56. Furman v. Georgia, 408 U.S. 238, 377 (1972), Burger, J., dissenting; *id.* at 260, Brennan, J., concurring. *See* 2. J. ELLIOT'S DEBATES 111 (2d ed. 1876).

57. Estelle v. Gamble, 429 U.S. 97, 104 (1976).

58. Atkins v. Virginia, 536 U.S. 304, 312 (2002).

59. Trop v. Dulles, 356 U.S. 86, 100–101 (1958).

60. ICCPR, *supra* note 10, Art. 10.

61. 138 CONG. REC. S4781–01 (daily ed., Apr. 2, 1992).

62. Concluding observations of the Human Rights Committee: United States of America, 03/10/95, A/50/40, para. 282.

63. *See Owen*, 445 U.S. at 650.

64. Michael Avery, *You Have a Right to Remain Silent*, 30 FORDHAM URB. L.J. 571, 589 (2003).

65. *Martinez*, 270 F.3d at 858.

7

Saucier v. Katz

Qualified Immunity as a Doctrine of Dilution
of Constitutional Rights.

David Rudovsky

Introduction

Most Americans would likely agree with the basic constitutional principle,
set forth by the first Chief Justice of the Supreme Court, John Marshall, that
"The very essence of civil liberty certainly consists of in the right of every
individual to claim the protection of the laws . . . [and] it is a general and in-
disputable rule that where there is a legal right, there is also a legal remedy."[1]
Yet, in many circumstances, there is no effective legal remedy for violations
of basic constitutional rights by government officials. Over the past 50
years, we have seen a substantial expansion of constitutional and statutory
protections of fundamental liberties, but at the same time, the Supreme
Court and Congress have limited the remedial powers of the federal courts.

While there are a number of potential remedies for governmental
misconduct, the principal remedy is money damages for injuries or losses
sustained as a result of the illegal actions of the government or its agents.
Thus, where a person has been subjected to excessive force or imprisoned
without cause, a court has the power to award damages to compensate the
victim of the misconduct for physical and psychological injuries, lost earn-
ings, and expenses related to the incident. For most people who have been
subjected to governmental misconduct, the only realistic remedy is money
damages. Other potential remedies, including an injunction against future
misconduct, internal disciplinary proceedings, or criminal prosecution of
the offending officer, will not compensate the victim and are very difficult
to achieve. Much has been written about the "exclusionary rule"—sup-
pressing illegally obtained evidence from criminal proceedings against the
person whose rights were violated. There are many exceptions to this rule,
and it does not apply at all with respect to a person who is not charged
with a criminal offense or where no evidence was obtained as a result of

police misconduct (e.g., where excessive force is used in an arrest). Accordingly, if limits are placed on the damages remedy, victims of governmental misconduct will often be left without any recourse for their injuries.

A principal means by which remedies for constitutional rights have been limited is the doctrine of official immunity. Thus, in many claims for damages resulting from the unconstitutional conduct of law enforcement officers, prosecutors, judges, and other officials, the injured party may be barred from recovery of damages even for proven violations. The Supreme Court has declared that some government officials, including the president, judges, and prosecutors, are *absolutely immune* from suits for money damages for conduct relative to their duties, regardless of how malicious or vindictive their actions. All other governmental officers enjoy a *qualified immunity* from suit. The immunity doctrines, which have been a matter of judicial creation (as opposed to legislation by Congress), prevent many persons from vindicating their rights in court.

In its current formulation, qualified immunity protects a police officer or other public official if the constitutional right at issue was not "clearly established" at the time of the incident or if a reasonable officer might have been mistaken about whether his or her actions would violate a clearly established right. It is a type of "mistake of law" defense not available to ordinary citizens in either civil or criminal cases. It might be argued that, since constitutional law is dynamic and evolving, the qualified immunity doctrine may be appropriate where the Supreme Court breaks with precedent or in an unexpected decision recognizes a new right *after* the officer has acted. There may also be a need for immunity in exceptional circumstances where a reasonable officer could not foresee that his conduct would be determined to be in violation of the Constitution. The Court, however, has provided a far broader immunity.

For example, even though the right to be free from an arrest or search by police who do not have probable cause to believe the suspect committed a crime has been part of the Fourth Amendment's protections for many years, an officer may avoid liability for an *unlawful* arrest or search if a reasonable officer could mistakenly have believed the conduct to be proper. Since conflicts between police and civilians are so diverse, it would not be unusual that a court had not previously addressed the officer's specific conduct in a new case. Thus, if immunity is available whenever an officer's specific conduct has not been the subject of a prior judicial decision, the scope of the protection afforded officers who are later determined to have violated the Constitution is very broad.

Qualified immunity defined that broadly provides an unnecessarily redundant layer of protection for police officers. The Fourth Amendment does not require perfection on the part of the police, and the probable cause standard itself provides a wide margin of error. The Constitution requires only that officers act reasonably in making an arrest or search. Thus, once it is determined that the officer acted "unreasonably," the case should be over. The immunity doctrine erroneously gives the officer a "second bite at the apple" at the expense of the rights of the citizen by allowing a court to conclude that a "reasonable" officer could have acted unreasonably.

There should be no misunderstanding the impact of the immunity doctrine. Police and governmental misconduct is a significant problem in our society. The pressure on law enforcement officials, including prosecutors and judges, to combat crime, terrorism, and other antisocial conduct is substantial, and there is often an incentive to cut constitutional corners and to use impermissible means to investigate alleged criminal acts. Even the metaphors we employ, such as the "war on drugs" and "war against terrorism," suggest a freedom for government to engage in extralegal methods to achieve "victory." The abuses of power associated with enforcement of drug laws and many of the post-9/11 efforts to prevent terrorist attacks reflect policies and practices that violate constitutional norms. To the degree that officials know that their conduct will not be punished, there is little reason for them to be concerned with constitutional rights. Thus, to the extent that immunity doctrine insulates these officials and officers from legal accountability, the abuses are likely to continue and citizens will continue to be deprived of legal recourse. An expansive immunity doctrine poses serious threats to the vindication of constitutional rights.

In 2001, the Supreme Court decided a case that presented the issue of whether the qualified immunity doctrine should apply where a police officer has used excessive force against a person being arrested. In *Saucier v. Katz*,[2] federal officials had arrested Elliot Katz, the president of the group In Defense of Animals, who was protesting at a political event where then Vice President Al Gore was speaking. Katz claimed that he was subjected to unreasonable force when he was thrown into a police van. The Supreme Court took the case to decide whether qualified immunity applied to excessive force claims. It assumed (without deciding) that the force used against Katz had been excessive under the Fourth Amendment.[3]

Katz argued that qualified immunity should not be applicable in excessive force cases. His main argument was that the defense was essentially redundant to any defense to the claim of excessive force: since permissible force must be "objectively reasonable" from the perspective of the police officer, once it has been concluded there was excessive force, by definition the force was unreasonable. Such force cannot be protected by qualified immunity, which protects only "objectively reasonable" conduct. Thus, once a court decides that the Fourth Amendment was violated by the use of excessive force, there should be no second layer of an immunity defense.

The Supreme Court rejected those arguments and decided that even where an officer violates the Fourth Amendment by using excessive or unreasonable force, the officer can still argue that under the circumstances his conduct was "objectively reasonable" and that a reasonable officer could have thought that the force was permissible. The Court stated:

> An officer might correctly perceive all of the relevant facts but have a mistaken understanding as to whether a particular amount of force is legal in those circumstances. If the officer's mistake as to what the law requires is reasonable, however, the officer is entitled to the immunity defense.
>
> *Graham* [the leading Supreme Court case on excessive force] does not always give a clear answer as to whether a particular application of force will be deemed excessive by the courts. This is the nature of a test which must accommodate limitless factual circumstances. This reality serves to refute respondent's claimed distinction between excessive force and other Fourth Amendment contexts; in both spheres the law must be elaborated from case to case. Qualified immunity operates in this case, then, just as it does in others, to protect officers from the sometimes "hazy border between excessive and acceptable force," . . . and to ensure that before they are subjected to suit, officers are on notice their conduct is unlawful.[4]

Three Justices (Ginsburg, Stevens, and Breyer) dissented and would not have recognized the qualified immunity defense in excessive force cases.

Dissent by David Rudovsky

The issue presented by this case is whether the qualified immunity defense should be available in cases where the plaintiff alleges a violation of the Fourth Amendment right to be free from excessive force by a police officer. The majority's determination that the defense is available is both illogical and unwise. The legal principle that excessive force violates the Fourth Amendment was clearly established by the Court's decision in *Graham v. Connor*.[5] Once a jury has determined that the force used was excessive, because the officer acted in an objectively unreasonable manner, allowing a defense of qualified immunity is entirely inconsistent with that determination. The standards for determining whether force was excessive and for deciding the qualified immunity issue are identical: was the force objectively reasonable under the circumstances. Given that, there is no reason to permit an officer to avoid liability once the jury has decided that he used excessive force.

A. The Development of the Qualified Immunity Defense

It is important to remember that the immunity doctrines are entirely a judicial invention. Section 1983 of Title 42 of the U.S. Code, which is the fountainhead for most civil rights litigation, makes no reference to any immunities. As Judge Easterbrook has noted, the statute provides for "liability in absolute terms. Public officials who violate the Constitution or laws must pay."[6] The Supreme Court has construed §1983 to incorporate common law immunities (i.e., immunities recognized in 1871 when the statute was adopted), and while there is legitimate debate as to whether Congress or the Court ought to be engaged in the immunity-drafting process, I am willing to accept the adoption of general common law immunities. However, we gain very little guidance from nineteenth-century law as to the scope of these immunities and, in particular, the scope of any qualified immunity from suit. Our first opinion discussing this doctrine in 1967 relied on early American and English cases and limited the immunity protection to officers who acted with "good faith and probable cause."[7] In that case, there was a strong claim for immunity since the officer had acted pursuant to a law that was only declared invalid *after* the arrest of the plaintiff. We recognized the inherent unfairness of holding an officer accountable in damages for conduct that was authorized by state statute at the time he made the arrest and became unconstitutional only by reason of a subsequent court decision.

We later broadened the defense to permit immunity where the officer held a good faith belief in the legality of his actions and where that belief was objectively reasonable.[8] Unfortunately, however, we subsequently made a wrong turn in 1982 in *Harlow v. Fitzgerald*,[9] when we permitted the defense even where the officer did not hold a subjective good faith belief that his actions were lawful. In *Harlow* we decided that qualified immunity was available unless the constitutional right that a plaintiff claims was violated had previously been "clearly established." Even so, this problematic standard could have been properly tailored to limit the defense to officers who could not fairly foresee that their conduct would be found to be illegal, because the applicable legal principles had never been clarified. Indeed, a number of lower federal courts applied *Harlow* in this manner and denied immunity to officers who made arrests or searches without probable cause, even though no court had previously addressed the exact facts involved in the case. Since the probable cause standard itself was "well established," these courts reasoned that such officers could not defeat a claim simply by asserting that they were faced with specific facts and circumstances that had not been previously addressed by a court.

The turning point came in 1987 in *Anderson v. Creighton*,[10] where the issue was whether an entry into a home without probable cause could be defended, not on the ground that the constitutional principle requiring probable cause was new or novel but on the theory that the "conduct" of the officers was "reasonable" since no court had ever expressly found a lack of probable cause on the facts presented by that case. We ruled that even where officers acted unreasonably in entering a home to search for a suspect (because there was not sufficient cause to permit such an entry given the information available to them), it was not unreasonable for them to have thought that they were complying with the Fourth Amendment.

It is not difficult to see the fallacy of this approach and the dangers of "double-counting" on the issue of reasonableness. Chief Judge Richard Posner of the Seventh Circuit Court of Appeals has characterized this standard as giving officers "two bites at the apple."[11] In the same vein, Chief Judge Newman of the Second Circuit has stated:

> It is not readily apparent how a police officer could have an objectively
> reasonable belief that conduct was lawful when the unlawfulness of
> that conduct rests on a determination that an objectively reasonable
> police officer would not have acted.[12]

Harlow provided a generous defense to the officers. *Anderson* went further and, in the words of the dissenting opinion in that case, "stunningly restricts the constitutional accountability of the police."[13] Not surprisingly, after *Anderson v. Creighton*, the lower courts started to grant immunity where the legal standard had been clearly established by previous cases, often where one would have thought the illegality of the officers' conduct was apparent. For example, in *Robles v. Prince George's County*,[14] police officers were holding a suspect wanted in another county but were not willing to wait for officers from that county to pick him up. They handcuffed the arrestee to a pole in the middle of a deserted shopping center parking lot at 3 a.m. and then notified the other jurisdiction where he could be located. The court had little difficulty determining that this action had no valid law enforcement purpose and thus violated the Constitution but quite extraordinarily ruled that the officers were entitled to qualified immunity since no court had previously proscribed this specific misconduct. It is difficult to believe that the court did not understand that the lack of a factually controlling precedent was the function of the truly unprecedented but nonetheless obvious illegality.

Similarly, in *Parrish v. Cleveland*,[15] the court granted qualified immunity, notwithstanding established law that prohibited the conduct in question. There, the defendant transported a highly intoxicated individual, already suffering bouts of vomiting, unattended and not observable in the back of a police wagon, with his head covered by a "spit-mask" designed to trap fluids from the mouth and nose. The court of appeals ruled that the officers had qualified immunity from suit, although the plaintiff's death from suffocation resulted from the forcible application of this mask.

In other cases, courts have found constitutional violations but have granted immunity from suit for misconduct that betrays the claim of a good faith attempt to comply with legal standards. Thus, immunity has been provided where school students were subjected to strip searches without sufficient cause on the ground that the conduct was not sufficiently "egregious" to warrant damages;[16] where a prosecutor personally attested to false information in opposition to a request for bail, having made no attempt to investigate the veracity of the statement, which itself came from a biased source;[17] for a search of password-protected computer files without the necessary judicial warrant;[18] where a police officer failed to intervene when a fellow officer fabricated a suspect's confession;[19] and where police shot a person who had initially intervened with a knife to try to stop a police dog from holding her brother but who was unarmed when shot.[20]

These—and many other similar rulings—make little sense. It is one thing to protect an officer from unforeseen changes in the law after he has acted; it is quite another to bar recovery for one whose rights were violated on the ever-expanding ground that a reasonable officer could have thought his conduct to be legal. We have widened the scope of immunity to protect "all but the plainly incompetent [officer] or those who knowingly violate the law."[21] The Civil Rights Act, however, is not limited to providing a remedy only where a plainly incompetent officer has violated a person's constitutional rights. A judicial gloss on a statute that was intended to provide relief for violations of rights that restricts its utility so radically is not warranted.

A reasonably trained police officer should be able to foresee that generally applicable legal principles will apply to his actions, even if he is unaware of a previous case where an officer acted in exactly the same way. Where the application of general principles leads to a result that a reasonable officer should have foreseen, there is no justification for denying relief to the person whose rights were violated. The law should require officers to hesitate to act where their conduct may violate rights and particularly where a court's declaration of such a violation is consistent with prior rulings.

Accordingly, I would reverse our decision in *Anderson* and limit the qualified immunity defense to those situations where a court decision finding the conduct to be unconstitutional was not fairly foreseeable by a reasonably trained officer. By "fairly foreseeable" I contemplate that trained officers should be able to anticipate most decisions in which constitutional violations are found by applying well-established legal principles, even to novel factual circumstances.

Even accepting our prior rulings, however, today's decision is still unjustified. If reasonableness is the key ingredient, I cannot see how one who acts unreasonably in the use of force could have "reasonably" thought that his conduct was justified.

B. Qualified Immunity Cannot Be a Defense to a Claim of Excessive Force Under the Fourth Amendment

Where the standard for qualified immunity is identical to that which governs the constitutional claim, qualified immunity cannot be a separate defense. In the excessive force context, once it is determined that an objectively reasonable officer would not have used the force in question, it makes no sense—indeed, it is conceptually incoherent—to assert that the very same objectively reasonable officer could have believed that the force was reasonable. In other words, a police officer cannot have an objectively reasonable belief that force was necessary when the same "reasonable" officer would not have acted in the same way in the same circumstances.[22]

In *Graham v. Connor*, the Court held that excessive force claims arising out of arrests or investigatory stops are to be analyzed under the Fourth Amendment's objective reasonableness standard. Reasonableness is to be determined by the "facts and circumstances of each particular case, including the severity of the crime at issue, whether the suspect poses an immediate threat to the safety of the officers or others, and whether he is actively resisting arrest or attempting to evade arrest by flight."[23]

Most significant, the Court defined "reasonableness" in a manner that gives the officers substantial latitude in determining whether and what type of force can be used. As the Court stated:

> The 'reasonableness' of a particular use of force must be judged from the perspective of a reasonable officer on the scene, rather than with the 20/20 vision of hindsight. . . .
>
> The calculus of reasonableness must embody allowance for the fact that police officers are often forced to make spit-second judgments—in circumstances that are tense, uncertain, and rapidly evolving—about the amount of force that is necessary in a particular situation.[24]

Graham provides officers with a substantial margin of error. Thus, even where the force used was unnecessary (for example, the suspect did not have the weapon the officer believed he possessed), there is no Fourth Amendment violation if the officer reasonably could have believed the force used was necessary. Accordingly, once a court has determined that force was excessive, it has of necessity made the judgment—with "allowance for the fact that police officers are often forced to make split-second judgments"—that an objectively reasonable officer could not have thought that the force used was necessary or reasonable.

The majority bases its decision in this case on *Anderson v. Creighton*, where this Court ruled that the qualified immunity doctrine is applicable in cases alleging Fourth Amendment violations for warrantless searches or arrests without probable cause. As explained earlier, I believe that *Anderson* was wrongly decided and would vote to overrule that decision, but even if *Anderson* were defensible, the majority decision in this case would still be incorrect.

In *Anderson*, the Court reasoned that where an officer is found to have violated the Fourth Amendment by making an arrest or conducting a search without sufficient cause, the officer is entitled to the defense of qualified immunity if an objectively reasonable officer could have believed that probable cause existed. The probable cause determination for a search or arrest requires an officer to decide whether the known facts show that a crime probably has been committed by the suspect or that a search would probably disclose contraband or material of evidentiary value. The Court put significant emphasis on the fact that in some cases the probable cause determination is made pursuant to evolving legal doctrine under the Fourth Amendment and may require the drawing of fine legal lines.

Even assuming that probable cause issues may present close and difficult legal issues, officers who must determine how much force to use in self-defense or in effectuating an arrest are not placed in an equivalent legal quandary, because they have a broad scope of discretionary powers. This Court ruled in *Graham* that police officers act consistently with the Fourth Amendment when their conduct is objectively reasonable—a nontechnical and deferential constitutional doctrine that reflects well-established and commonly held judgments on the limits of police force. This standard provides a margin of error, precludes "Monday morning quarterbacking" by a court, permits the officer a wide range of reasonable responses, and does not require the officer to make finely tuned legal determinations.

Reasonable force includes a range of options or responses. Different officers in the identical situation, each behaving reasonably, might elect to use a baton, a chemical agent, a take-down hold, or a different technique; each might use greater or lesser force, within a reasonable range, in employing the chosen technique.[25] Thus, once it has been determined that an officer has acted in an excessive fashion, it means that he has acted outside the entire range of options that reasonable officers might have chosen. Thus, it is not possible to claim that an objectively reasonable officer could have thought the challenged actions to be proper.

The critical point is that where the standard for determining qualified immunity is the same as that for deciding the constitutional question itself, the defense is redundant. This is not a matter of semantics; rather, in determining whether an officer's use of force was within a range of reasonable options, the jury is also (and necessarily) answering the question whether a reasonable officer "could have believed" his use of force "to be lawful."[26] The existence of such broad protection in the Fourth Amendment itself eliminates any fear that officers will be unreasonably chilled from acting in the absence of a separate qualified immunity defense.

It is illogical to suggest that where the use of force is excessive that an "appropriately competent officer could reasonably believe" that such excessive force was reasonable. Put another way, the law ultimately may permit only a single right answer to the question of whether probable cause exists with respect to any particular arrest or search, but not every wrong answer is therefore unreasonable. By contrast, there is rarely a single appropriate use of force, and there is a range of reasonable responses. However, once the force used is determined to be unreasonable for Fourth Amendment purposes, an officer's use of excessive force cannot later be characterized as reasonable for qualified immunity purposes.

The Court fails to explain how an officer could act in an objectively unreasonable manner for Fourth Amendment purposes but could still have reasonably believed that his conduct was lawful. The Court says that "*Graham* does not always give a clear answer as to whether a particular application of force will be deemed excessive," but that assertion ignores the fact that the *Graham* standard for determining what force is appropriate is sufficiently particularized to provide officers fair notice of what force is permissible. Accordingly, qualified immunity in this context permits double-counting and stretches the immunity doctrine well beyond necessary limits.

C. The Dangers of an Expansive Qualified Immunity Doctrine

Qualified immunity has been justified as necessary (1) to protect officers who have to make "difficult" legal judgments, (2) to prevent overdeterrence of officers, and (3) to encourage courts to announce new constitutional principles they might otherwise reject.

The rationales for the doctrine are seriously overstated and not well supported. First, as I have detailed, where an officer has reason to know that a court may find his conduct unlawful, he *should* hesitate and resolve so-called difficult legal issues on the side of protecting constitutional rights. There is no empirical support for the argument that officers must always choose greater force over lesser force or delay in order to have sufficiently vigorous enforcement of the criminal law or to protect the public.

Second, there is no strict liability in constitutional tort litigation. Officers are never found liable for constitutional violations in the absence of evidence of culpable conduct. For example, a search is not illegal simply because it turns up no contraband; the officer needs only a "fair probability" of finding contraband. Nor would an innocent person convicted of a crime have a civil remedy following her exoneration unless she could prove wrongful conduct by a state official.[27] The argument that qualified immunity is necessary to avoid the overdeterrence of officers suggests that we must protect officers who have been found to have engaged in culpable conduct in order to encourage them to enforce the law. This is a cynical argument for which there is no empirical support. No one has made the case, for example, that, prior to this Court's decision in *Anderson v. Creighton*, officers were failing to make arrests or searches or using too little force in subduing suspects because of a fear of civil liability.

Moreover, denying a remedy to persons whose rights have been found to have been violated is not a good way to achieve effective law enforcement while protecting constitutional rights. To the degree that government agencies believe that police officers require enhanced protection against damages, having the governmental employer indemnify officers for damages judgments can provide it. If the Court is concerned about the cost of providing a remedy for rights violations where an officer would be left holding the "tab," we could permit recovery directly against the municipal employer where the officer acts improperly.[28] This would place the burden of payment on the government and, in turn, act as an incentive for the adoption of measures aimed at reducing future violations.

Third, the argument that qualified immunity is needed to permit the development of constitutional law, while of some surface appeal, is ultimately unpersuasive. Indeed, this Court has been careful not to give retroactive effect to constitutional rulings that make a sharp break with past practices and would jeopardize the status of convictions fairly obtained under then existing constitutional standards. Thus, we have applied the Fourth Amendment exclusionary rule in state criminal prosecutions, the *Miranda* warnings, and new standards for ensuring counsel at lineups prospectively. By contrast, where the right recognized is essential to a fair trial, as in *Gideon*, where we required appointment of counsel for indigent criminal defendants in felony cases, we have applied the rule retroactively out of a sense of fairness and the need for reliability of verdicts in criminal cases.

In the same fashion, qualified immunity can provide protection from civil liability where a court announces "new" constitutional law. If a court ruling deviates from prior principles and a new right is recognized, only officers who violate that right in the future are at risk of being held liable in damages. Qualified immunity will protect the officer in the case in which the new and unanticipated principle is articulated. There is a critical difference between protecting officers from liability as a result of new or otherwise unforeseeable decisions and protecting them from liability where the correct result was foreseeable based on prior decisions.

It should also be noted that police officers are also protected by other limits on civil rights suits for misconduct in criminal proceedings. A plaintiff who complains about such misconduct will usually be required to first secure the reversal of her criminal conviction.[29] Moreover, unless the alleged misconduct is serious, it is unlikely that a claim will be brought, as lawyers will carefully screen these claims. Suits by prisoners are subject to the very severe restrictions in filing suits that were instituted by Congress in the Prison Litigation Reform Act.[30]

The fact is that the constitutional costs of an expansive qualified immunity doctrine far exceed its benefits. By providing the police with a broad defense of qualified immunity, we can fully expect officers to apply the lesser Fourth Amendment protections of the immunity doctrine in their street-level decisions to arrest, search, and use force. After all, if a court will demand only "arguable probable cause" for a search or arrest or will permit "reasonable" unreasonable force, there is little reason for the officer not to apply these subconstitutional standards in their everyday policing. In these circumstances, deviance is defined downward and officers may well continue to operate on this subconstitutional level. As Professor Levinson states:

> [O]ne might doubt the extent to which governmental officials whose behavior is governed by constitutional law care much about constitutional rights except as predictors of legal risk, which is a function of remedies – especially in the context of criminal justice where there are strong normative reasons for pushing against constitutional limits.[31]

Finally, while this Court has frequently asserted that limitations on damages are justified on the grounds that alternative remedies exist for both deterrence and compensation, there are significant limitations on the supposed alternatives. Thus, the exclusionary rule has been substantially reduced in scope, the structural injunction remedy is available only under very limited circumstances, and internal discipline is hardly universal. These developments reflect a remedial "shell game" in which, as discrete remedies are reduced or limited, we are told that equally effective alternatives exist. Nevertheless, when implementation of those remedies is at issue, the same justifications are provided for limiting those remedial measures.

Damages can play a vital role in deterring both individual and governmental misconduct, but only if the damages assessment reflects the seriousness of the proven misconduct and the injuries that are suffered, government officials take necessary steps to reform practices and procedures that cause constitutional violations, and individual officers are properly disciplined, retrained, and supervised as a result of findings of misconduct. Some jurisdictions view money damages simply as a cost of doing business, and, as long as the amounts that are awarded or paid by way of settlement do not exceed budgetary limits, the "benefits" achieved by aggressive policing or other governmental operations that result in constitutional violations are seen as worth the price. But this fact does not prove that damages cannot deter. There are situations in which governmental units have changed practices and policies in the wake of large damage awards.[32] Further, the fact that some damage awards have not had a deterrent effect may well be a function of the limitations that courts and legislatures have imposed on damages in civil rights cases. Thus, if damages were permitted on the basis of the inherent value of rights (without a showing of injury or other losses) and punitive damages were recoverable from municipalities, it would be more difficult for government to consider damages simply as a cost of doing business. Surely, at some level, the cost of doing business in violation of the Constitution will be simply too great for the municipal budget, and practices will change.

As this Court stated in *Bivens v. Six Unknown Named Agents of the FBI*, for many plaintiffs "it is damages, or nothing."[33] To deprive a person whose constitutional rights have been violated of a judicial remedy for a proven violation is an extraordinary step. It may be justified in some narrow set of circumstances, but not under the ever-expanding umbrella of qualified immunity as defined by the majority in this case.

I dissent.

NOTES

1. Marbury v. Madison, 5 U.S. 137, 163 (1803)

2. Saucier v. Katz, 533 U.S. 194 (2001).

3. Normally, the Court would first decide whether any violation occurred and reach the immunity issue only if there was a violation. Here, the Court skipped the first step, but it seems clear from the Court's Opinion that none of the Justices believed that the force used was unreasonable from a constitutional perspective. That fact no doubt contributed to the majority's decision to grant immunity.

4. *Katz*, 533 U.S. at 205–206.

5. Graham v. Connor, 490 U.S. 386 (1989).

6. McNair v. Coffey, 234 F.3d 352, 356 (7th Cir. 2000).

7. Pierson v. Ray, 386 U.S. 547 (1967).

8. *See*, e.g. Wood v. Strickland, 420 U.S. 308 (1975).

9. Harlow v. Fitzgerald, 457 U.S. 800 (1982).

10. Anderson v. Creighton, 483 U.S. 635 (1987).

11. Llaguno v. Mingey, 763 F.2d 1560, 1569 (7th Cir. 1985).

12. Oliveira v. Mayer, 23 F.3d 642, 648 (2d Cir. 1994).

13. *Anderson*, 483 U.S. at 647 (dissenting op. by Justice Stevens, joined by Justices Brennan and Marshall).

14. Robles v. Prince George's County, 302 F.3d 262 (4th Cir. 2002).

15. Parrish v. Cleveland, 372 F.3d 294 (4th Cir. 2004).

16. Thomas v. Roberts, 323 F.3d 950 (11th Cir. 2003).

17. Trulock v. Freeh, 275 F.3d 391 (4th Cir. 2001).

18. Cruz v. Kauai Cy., 279 F.3d 1064 (9th Cir. 2002).

19. Jones v. Cannon, 174 F.3d 1271 (11th Cir. 1999).

20. *Id.* at 397.

21. Hunter v. Bryant, 502 U.S. 224, 229 (1991). The notion that qualified immunity protects all but "plainly incompetent" officers was originally invoked in a very specific context. In *Malley v. Briggs*, 475 U.S. 335 (1986), the Court decided that in a rare case, a police officer could be held liable for an unconstitutional search, even though the officer had obtained a search warrant from a court, if no reasonably competent officer would have concluded that the court should issue the warrant. The Court rejected the officer's argument that he should have been entitled to absolute immunity because he sought a warrant from a court and obtained one. The Court concluded that qualified immunity provided sufficient protection. There is greater reason to protect police officers from liability when they have sought court permission before taking action than when they act entirely on their own. We should have limited the notion that the qualified immunity doctrine protects all but "plainly incompetent" officers to cases in which the officer is acting under the authority of a warrant.

22. A number of lower federal courts have held that the Fourth Amendment and the qualified immunity doctrine pose precisely the same legal issue and that any differing determinations would be irreconcilable. *See, e.g.,* Frazell v. Flanagan, 102 F.3d 877, 886–87 (7th Cir. 1966)("once a jury has determined under the Fourth Amendment that the officer's conduct was objectively unreasonable, that conclusion necessarily resolves for immunity purposes whether a reasonable officer could have believed that his conduct was lawful"); Roy v. City of Lewiston, 42 F.3d 691 (1st Cir. 1994); Alexander v. County of Los Angeles, 64 F.3d 1315 (9th Cir. 1995); Scott v. District of Columbia, 101 F.3d 748 (D.C.Cir. 1996); Ramirez v. City of Reno, 925 F.Supp. 681, 687–89 (D.Nev. 1996)("intrinsic analytical incompatibility of an excessive force claim with a qualified immunity claim" given the objective reasonableness test; the "two lines of inquiry converge"); McNair v. Coffey, 234 F.3d 352 (7th Cir. 2000).

23. *Graham*, 490 U.S. at 396.

24. Id. at 396–97.

25. Under *Graham*, police are not held to a "least amount of force" test. Rather, as long as the force used was within a range of objectively reasonable options, the Fourth Amendment is satisfied. See Forrett v. Richardson, 112 F.3d 416, 420–21 (9th Cir. 1997)(shooting violent felony suspect was reasonable even if his capture through other means was inevitable); Scott v. Henrich, 39 F.3d 912, 915 (9th Cir. 1994) (reasonable to shoot armed man who confronted police at door).

26. *Anderson*, 483 U.S. at 638.

27. Indeed, for many constitutional violations the plaintiff must prove a very high level of culpability. *See, e.g.,* County of Sacramento v. Lewis, 523 U.S. 833 (1998) (no liability for officers in high-speed chase unless they acted in a manner that "shocks the conscience" by *intending* to cause harm to a person injured during the chase).

28. Although recovery against an employer for the torts committed by employees is routinely afforded under the doctrine of respondeat superior, this Court has held that doctrine inapplicable to civil rights claims. Monell v. Department of Social Services, 436 U.S. 658 (1978). We could, however, overrule that decision, as several Justices of this Court have suggested.

29. Heck v. Humphrey, 512 U.S. 477 (1994).

30. 42 U.S.C. § 1997e.

31. Daryl J. Levinson, *Rights Essentialism and Remedial Equilibration,* 99 Colum. L. Rev. 857, 911 (May 1999).

32. As one example, in Philadelphia, in 1996, in the wake of a police abuse scandal and the payment of several million dollars in settlements to persons who were wrongfully arrested and prosecuted on false narcotics charges, the city agreed to a settlement agreement in a federal lawsuit that mandated extensive changes in the operation, policies, and practices of the police department (including computerization of almost all records and data in the department, extensive use of force reporting, changes in internal affairs investigative procedures, heightened supervision of narcotics law enforcement, new policies to address racial profiling and unjustified stops of cars and pedestrians, and new hiring procedures). See Settlement Agreement, *NAACP v. City of Philadelphia,* C.A. No. 96-6045 (E.D. Pa.).

33. Bivens v. Six Unknown Named Agents of the FBI, 403 U.S. 388, 410 (1971).

8

Strickland v. Washington

Gutting *Gideon* and Providing Cover
for Incompetent Counsel

Abbe Smith

Introduction

The Sixth Amendment to the U.S. Constitution provides that "[i]n all criminal prosecutions, the accused shall enjoy the right . . . to have the Assistance of Counsel for his defence." Although the right to counsel in federal proceedings was well established early in the country's history, there was no corresponding right in state courts until well into the twentieth century. Instead, most states relied on volunteer lawyers to represent criminal defendants who could not afford counsel.[1]

The right to counsel has been called "the most precious"[2] and "fundamental"[3] of constitutional rights. This is because lawyers are often crucial to the assertion of other rights.[4] It has also been said that the right to counsel "makes the promise of equality in the criminal justice system possible."[5] It is through counsel that the poor and marginalized have access to justice.

The landmark case of *Gideon v. Wainwright*, which held that a poor person charged with a felony was entitled to counsel at state expense, recognized the crucial role lawyers play in our criminal justice system:

> [R]eason and reflection require us to recognize that in our adversary system of criminal justice, any person haled into court, who is too poor to hire a lawyer, cannot be assured a fair trial unless counsel is provided for him. This seems to us to be an obvious truth. . . . That government hires lawyers to prosecute and defendants who have the money hire lawyers to defend are the strongest indications of the widespread belief that lawyers in criminal courts are necessities, not luxuries. The right of one charged with crime to counsel may not be deemed fundamental and essential to fair trials in some countries but it is in ours.[6]

The 1963 *Gideon* decision is the starting point—and the high-water mark—for any discussion of the right to counsel. Unlike other Warren Court criminal procedure decisions, *Gideon* enjoyed support across the ideological spectrum when it was decided and remains uncontroversial today. Most Americans would find it unthinkable to face serious criminal charges without a lawyer.[7]

Gideon occupies a special place in our law and culture in part because it is a classic American story.[8] Clarence Earl Gideon, a poor drifter who had been in and out of jail, was charged with breaking and entering into a pool hall. He denied the crime. When his case was called to trial, he asked the court to appoint a lawyer because he had no money to hire one himself. The court denied his request, and Gideon reluctantly went to trial without a lawyer. He was quickly convicted and sentenced to five years in prison.

From prison, Gideon sent a handwritten note to the Supreme Court asking that it hear his case. Against the odds—for many prisoners write such pleas—the Justices agreed. The Court appointed Abe Fortas, one of the country's most prominent lawyers, to represent Gideon.[9] On March 18, 1963, the Court overruled an earlier decision guaranteeing counsel only in capital cases and held that there could be no fair trial in serious cases without a right to counsel for the defendant.

It is sometimes easy to forget the difference good counsel can make. At his new trial, Gideon was represented by an experienced court-appointed lawyer. He was acquitted.[10]

Gideon promised so much. But the vision of a "vast, diverse country in which every man charged with crime will be capably defended, no matter what his economic circumstance, and in which the lawyer representing him will do so proudly, without resentment at an unfair burden, sure of the support needed to made an adequate defense," has not come to pass.[11] As one commentator observed, "No constitutional right is celebrated so much in the abstract and observed so little in reality as the right to counsel."[12]

Although there are political reasons for *Gideon*'s unmet promise, the case of *Strickland v. Washington*[13] is also to blame. It is the low-water mark in the legal evolution of the right to counsel. *Strickland* set the legal standard for constitutionally acceptable legal representation (the "effective assistance of counsel") so low that Justice Harry Blackman once lamented that *Strickland* requires only that a defendant be represented by a "person who happens to be a lawyer."[14] Public defenders refer to the *Strickland* standard as the "warm body" or "pulse" test—in all but the most outrageous cases, any lawyer "capable of fogging a mirror" will be deemed effective.[15]

Strickland was the first case in which the Supreme Court addressed the meaning of constitutionally effective representation. Prior to *Strickland*, lower courts established their own standards for determining what constituted effective representation. In 1945, the Court of Appeals for the District of Columbia Circuit held that a constitutional violation would be found where the circumstances surrounding the trial "shocked the conscience of the court" and "made the proceedings a farce and mockery of justice."[16] The Supreme Court declined to review the D.C. case, and most circuits adopted this low standard. The 1970 case of *McMann v. Richardson*, in which the Supreme Court found that the Sixth Amendment right to counsel specifically contemplated the *effective* assistance of counsel, caused many courts to reconsider the "farce and mockery" standard.[17]

Gideon and *McMann* led to efforts to systematize and standardize the provision of indigent defense services in the early 1970s. In 1973, the National Advisory Commission on Criminal Justice Standards and Goals wrote a basic set of standards governing indigent defense systems. The next year, the U.S. Justice Department convened the National Study Commission on Defense Services, which issued its comprehensive *Guidelines for Legal Defense Systems in the United States* soon thereafter. Soon, a web of standards at the national, state, and local levels would govern the provision of indigent defense across the country.

Then came *Strickland*, in 1984.

The facts in *Strickland* are memorable. David Leroy Washington, a hard-working, church-going family man, was living with his wife and his newborn child in a blighted Miami neighborhood when his life fell apart in 1976.[18] He lost his job and was having trouble supporting his family. He was becoming increasingly distraught when a man, claiming to be a minister, approached him in a laundromat. When the man invited Washington to have sex in exchange for money, Washington "snapped" and stabbed him to death. Within a ten-day period, he killed twice more and committed other crimes.[19] When the crime spree was over,[20] Washington surrendered and gave a lengthy confession to one of the killings. Against his court-appointed lawyer's advice, he later confessed to the other crimes as well, waived his right to a jury trial, and pleaded guilty to three capital murder charges.

Washington's lawyer felt discouraged about the case, especially after the confessions. He did not believe "there was anything [he] . . . could do . . . to save David Washington from his fate."[21] As a result of his "sense of hopelessness," he filed a couple of perfunctory pretrial motions and essentially stopped working on the case.[22] The lawyer's investigation consisted only of talking with Washington a couple of times at the jail and speaking on the telephone with his wife and his mother. After one failed attempt at a face-to-face meeting with the family, he made no further efforts to meet with them.[23] He made no effort to seek out his client's friends, neighbors, co-workers, members of his church, or members of his extended family who might have provided important testimony about Washington's character and background or who would have at least presented a different side of his life at sentencing.[24]

The lawyer also made no effort to consult with a psychiatrist or psychologist or to secure a mental health examination for Washington because he believed his client had no psychological problems.[25] He apparently did not think a mental health professional might help explain the "inexplicable difference" between the man he had come to know in prison and the crimes he had committed.[26] The lawyer did not even request a presentence investigation report, which is ordinarily prepared in criminal cases and which might have uncovered important information about Washington's life history.

Such investigative efforts would have been valuable. The record at a later federal habeas proceeding established that there was a substantial amount of mitigating evidence. For the habeas proceeding, a new lawyer secured 14 affidavits from the defendant's family, friends, neighbors, former employees, and community members. All of the witnesses said they would have testified at trial had they been contacted by counsel. All described Washington as responsible, peaceful, and hardworking, a loving husband and father, and a man of conviction and faith.[27] Many remarked that the crimes were completely out of character for him.[28]

Moreover, at the habeas proceeding, a psychiatrist and a psychologist testified that Washington's violent actions were attributable to an eruption of long-suppressed feelings due to extensive child abuse, incest, and having grown up in a broken and violent family. Washington was also suffering from a severe depression because of his financial situation. Both mental health professionals attested to the defendant's substantial and sincere remorse.[29]

Washington's appeal to the Court of Appeals was heard in a special proceeding that included all the judges of that court. It established a new standard for determining ineffective assistance of counsel. The Court held that criminal defendants have a right to "counsel reasonably likely to render and rendering reasonably effective assistance given the totality of the circumstances."[30] The standard included a duty to investigate in order for counsel to make informed choices.[31] A defendant claiming ineffective assistance was required to show that the counsel had made errors "resulting in actual and substantial disadvantage to the course of his defense."[32] The Court of Appeals explicitly rejected the argument that a defendant should have to show that the outcome of the trial was affected by counsel's ineffective assistance.[33]

The Supreme Court granted certiorari to review the standard set by the Court of Appeals.[34] Justice O'Connor, writing for the majority, established a two-pronged test for finding a lawyer's performance constitutionally defective: first, that counsel had made errors so serious that the lawyer was not functioning as the "counsel" guaranteed by the Sixth Amendment, and, second, that the deficient performance prejudiced the defense.[35]

The opinion began by formally reaffirming the rights guaranteed by the Sixth Amendment. The Court noted that mere presence by counsel— the "warm body" standard—was not enough: "That a person who happens to be a lawyer is present at trial alongside the accused . . . is not enough to satisfy the constitutional command."[36] The Court reiterated that "the right to counsel is the right to the effective assistance of counsel."[37]

However, the standard for attorney performance actually adopted by the Court was not effective assistance of counsel but *"reasonably effective assistance."*[38] The Court held that a defendant challenging his counsel's performance must show that the "representation fell below an objective standard of reasonableness."[39] The Court declined to provide guidelines for what might constitute reasonable representation, reasoning that the Sixth Amendment did not enumerate any particular requirement.[40]

Although the Court suggested that prevailing norms of practice such as the American Bar Association's *Standards for Criminal Justice* might be helpful in determining what is reasonable, they were only "guides" and had no constitutional force.[41] The Court rejected the idea that specific guidelines for attorney performance were essential to the right to counsel, because of the variety of circumstances that different cases present. Guidelines would not reflect the "range of legitimate decisions regarding how best to represent a criminal defendant."[42] Indeed, the Court suggested that detailed guidelines could "distract" a defense lawyer from the vigorous advocacy required.[43] The Sixth Amendment, the majority concluded, does not have the purpose of improving the quality of legal representation. Its purpose is merely to ensure that defendants receive a fair trial.[44]

The Court concluded that judicial scrutiny of a defense lawyer's performance "must be highly deferential."[45] A court must "eliminate the distorting effects of hindsight" and evaluate performance from the counsel's perspective at the time of the trial or proceeding. In sum, "a court must indulge a strong presumption that counsel's conduct falls within the wide range of reasonable professional assistance; that is, the defendant must overcome the presumption that, under the circumstances, the challenged action 'might be considered sound trial strategy.'"[46]

This presumption in favor of finding the defense lawyer's performance "reasonably effective" is almost impossible to overcome.

The second prong of the test requires that even where counsel's performance was deficient, to obtain a new trial a defendant must show that "there is a reasonable probability that, but for counsel's unprofessional errors, the result of the proceeding would have been different."[47] The Court defined "reasonable probability" as "a probability sufficient to undermine the confidence in the outcome."[48]

In this case, the Court concluded that the conduct of Washington's counsel at and before the sentencing proceeding was a reasonable "strategy."[49] Even if counsel's conduct was unreasonable, the Court found insufficient prejudice to justify setting aside the death sentence, because Washington was probably going to get the death penalty no matter what counsel did.[50]

All good defenders know the story of *Gideon* and find inspiration in it. When *Strickland* came down, practitioners and scholars immediately knew it dealt a body blow to *Gideon*.[51] In the twenty years since *Strickland* was decided, things have only gotten worse.

While some indigent defendants are well represented—some of the best lawyers in the country are public defenders—many are so badly represented they might as well have no lawyer at all. In addition, even the most devoted public defenders experience an "unfair burden" because they have too many cases, too little time, and too few resources. Even adequately paid defenders cannot provide effective assistance of counsel without caseload limits and adequate funding for investigative and expert services.

In order to understand the significance of *Strickland* to the right to counsel, it is important to recognize that criminal defense in this country is, by and large, indigent defense. It has always been so. As Clarence Darrow told inmates at the Cook County Jail more than a hundred years ago: "Nine-tenths of you . . . are in jail because you did not have a good lawyer and, of course, you did not have a good lawyer because you did not have enough money to pay a good lawyer." The vast majority of defendants cannot afford to hire their own lawyers and are represented by appointed counsel.[52]

In the years since *Strickland* was decided, the Supreme Court has found ineffective assistance of counsel in only three cases, all capital cases.[53] Not a single noncapital ineffective assistance of counsel case— where ineffectiveness was the main issue the Court sought to review—has been heard by the Supreme Court since *Strickland* was decided.[54] Given the special scrutiny capital cases receive, the numbers of such cases seeking Supreme Court review, and the notoriously shoddy lawyering that many capital defendants receive,[55] it is remarkable that the Supreme Court has found only three cases worthy of relief.

Since *Strickland* was decided, lower courts have also been reluctant to find ineffective assistance of counsel in even the most shameful cases. Courts have declined to find ineffectiveness where defense counsel slept during the trial,[56] where counsel used heroin and cocaine throughout the trial,[57] where counsel allowed his client to wear the same clothes in court that the perpetrator was alleged to have worn at the crime,[58] and where counsel appointed in a capital case was unable to name a single Supreme Court decision on the death penalty.[59] In one capital case, the attorney was found effective even though he "consumed large amounts of alcohol each day of the trial . . . drank in the morning, during court recess, and throughout the evening . . . [and] was arrested during the trial for driving to the courthouse with a .27 blood-alcohol content."[60] In another case, an attorney suffering from Alzheimer's disease was found effective even though he failed to make an opening statement and made no objection when the prosecutor introduced evidence of his client's inadmissible prior convictions.[61]

There are more examples.

In a Texas case, the Fifth Circuit found that appointing a lawyer on the morning of a noncapital trial comported with *Strickland*.[62] The Court pointed out that the prosecutor's case was "straightforward," and there was a positive eyewitness identification of the defendant at trial.[63]

In another Texas case, the defense lawyer failed to introduce any evidence about his client at the penalty phase of a capital trial. The attorney's entire summation in the penalty phase was: "You are an extremely intelligent jury. You've got that man's life in your hands. You can take it or not. That's all I have to say." A federal district court granted the convicted man's petition for a writ of habeas corpus because of the lawyer's failure to present or argue mitigating evidence, but the Fifth Circuit found that the attorney's lack of argument was a "dramatic ploy" that satisfied *Strickland*. The lawyer was later suspended for other reasons. The defendant was executed.[64]

In a Georgia case, a man accused of capital murder was represented by an attorney who, at the guilt phase, gave no opening statement, presented no defense, conducted scant cross-examination, made no objections, and emphasized the heinousness of the crime in brief closing remarks that could hardly be called a "closing argument." Even though the defendant was severely mentally impaired, the lawyer presented no evidence of this at either the guilt or penalty phase. At the penalty phase, he also offered no evidence of his client's steady work history, service in the military, church involvement, and cooperation with police. In his summation, the lawyer suggested that death might be the most appropriate punishment for his own client. This representation was deemed effective enough. The defendant was executed.[65]

In another infamous Texas case, in which defense counsel kept dozing off during his client's capital trial—so noticeably that the bailiff had to repeatedly come around to defense table and kick him—no fewer than five federal appeals judges ruled that sleeping during a capital trial does not violate *Strickland*.[66]

An example of the extraordinary lengths to which some courts go to avoid finding ineffective assistance is the case of *Rogers v. Zant*.[67] In *Rogers*, the defendant, who had smoked a PCP-laced cigarette the day of the offense, was charged with the capital murder of his neighbor. His lawyer failed to investigate the effects of PCP, a drug associated with aggression. The federal appeals court, reversing a finding of ineffectiveness by the district court, stated, "Even if many reasonable lawyers would not have done as defense counsel did at trial, no relief can be granted on ineffectiveness grounds unless it is shown that *no* reasonable lawyer, in the circumstances, would have done so."[68] Rejecting decisions by other panels of the same court which held that strategic decisions must be based on some investigation, the panel in *Rogers* determined that "'strategy' can include a decision not to investigate" and that "once we conclude that declining to investigate further was a reasonable act, we do not look to see what a further investigation would have produced."[69]

Although *Gideon* was based on the recognition that lawyers are "necessities, not luxuries," representation by a capable, dedicated, experienced lawyer with adequate time and resources is in fact a luxury for many accused. As one scholar has written, the "differences in the quality of legal assistance available to the rich and poor play probably the most significant systemic role in maintaining a double standard in criminal justice. A constitutional right is only as good as the lawyer one has to assert it."[70]

The legacy of *Strickland* has been that every mistake by counsel, no matter how egregious, is a "judgment call," a matter of "strategy," or a "tactical" decision, all of which are beyond review. *Strickland* has also allowed inadequate representation by underfunded and overwhelmed public defenders and court-appointed counsel.

Strickland stands as a cynical reminder that rights, no matter how fundamental, and no matter how closely tied to our sense of ourselves as a nation, can be rendered empty.

In her dissent, Professor Abbe Smith argues that whether a criminal defense lawyer provided constitutionally adequate representation should be judged by professional standards. She concludes that the established ethical rules and standards for conducting the defense of a person charged with crime are sufficiently well established and accepted that we should explicitly incorporate them into Sixth Amendment jurisprudence. In particular, she would have held that the Sixth Amendment imposes on counsel a duty to investigate, because reasonably effective assistance must be based on professional decisions, and informed legal choices can be made only after investigation of options. Prof. Smith would not impose the burden on the defendant of proving that a competent performance by counsel would have resulted in a different outcome. She concludes that a showing of incompetence on the part of defense counsel should automatically require reversal of the conviction without regard to proof of prejudice to the defendant.

Dissent by Abbe Smith

The right to counsel is at the heart of our system of justice. The right arose out of the founders' dislike for the English practice of prosecuting people without representation. Believing that those charged with felonies—usually defined as crimes carrying a penalty of a year or more in prison—should have counsel, several American colonies also created a right to counsel in their state constitutions.[71]

Roots of the modern right to counsel can be found more than a century ago. In 1853, the Indiana Supreme Court recognized a right to an attorney at public expense for an indigent person accused of crime. "It is not to be thought of in a civilized community for a moment that any citizen put in jeopardy of life or liberty should be debarred of counsel because he is too poor to employ such aid," the Indiana court wrote in *Webb v. Baird*. "The defense of the poor in such cases is a duty which will at once be conceded as essential to the accused, to the court and to the public."[72]

The *Webb v. Baird* decision was the exception rather than the rule in the states. For much of the twentieth century, most states relied on volunteer lawyers to defend the accused, even those charged with serious crimes. While some private programs, such as the New York Legal Aid Society, were active as early as 1896 in providing counsel to needy immigrants and others, the first public defender's office did not begin operations until 1914 in Los Angeles. Such offices did not exist outside of the largest cities.

The right to counsel in federal court was well established by statute early in the country's history and was reaffirmed by this Court in 1938 in *Johnson v. Zerbst*.[73] The right to counsel in state courts was developed more gradually. In 1932, the Court made its first major statement about the right to counsel in the "Scottsboro Case," *Powell v. Alabama*, in which seven young black men, some of them only boys, had been convicted and sentenced to death without counsel for the rape of two white women in a small Alabama town.[74] The trial occurred only six days after the indictment and twelve days after the alleged offense. Reversing the convictions, the Court held that counsel was required in all state capital proceedings. Writing for the majority, Justice Sutherland discussed the importance of defense counsel in words that hold true today:

> The right to be heard would be, in many cases, of little avail if it did not comprehend the right to be heard by counsel. Even the intelligent and educated layman has small and sometimes no skill in the science of law. If charged with crime, he is incapable, generally, of determining for himself whether the indictment is good or bad. He is unfamiliar with the rules of evidence. Left without the aid of counsel he may be put on trial without a proper charge, and convicted upon incompetent evidence, or evidence irrelevant to the issue or otherwise inadmissible. . . . He requires the guiding hand of counsel at every step in the proceedings against him. Without it, though he be not guilty, he faces the danger of conviction because he does not know how to establish his innocence.[75]

Only a decade later, in *Betts v. Brady*,[76] the Court declined to extend the Sixth Amendment right to counsel to serious noncapital state proceedings. It was not until 21 years after *Betts* that the Court again considered the issue of the right to counsel in noncapital felony proceedings. In a series of decisions, beginning with *Gideon v. Wainwright*,[77] in 1963, this Court firmly established the right to counsel in nearly all aspects of state criminal proceedings.

In 1967, in *In re Gault*,[78] the Court extended *Gideon* to juvenile delinquency proceedings. In 1972, in *Argersinger v. Hamlin*,[79] the right to counsel was extended to all misdemeanor state proceedings in which there was a potential loss of liberty.

Gideon, Gault, and *Argersinger* are the best known of the right to counsel cases, but they were part of a broader array of decisions. The Court recognized a defendant's right to counsel at such critical stages of criminal proceedings as postarrest interrogation, in *Miranda v. Arizona*, in 1966; at lineup, in *United States v. Wade* in 1967; a preliminary hearing, in *Coleman v. Alabama* in 1970; and a plea negotiation, in *Brady v. United States* and *McMann v. Richardson*, both in 1970.

After conviction, defendants are entitled to counsel in an appeal of right under *Douglas v. California*[80] and in some probation and parole proceedings under *Mempa v. Rhay*.[81]

This Court has repeatedly recognized that an accused's right to be represented by counsel is a "fundamental component of our criminal justice system."[82] Without the "guiding hand" of counsel—competent, devoted, zealous counsel[83]—many other rights would go unprotected, because lawyers "are the means through which the other rights of the person on trial are secured."[84] As Professor Walter Schaefer has observed, "Of all the rights that an accused person has, the right to be represented by counsel is by far the most pervasive, for it affects his ability to assert any other rights he may have."[85]

In *United States v. Cronic*, an ineffective assistance-of-counsel case also decided today,[86] the Court cites with approval the words of Professor Schaefer, affirming the critical role of counsel in ensuring a fair trial.[87] Yet, the Court fails to create a standard for the performance of counsel that reflects the crucial role that counsel plays in our adversary system of justice. Instead, in both *Cronic* and this case, the Court has created such a low standard as to subvert the right to counsel and the adversary system. Worse, the majority establishes a nearly impossible-to-meet two-pronged test: that a defendant must show that his lawyer "made errors so serious that counsel was not functioning as the 'counsel' guaranteed by the Sixth Amendment" and that his lawyer's deficient performance so prejudiced the defense that, but for counsel's incompetence "there is a reasonable probability that . . . the result . . . would have been different."

I would hold instead that whether a criminal defense lawyer provided constitutionally adequate representation should be judged chiefly by professional standards. There are well-established ethical rules and standards for conducting the defense of a person charged with crime. The rules are sufficiently accepted that we should explicitly incorporate them into Sixth Amendment law. If a lawyer's performance falls so short of professional norms as to subject the lawyer to disciplinary action, that performance should be held to violate the Sixth Amendment's guarantee of effective assistance of counsel. It is disgraceful that the constitutional standard for judging the competence of lawyers in cases where life or liberty is at stake is less than the standard for malpractice.[88]

Here, Washington's lawyer's conduct clearly fell short of professional norms as established by the *ABA Standards for Criminal Justice*:

> It is the duty of the lawyer to conduct a prompt investigation of the circumstances of the case and to explore all avenues leading to facts relevant to the merits of the case and the penalty in the event of conviction. . . . The duty to investigate exists regardless of the accused's admissions or statements to the lawyer of facts constituting guilt or the accused's stated desire to plead guilty.[89]

The standards could not be clearer or more in line with the facts of this case. The "hopelessness" of the cause, heinousness of the crime, or guilt of the accused does not excuse the lawyer from investigating and preparing a defense. In failing to do these things, Washington's lawyer abandoned his professional duty to his client and violated the Sixth Amendment.

The Court's vague, malleable legal standard for effective assistance of counsel does not comport with the recognition of the crucial role counsel plays in ensuring fairness. The Court's denigration of professional standards as mere "guides" fails to give proper respect to the principles that such standards establish. It also fails to provide clear direction to the lower courts and defense bar as to the difference between adequate and inadequate representation. I would adopt the reasoning of the United States Court of Appeals for the Fifth Circuit with regard to the performance in this case: the Sixth Amendment imposes on counsel a duty to investigate because reasonably effective assistance must be based on professional decisions, and informed legal choices can be made only after investigation of options.[90] The complete failure to investigate necessarily "undermine[s] confidence in the outcome."[91]

However, I would go further than the Fifth Circuit's prejudice test, under which the defendant must show that counsel's deficient performance "resulted in actual and substantial disadvantage to the course of his defense."[92] Although this standard is preferable to the majority's test, I agree with Justice Marshall that a showing of incompetence on the part of defense counsel should automatically require reversal of the conviction regardless of the injury to the defendant.[93]

Even if a prejudice requirement is justifiable, placing the burden of proving prejudice on the defendant is inappropriate and undermines the presumption of innocence. As Judge David Bazelon of the United States Court of Appeals for the D.C. Circuit has noted:

> A requirement that the defendant show prejudice . . . shifts the burden
> [of proving his case] to him and makes him establish the likelihood
> of his innocence. It is no answer to say that the appellant has already
> had a trial in which the government was put to its proof because the
> heart of his complaint is that the absence of the effective assistance of
> counsel has deprived him of a full adversary trial.[94]

The majority's prejudice test implies that only the innocent deserve competent counsel. But the guarantee of effective assistance of counsel also functions to ensure that convictions "are obtained only through fundamentally fair procedures."[95] I agree with Justice Marshall that "[e]very defendant is entitled to a trial in which his interests are vigorously and conscientiously advocated by an able lawyer. A proceeding in which the defendant does not receive meaningful assistance in meeting the forces of the State does not . . . constitute due process."[96]

The majority's position—that "the Sixth Amendment is not violated when a manifestly guilty defendant is convicted after a trial in which he was represented by a manifestly ineffective attorney"—is inconsistent with the fundamental principles underlying our system of justice. This "guilty anyhow" way of thinking "has played a major role in perpetuating ineffective representation."[97] In this country, we respect the rights even of the guilty:

The presumption of innocence, the rights to counsel and confrontation, the privilege against self-incrimination, and a variety of other trial rights, matter not only as devices for achieving or avoiding certain kinds of trial outcomes, but also as affirmations of respect for the accused as a human being—affirmations that remind him and the public about the sort of society we want to become and, indeed, about the sort of society we are.[98]

It is clear that Washington's Sixth Amendment rights were violated by incompetent counsel. Defense counsel failed to investigate because he felt "hopeless . . . about overcoming the evidentiary effect of [Washington's] confessions to the gruesome crimes."[99] This is simply unacceptable as a matter of professional responsibility and constitutional law, notwithstanding the majority's strange sympathy for the lawyer.[100]

No doubt an acquittal at trial was hopeless, but there are two separate phases in a capital murder trial. In addition to the guilt phase, there is the critically important penalty phase. The latter was the only contested proceeding for Washington. At the penalty phase, any evidence that might support a decision not to execute is allowed, including the circumstances of the crime, the defendant's history, character, and intelligence, and the defendant's psychological profile. This is specifically set forth in the Florida statutes.[101]

Even the most despised defendant has a life story. Competent capital defenders—whether hopeful or despairing—find the story, put it together as forcefully as possible, and use it to argue against execution.[102] Washington's lawyer decided to rely on the defendant's "sincerity and frankness" in pleading guilty. He put on no evidence at sentencing except Washington's brief statements during the guilty plea. Appallingly, the defendant's closing argument took up only three pages of the sentencing transcript.[103]

It "shocks the conscience" of at least this member of the Court that Washington's lawyer called no character witnesses to testify to his good moral character, no mental health experts to explain the defendant's mental and emotional state at the time of his crimes, and no family members to beg for lenience.[104] Yet, the majority finds counsel's decision to put on no case at all a perfectly rational judgment:

It . . . reflected the judgment that it was advisable to rely on the plea colloquy for evidence about respondent's background and about his claim of emotional stress: the plea colloquy communicated sufficient information about these subjects, and by forgoing the opportunity to present new evidence on these subjects, counsel prevented the State from cross-examining respondent on his claim and from putting on psychiatric evidence of its own.[105]

The majority gives counsel too much credit. The plea colloquy to which the majority refers consisted of respondent stating that, aside from a string of burglaries, he had no significant criminal record prior to the crime spree and that he was "under extreme stress caused by his inability to support his family."[106] This barely establishes, much less "*sufficiently communicates*," a reason to spare respondent's life in the face of multiple killings. The majority seems to agree with trial counsel that respondent's "owning up" to his crimes was his best strategy, largely because the trial judge praised respondent for "step[ping] forward and admit[ting] . . . responsibility."[107] However, the trial judge also cautioned respondent that his "great deal of respect" for respondent and others who "step forward" should not be taken as an indication of his likely sentencing decision.[108]

The majority makes more of what respondent's counsel actually did—which was paltry—than what he failed to do. The majority refers to counsel's "active pursuit" of pretrial motions (which were of a boilerplate nature) and discovery (which was a form letter). It notes counsel's efforts to advise his client against confessing, waiving his right to a trial by jury, and waiving his right to an advisory jury at his capital sentencing hearing. It notes counsel's successful motion to exclude respondent's "rap sheet" from the sentencing hearing. The majority considers counsel's failure to request a presentence report a wise strategic move: "Because he judged that a presentence report might prove more detrimental than helpful, as it would have included respondent's criminal history and thereby would have undermined the claim of no significant history of criminal activity, he did not request that one be prepared."[109]

But this was not a shoplifting case, where such a gambit might pay off. When the crime is minor, it might make sense to move quickly to sentencing without the benefit of a presentence report lest it reveal more criminal history than is known to the court.[110] This was a capital murder case where the crimes were "gruesome,"[111] and Washington's criminal history was a matter of public record. A favorable or sympathetic presentence report might have helped. Counsel certainly knew that there were many aggravating circumstances in the three murders. Furthermore, the trial court readily found these circumstances: that the murders were "especially heinous, atrocious, and cruel, all involving repeated stabbings"; that the murders were committed in the course of at least one other dangerous and violent felony; that the murders were for pecuniary gain, as they were connected to robberies; and that all the murders were committed to avoid apprehension and hinder law enforcement.[112] The trial court found no mitigating circumstances because none were presented by the lawyer.

My own review of the facts in this case is not meant to second-guess counsel or impose my own standards for criminal defense. I agree with the majority that hindsight can be distorting. I also agree that "[n]o particular set of detailed rules for counsel's conduct can satisfactorily take account of the variety of circumstances faced by defense counsel or the range of legitimate decisions regarding how best to represent a criminal defendant."[113] I acknowledge that even "the best criminal defense attorneys would not defend a particular client in the same way."[114] However, Washington's counsel did virtually *nothing* to defend his client here. There is no way this meets even the majority's tepid rule that counsel's assistance be "reasonable considering all of the circumstances."[115] Here is the principal problem with the majority's standard. In the name of protecting the "independence of counsel" and not restricting the "wide latitude counsel must have in making tactical decisions," the majority offers virtually no standard at all. The only situations the majority cites in which counsel might be presumptively ineffective are where there is a conflict of interest,[116] substantial state interference with the defense lawyer,[117] or "a complete denial of counsel."[118] Although the majority in *Cronic* referred to circumstances approximating the complete denial of counsel—"when although counsel is available to assist the accused during trial, the likelihood that any lawyer, even a fully competent one, could provide effective assistance is so small that the presumption of prejudice is appropriate without inquiry into the actual conduct of the trial"—it seems unlikely that the Court will ever find such a case.[119]

While the majority recognizes that "[r]epresentation of a criminal defendant entails certain basic duties," such as consulting with a client, keeping the client informed of important developments, and "bring[ing] to bear such skill and knowledge as will render the trial a reliable adversarial testing process,"[120] it goes no further than this general acknowledgment. The majority disparages the notion of a "checklist for judicial evaluation of attorney performance" and holds that prevailing norms of practice as reflected in the *ABA Standards,* are "guides to determining what is reasonable, but . . . only guides."[121]

The majority makes the unpersuasive assertion that "detailed guidelines for representation" would only "distract counsel from the overriding mission of vigorous advocacy of the defendant's cause."[122] But how could such guidelines be a distraction? Every state has ethical codes, rules, standards, and guidelines governing lawyers' professional conduct.[123]

The majority is at its most wrongheaded when it attempts to parse the purpose of the effective assistance guarantee of the Sixth Amendment. It dismisses the notion that the effective assistance guarantee has anything to do with the quality of legal representation and proclaims instead that the "purpose is simply to ensure that criminal defendants receive a fair trial."[124] But a criminal defendant cannot receive a fair trial in the absence of competent counsel. If the counsel's assistance is of "vital importance" and the "right to counsel plays a crucial role in the adversarial system embodied in the Sixth Amendment, since access to counsel's skill and knowledge is necessary to accord defendants the 'ample opportunity to meet the case of the prosecution' to which they are entitled,"[125] it follows that fairness and competent counsel are inextricably linked.

The majority seems to understand this connection when it states that "a person who happens to be a lawyer [being] present at trial alongside the accused . . . is not enough to satisfy the constitutional command."[126] But it fails to recognize that respondent's counsel in the case at bar was essentially that. It is not enough for a person who happens to be a lawyer to do nothing more than accompany the accused to the gallows. As the majority states, the Sixth Amendment "recognizes the right of the assistance of counsel because it envisions counsel's playing a role that is critical to the ability of the adversarial system to produce just results. An accused is entitled to be assisted by an attorney . . . who plays the role necessary to ensure that the trial is fair."[127]

It is well settled that "the right to counsel is the right to the effective assistance of counsel."[128] The text of the Sixth Amendment itself makes this plain. "The Amendment requires not merely the provision of counsel to the accused, but 'Assistance,' which is to be 'for his defence.'"[129] The "core purpose of the counsel guarantee was to assure 'Assistance' at trial, when the accused was confronted with both the intricacies of the law and the advocacy of the public prosecutor."[130] If no actual "Assistance" "for" the accused's "defence" is provided, then the constitutional guarantee has been violated.[131]

The mere appointment of counsel—the so-called warm body test[132]—is not enough to satisfy the effective assistance guarantee. To hold otherwise would "convert the appointment of counsel into a sham and nothing more than a formal compliance with the Constitution's requirement that an accused be given the assistance of counsel. The Constitution's guarantee of assistance of counsel cannot be satisfied by mere formal appointment."[133]

And yet, "inexperienced, incompetent, [and] indifferent" counsel—"walking violations of the Sixth Amendment"—can be found in every courthouse in this country.[134] Examples of incompetent or marginal defense counsel are plentiful: counsel not knowing that the court keeps records of prior convictions; counsel advising a judge that he could take only a few minutes for summation because he had to move his car by a certain time; counsel inviting the jury to draw a negative inference from the fact that there were no corroborating witnesses to his client's alibi; counsel telling the jury he had done the best job he could "with what he had to work with."[135]

Just as one would not want a doctor inexperienced or incompetent in surgery to remove one's appendix, an inexperienced or incompetent trial lawyer should not represent defendants facing imprisonment or death. This is not simply a goal for the legal profession but a matter of constitutional right.

The majority's two-pronged "performance and prejudice test" for ineffective assistance of counsel—that the attorney's conduct must fall "outside the wide range of professional competence" and the attorney's incompetence be so deficient as to "undermine confidence in the outcome"—reflects a greater concern for the reputation of incompetent lawyers than for the rights of the accused.[136] This is not simply wrong as a matter of law; it is immoral.

Under the majority's test, it will be nearly impossible for a convicted defendant to establish constitutionally defective counsel. Even if counsel is demonstrably physically or mentally impaired, a defendant "must show that there is a reasonable probability that, but for counsel's unprofessional errors, the result of the proceeding would have been different." In other words, where the Government's case is strong, a showing that defense counsel was wholly inadequate will never be enough to make out a Sixth Amendment violation.

This Court can and should do better. We have an obligation to put forth a vision of legal representation that commands respect. Feckless, reckless lawyers who neglect their professional responsibilities and threaten the proper functioning of the adversary system[137] should not be protected by a presumption that their conduct is reasonable. They should be disciplined and their clients should receive a new trial or sentencing.

At the very least the Court should be honest about the sad reality of *Gideon* 20 years after it was decided. As Anthony Lewis predicted, it is "an enormous social task to bring to life the dream of *Gideon v. Wainwright*—the dream of a vast, diverse country in which every man charged with crime will be capably defended, no mater what his economic circumstance."[138] The task will never be accomplished without strong backing from the Court. The Court today not only fails to live up to the promise of *Gideon*; it abandons it completely.

Although hard data are difficult to amass,[139] the issue of deficient representation in indigent criminal defense is serious enough to call into question the "legal and moral foundations of the criminal process."[140] Recently, an American Bar Association study found that "millions of persons in the United States who have a constitutional right to counsel are denied effective legal representation."[141] Respected scholars, judges, and lawyers agree.[142] These observers have nothing to gain by casting shame on the American legal profession.

There are many reasons for the unfulfilled promise of *Gideon*. Some are political and institutional. Shamefully low fees for appointed counsel in many jurisdictions,[143] pay schemes that encourage guilty pleas over trials,[144] crushing caseloads for public defenders,[145] and busy urban courts that value speed above all else[146] contribute to poor lawyering. Some are cultural. As Justice Brennan has written: "How can we blame laymen for their impatience with procedural safeguards when so many *lawyers* believe that contributing one's legal services to an unpopular or unremunerative cause is dirty, or nasty, or opprobrious?"[147] The legal profession does not do enough to encourage talented young lawyers to represent the poor accused, promote pro bono defense work by large firms, or support the existing indigent defense bar.

It is essential that the accused be represented by able counsel whether they have been charged with capital murder or an ordinary street crime. I agree with the majority in this regard and disagree with Justices Brennan and Marshall. As the majority states, "[f]or purposes of describing counsel's duties," a capital sentencing proceeding "need not be distinguished from an ordinary trial."[148] Although "the penalty of death is qualitatively different form a sentence of imprisonment, however long,"[149]—and courts would be wise to appoint the most experienced and skilled counsel to capital cases—the right to counsel is important in all criminal trials.

The rate of incarceration in this country is unprecedented and still rising. According to Department of Justice data, the United States imprisoned a record-high 412,303 inmates in 1982.[150] The growing number of incarcerated is largely due to so-called sentencing reforms, such as mandatory minimum sentencing, sentencing guidelines, statutory sentencing enhancement schemes, and restrictions on parole.[151] Already bursting American prisons and jails can barely contain the growing number of inmates.[152] In many jails and prisons, inmates sleep in the gymnasium or on the floor and are double- and triple-bunked in cells meant for one inmate.[153]

Prison has become the favored approach to addressing complex social problems. The disproportionate number of poor and nonwhite prisoners[154] suggests the incarceration of whole communities of already marginalized citizens. One can only imagine the ancillary consequences of so much incarceration—to our sense of ourselves as a free nation, to the struggling economy of our poorest neighborhoods, to the family members left behind, and to the prisoners themselves.

The lengthy sentences now being served, not just by those convicted of murder but by street level drug dealers, have changed the nature and purpose of incarceration, making the distinction between a prison sentence and a death sentence not so far apart. People die in prison.

I would add just a few words on the majority's treatment of the question of "finality." Though a jury verdict should not be lightly overturned, the importance of finality does not justify trampling on fundamental rights. Even the majority concedes that "finality concerns are . . . weaker" when counsel—a "crucial assurance[] that the result of the proceeding is reliable"—is ineffective.[155]

An attorney who conducts no investigation in a capital case is constitutionally ineffective. An attorney who fails to put on evidence at the penalty phase of a capital murder trial is constitutionally ineffective. David Washington had what amounted to no counsel at all in this case. He will likely be put to death as a result.

The majority decision does more than permit an incompetently represented man to be executed. It creates a shamefully low standard for an essential American right, effectively eviscerating that right. It takes the heart out of *Gideon*, the case that reflects the highest aspirations of American law and society. It does so blithely, as if justice has been done.

It ushers in an era not of equal justice, but justice on the cheap.

I find that a clear violation of the Sixth Amendment has been established here, requiring a new sentencing proceeding.

I dissent.

Epilogue

Since both *Gideon* and *Strickland* were decided, public defender caseloads remain high, indigent defense contracts continue to be awarded to the lowest bidder without regard to quality, and defense funding has not kept pace with other components of the criminal justice system. These problems have serious consequences. As former Attorney General Janet Reno has stated, "[T]he lack of competent, vigorous legal representation for indigent defendants calls into question the legitimacy of criminal convictions and the integrity of the criminal justice system as a whole."[156]

The chief problem is, and has always been, underfunding. Every couple of years, a new national study decries the inadequate funding of indigent defense.[157] Theses studies and the commentary that accompanies them invariably comment on the deficient representation provided by inexperienced, ineffectual, overburdened, and underfunded defense counsel.[158]

The fact that the defense bar consists mostly of publicly financed lawyers does not have to spell its doom. Many devoted, experienced, and skilled lawyers are public defenders and "panel" lawyers.[159] However, very real constraints prevent even the most devoted lawyers from providing provide high-caliber criminal defense.

Notwithstanding the good will that *Gideon* generated when it was decided, there has never been any political will behind it. Courts can establish certain constitutional procedural rights, but legislative underfunding undercuts these guarantees in practice.[160]

The unmet promise of *Gideon* is not an abstract legal problem. Where there is no meaningful right to counsel, the poor accused are demonstrably harmed. According to the Justice Department, 88 percent of defendants with public counsel but only 77 percent of defendants with private counsel received a prison sentence in federal court, and 71 percent of defendants with public counsel but 54 percent of defendants with private counsel received a prison sentence in state court.[161]

There is also a racial dimension to inadequate indigent defense services. More nonwhites than whites tend to have publicly funded counsel.

In state prison, 77 percent of black inmates, 73 percent of Hispanic inmates, and 69 percent of white inmates had court-appointed counsel. In federal prison, 65 percent of blacks, 56 percent of Hispanics, and 57 percent of whites had court-appointed counsel.[162]

Funding for defense services is often the first thing to go when state budgets are tight—and not just in the Deep South. In 2004, Minnesota laid off large numbers of public defenders because of a budget crisis. The defenders who managed to hold on to their jobs had to cover their own caseloads along with those of their departed colleagues with no money to pay for basics like hearing transcripts, not to mention investigative or expert services.[163] In Pittsburgh, the county commission cut funding for the public defender office in 1996, resulting in the loss of 12 lawyers and eight investigators.[164] In 1995, Governor Tommy Thompson of Wisconsin proposed and obtained significant cuts to the state public defender's budget, increases in public defender caseloads, limits on how much court-appointed lawyers could spend on court documents and investigative services, and flat rate payments to appointed counsel.[165] Even in our nation's capital, court-appointed attorneys often go unpaid during budget crises.[166]

Most state and local governments have never provided the funds necessary to provide effective assistance of counsel to the poor consistent with the Sixth Amendment.[167] In some places, the hourly pay rate for legal services is less than the cost of a haircut. Many jurisdictions allow court-appointment schemes built on cronyism, not quality of counsel. One Texas lawyer who was routinely appointed to capital cases by judges who liked the way he helped move their dockets used to boast of hurrying through capital trials like "greased lightening."[168]

Lack of pay parity with the local prosecuting agency and the failure to adequately compensate experienced lawyers make it hard for public defender offices to retain the best staff. In Alabama, indigent defense attorneys receive less than one-quarter the funding that prosecutors receive. This figure does not include money given to police and other law enforcement services who work with prosecutors to investigate and develop cases.[169] In Mississippi, compensation is fixed at a flat amount based on the charge, notwithstanding the complexity of the cases, and the fee for a capital case is limited at one thousand dollars. A judge noted in one capital case that "the court reporter was paid far more than the defense counsel."[170]

Lack of money for full-time investigators for public defender offices and insufficient funding of private investigators for court-appointed lawyers has a clear effect on the quality of representation. A Phoenix study revealed that only about 55 percent of defense lawyers viewed the crime scene before trial in felony cases, and only 31 percent interviewed prosecution witnesses who testified at trial. Almost 50 percent of lawyers entered plea agreements without interviewing any prosecution witnesses, while 30 percent entered plea agreements without interviewing any defense witnesses.[171]

In New York City, things are even worse. Assigned counsel in homicide cases visited the crime scene in only 12 percent of their cases and conducted pretrial interviews of only 21 percent of witnesses and 25 percent of their own clients. In felonies—including serious cases like rape, kidnapping, aggravated assault, and child abuse—these attorneys interviewed witnesses in only around 4 percent of their cases and their clients in only 18 percent.[172]

Jonathan Casper's well-known study of criminal defense found that 27 percent of public defenders spend less than 10 minutes with their clients, while 59 percent spend less than half an hour.[173] This conduct is contrary to well-established criminal defense standards on investigation and client interviewing and counseling.[174] It is also contrary to the most basic—and perfectly reasonable—expectations by clients of their lawyer's performance. In a word, such conduct is unethical.[175] It is no wonder that the "grim reality of indigents' pervasive mistrust of their lawyers" persists.[176]

Anyone who has ever stepped foot in a criminal courthouse has observed painful scenes of incompetent court-appointed lawyers providing "legal assistance" to hapless clients. Professor Vanessa Merton offers a brilliant description of one such lawyer:

> All along, he had been leaning against a wall, scribbling with a pencil on a stack of files. He had no brief case or satchel or backpack to hold a handy CPL or Penal Law. He was, to put it politely, unkempt: flushed, uncombed, unshaven, shirt-tails hanging out of his trousers, and extremely distracted looking. My first thought was he must be unusually dedicated to come to court when he was so obviously sick with the flu.
>
> As it developed, that didn't seem to be the problem. . . .
>
> "OK, here it is–Sanchez, yeah, another car thief. Probably young, though, you know? Maybe not such a bad kid–maybe he does it to support his dear mother. (Head thrown back in, a gleeful guffaw over his own wit.) What are you looking for? These guys don't care if they get

a conviction as long as there's no jail. How 'bout a fine? He can always steal another car to pay it." (Another raucous guffaw that descended into a giggle. Then he started working on something in his ear.)[177]

There is some good news.

In 2002, the Court denied certiorari on a high-profile sleeping lawyer case, letting stand an appellate ruling that a Texas death row inmate is entitled to a new trial because his lawyer fell asleep repeatedly during his 1983 trial. It is to be hoped that the Court was suggesting that the sleeping lawyer met the Court's stringent test for *per se* prejudice and automatic reversal.[178] Many scholars have called for such a *per se* finding of prejudice for sleeping lawyers or lawyers under the influence of alcohol or drugs under both *Strickland* and *Cronic*.[179]

In 2005, in *Rompilla v. Beard*,[180] the Court reversed on ineffectiveness grounds the death sentence of a Pennsylvania man because his lawyer had failed to search his criminal record for evidence that might have persuaded the jury to spare his life. The Court found that counsel had failed to make "reasonable efforts to obtain and review material that counsel knows the prosecution will probably rely on as evidence of aggravation at the sentencing phase of trial."[181]

Significantly, the Court, in a decision by Justice Souter, cited the *ABA Standards for Criminal Justice*:

> It is the duty of the lawyer to conduct a prompt investigation of the circumstances of the case and to explore all avenues leading to facts relevant to the merits of the case and the penalty in the event of conviction. The investigation should always include efforts to secure information in the possession of the prosecution and law enforcement authorities. The duty to investigate exists regardless of the accused's admissions or statements to the lawyer of facts constituting guilt or the accused's stated desire to plead guilty.[182]

In *Rompilla*, the Court cites another recent reversal on ineffectiveness grounds, *Wiggins v. Smith*, to support its use of the *ABA Standards* as "'guides to determining what is reasonable.'"[183] Justice Souter states that the *Standards* "describe[] the obligation in terms no one could misunderstand in the circumstances of a case like this."[184]

Occasionally, lawyers and judges play a heroic role in ensuring a meaningful right to counsel. In Louisiana, for example, when an overworked public defender named Rick Teissier filed a pretrial motion asking that his own legal assistance in a murder case be declared ineffective prior to trial because of his caseload, the trial judge agreed. The judge then declared the entire Orleans public defender system unconstitutional and ordered the legislature to come up with sufficient funding to bring it up to constitutional standards. On appeal, the Louisiana Supreme Court agreed and found that "because of excessive caseloads and insufficient support, indigent defendants are generally not provided effective assistance in New Orleans." While it declined to find the entire defender system unconstitutional, it created a rebuttable presumption that indigent defendants represented by the Orleans public defender officer were receiving ineffective assistance of counsel.[185]

NOTES

1. *See* www.nlada.org/About/About_HistoryDefender [last visited Nov. 12, 2007].

2. Walter V. Schaefer, *Federalism and State Criminal Procedure*, 70 Harv. L. Rev. 1, 8 (1957).

3. United States v. Cronic, 466 U.S. 648, 653 (1984).

4. *Id.*, 466 U.S. at 654.

5. David Cole, No Equal Justice 63 (New York: The New Press, 1999).

6. Gideon v. Wainwright, 372 U.S. 335, 344 (1963).

7. A stunning exception is the prosecution of alleged terrorists held at Guantanamo Bay, Cuba. *See generally* Joseph Margulies, Guantanamo and the Abuse of Presidential Power (New York: Simon & Schuster, 2005) (discussing the lack of basic rights at Guantanomo); Clive Stafford Smith, Ferry (New York: Nation Books, 2007) (same).

8. Anthony Lewis's award-winning book *Gideon's Trumpet*, which tells the story of *Gideon*, is required reading in high schools, colleges, and law schools across the country. The television movie version of *Gideon's Trumpet* starred no less than Henry Fonda. *See* Anthony Lewis, Gideon's Trumpet (New York: Random House, 1964); "Gideon's Trumpet" (CBS Television, Hallmark Hall of Fame Productions, Apr. 30, 1980).

9. Twenty-two state attorneys general (led by Minnesota Attorney General Walter Mondale, who would later serve as Vice President) joined Gideon in arguing that Sixth Amendment protection be extended to all defendants charged with felonies in state courts.

10. *See* Cole, *supra* note 5 at 63.

11. Lewis, *supra* note 8, at 205, n. 3; *see also* Stephen B. Bright, *Counsel for the*

Poor: The Death Sentence Not for the Worst Crime but for the Worst Lawyer, 103 YALE L.J. 1835, 1837 (1994) [hereinafter *Worst Lawyer*] ("More than sixty years after *Powell* and thirty years after *Gideon*, this task remains uncompleted, the dream unrealized.").

12. Stephen Bright, *Turning Celebrated Principles into Reality*, THE CHAMPION: NAT'L ASS'N OF CRIM. DEF. LAW, Jan.–Feb. 2003, at 6.

13. Strickland v. Washington, 466 U.S. 668 (1984).

14. McFarland v. Scott, 512 U.S. 1256, 1259 (1994) (Blackmun, J., dissenting).

15. David Luban, *Are Criminal Defenders Different?*, 91 MICH. L. REV. 1729, 1740 (1995).

16. Diggs v. Welch, 148 F.2d 667, 670 (D.C. Cir. 1945).

17. McMann v. Richardson, 397 US. 759 (1970).

18. Some of the facts that follow are taken from materials in the Joint Appendix (hereinafter "J.A.") filed by the parties in the Supreme Court. *See* J.A., at 338–65.

19. The following materials not available in 1984 were helpful in constructing a narrative of David Leroy Washington's life and crimes: DAVID VON DREHLE, AMONG THE LOWEST OF THE DEAD, 134–35 (1995); DAVID J. KEEFE, SENTENCING ADVOCACY AND THE RIGHT TO EFFECTIVE ASSISTANCE OF COUNSEL: THE PROSPECTS FOR SENTENCING ADVOCACY IN NONCAPITAL STATE COURT SENTENCING PROCEEDINGS 2 (The Sentencing Project, July 2003).

20. In addition to the three murders, Washington allegedly committed multiple counts of robbery, torture, kidnapping, attempted murder, assault, attempted extortion, and theft. Strickland v. Washington, 466 U.S. 668, 669 (1984).

21. J.A., at 400.

22. Counsel admitted as much: he said that his despair over the confessions resulted in a "cessation and end" to his preparation. J.A., at 426.

23. Some of the facts are taken from the Appendix filed in the Supreme Court by the Petitioner Strickland (hereinafter "P.A."). *See* P.A., at 264–65.

24. P.A., at 265.

25. P.A., at 264–65.

26. P.A., at 266, quoting the trial lawyer.

27. J.A., at 338–65.

28. A Dade County police officer stated that in his years in law enforcement he had "never seen anyone do something like David has done with the history and character that David has." J.A., at 365.

29. Transcript of habeas corpus proceeding at 6–9, 10–15, *Strickland*.

30. *Strickland*, 466 U.S. at 680 (quoting the appellate decision, 693 F.2d 1243, 1250 (1982)).

31. *Id.*

32. *Id.* at 682 (quoting the appellate decision 693 F.2d at 1262).

33. *Id.* at 684.

34. *Id.*

35. *Strickland,* 466 U.S. at 687.
36. *Id.* at 685.
37. *Id.* at 686.
38. *Id.* at 687 (emphasis added).
39. *Id.* at 688.
40. *Id.*
41. *Id.*
42. *Id.* at 689.
43. *Id.*
44. *Id.*
45. *Id.*
46. *Id.*
47. *Id.* at 694.
48. *Id.*
49. *Id.*
50. *Id.* at 699.

51. *See generally* Vivian O. Berger, *The Supreme Court and Defense Counsel: Old Roads, New Paths—A Dead End?,* 86 COLUM. L. REV. 9 (1986). Two years after *Strickland,* Professor Berger was somewhat forgiving of the Court, noting the institutional constraints that made it "very hard for the justices to project a vision of counsel that can both command respect and be realized in practice." *Id.* at 13. Still, Berger lamented the Court's missed opportunity to play a leadership role:

> When [the Court] refuses to take serious issues seriously . . . the Court impoverishes the moral and intellectual discourse within the profession and betrays its leadership role. When it generally eulogizes counsel and stresses the need for effective assistance yet disparages the lawyer-client relationship . . . and overtly encourages dismissive treatment by lower courts of challenges to counsel, as in *Strickland,* one wonders whether the majority are being hypocritical or merely nodding. At a minimum, the Court could have stated frankly that inept performance by defense counsel is no rarity, but indicated that other institutions would have to carry the lion's share of the remedial burden.

Id. at 115.

52. As a Justice Department report stated, "Court-appointed legal representation for indigent criminal defendants plays a critical role in the Nation's criminal justice system." DEP'T OF JUSTICE, BUREAU OF JUSTICE STATISTICS, INDIGENT DEFENSE SERVICES IN LARGE COUNTIES, 1999, 1 (Nov. 2000). For data on the percentage of criminal defendants who are indigent, *see* DEP'T OF JUSTICE, BUREAU OF JUSTICE STATISTICS SPECIAL REPORT, DEFENSE COUNSEL IN CRIMINAL CASES 1 (Nov. 2000) [hereinafter DEFENSE COUNSEL IN CRIMINAL CASES] (reporting that 82 percent of felony state defendants and 66 percent of felony

federal defendants were represented by court-appointed counsel); *see also* Note, *Gideon's Promise Unfulfilled: The Need for Litigated Reform of Indigent Defense*, 113 HARV. L. REV. 2062, 2065 (2000) (reporting that indigent defendants represent about 80 percent of all criminal defendants).

53. *See* Rompilla v. Beard, 545 U.S. 374 (2005) (counsel ineffective for failing to make reasonable efforts to obtain and review material the prosecution would likely rely on as evidence of aggravation at penalty phase); Wiggins v. Smith, 539 U.S. 510 (2003) (counsel ineffective for failing to investigate and present mitigating evidence at penalty phase); Williams v. Taylor, 529 U.S. 362 (2000) (counsel ineffective for failing to investigate and present mitigating evidence at penalty phase).

54. Two noncapital cases, *Dretke v. Haley*, 541 U.S. 386 (2004), and *Daniels v. United States*, 532 U.S. 374 (2001) made it to the Supreme Court on other grounds but also had ineffective assistance claims. The Court denied relief.

55. *See generally* Bright, *Worst Lawyer, supra* note 11 (describing the pervasiveness of deficient representation in capital cases and offering examples); James S. Liebman, *The Overproduction of Death*, 100 COLUM. L. REV. 2030, 2102–9 (2000) (discussing the role that ineffective defense lawyers play in the "overproduction" of death sentences in the United States).

56. *See* People v. Tippins, 570 N.Y.S. 2d 581 (1991); *see also* Burdine v. Johnson, 231 F.3d 950 (5th Cir. 2000), *vacated and remanded*; Burdine v. Johnson, 262 F.3d 336 (5th Cir. 2001), *rehearing en banc, affirmed*; Cockrell v. Burdine, 122 S. Ct. 2347 (2002), *cert. denied*. Although the district court in *Burdine* had found that "[a sleeping counsel is equivalent to no counsel at all," Burdine v. Johnson, 66 F.Supp. 2d 854, 866 (S.D. Tex. 1999) (quoting Javor v. United States, 724 F.2d 831, 834 (9th Cir. 1984)), a Fifth Circuit panel in a 2-1 one decision reversed because the trial record did not indicated when the court-appointed attorney, Joe Frank Cannon, slept, so the court could not presume that his sleeping affected the trial. In the *en banc* decision, the Fifth Circuit reversed Burdine's capital murder conviction. Still, it is important to note that five of 14 federal appeals court judges believed that a lawyer sleeping during a capital murder case is not *per se* ineffective under *Strickland* and would have allowed Burdine's execution to go forward. For a discussion of another sleeping lawyer case, *see* Bruce Shapiro, *Sleeping Lawyer Syndrome*, THE NATION, Apr. 7, 1997 (discussing McFarland v. State, 928 S.W.2d 482 (Tex. Crim. App. 1996), overruled on other grounds by Mosley v. State, 983 S.W.2d 249, 263 (Tex. Crim. App. 1998)). When asked why he slept through most of his client's 1992 capital murder trial, the Texas lawyer John Benn said, "I'm seventy-two years old. I customarily take a short nap in the afternoon." The bailiff kicked Benn's chair several times but eventually gave up trying to keep Benn awake.

57. People v. Badia, 552 N.Y.S.2d 439 (1990).

58. People v. Murphy, 464 N.Y.S.2d 882 (1983).

59. *See* Bright, *Worst Lawyer, supra* note 11, at 1839 (describing Birt v. Montgomery, 725 F.2d 587, 601 (11th Cir. 1984); 469 U.S. 874 (1984), *cert. denied.*

60. People v. Garrison, 76 P.2d 419 (Cal. 1989).

61. Pilchak v. Camper, 741 F.Supp. 782 (W.D. Mo. 1990), *aff'd*, 935 F.2d 145 (8th Cir. 1991).

62. Avery v. Procunier, 750 F.2d 444 (5th Cir. 1985).

63. Of course, most competent defenders—and knowledgeable courts—recognize that eyewitness identification is fallible and can be effectively challenged through cross-examination and the presentation of expert testimony. *See* Abbe Goodnough & Terry Aguayo, *25 Years Later, DNA Test Comes to a Man's Defense,* N.Y. TIMES, Aug. 3, 2005, at A11 (recounting the story of Luis Diaz, who was wrongfully convicted of multiple rapes in the 1970s on the basis of a series of mistaken identifications and noting that mistaken witness identification accounted for the majority of wrongful convictions subsequently overturned due to DNA testing between 1989 and 2005).

64. Bright, *Worst Lawyer, supra* note 11, at 1858 (citing Romero v. Lynaugh, 884 F.2d 871, 875, 877 (5th Cir. 1989).

65. *Id.* at 1859–60 (citing Messer v. Kemp, 760 F.2d 1080, 1096 n. 2 (11th Cir. 1985) (Johnson, J., dissenting), *cert. denied*, 474 U.S. 1008, 1090 (1986) (Marshall, J., dissenting from denial of certiorari), and Messer v. Kemp, 831 F.2d 946, 951 (11th Cir. 1987) (*en banc*), *cert. denied*, 485 U.S. 1029 (1988)).

66. Burdine v. Johnson, 262 F.3d 336 (5th Cir. 2001) (*en banc*), *cert. denied*, 535 U.S. 1120 (2002).

67. Rogers v. Zant, 13 F.3d 384 (11th Cir. 1994), *cert. denied* 513 U.S. 899 (1994).

68. *Id.* at 386.

69. *Id.* at 388.

70. COLE, *supra* note 5, at 95.

71. *See* Powell v. Alabama, 287 U.S. 45, 599–61, 61–64 (1932); Bruce A. Green, *Lethal Fiction: The Meaning of "Counsel" in the Sixth Amendment,* 78 IOWA L. REV. 433, 439 & n.12 (1993) [hereinafter *Lethal Fiction*].

72. Webb v. Baird, 6 Ind. 11, 15 (1854).

73. Johnson v. Zerbst, 304 U.S. 458 (1938).

74. Powell v. Alabama, 287 U.S. 45 (1932). In the "Scottsboro Boys" case, nine young blacks were originally accused of raping two white women. On the day of trial, a lawyer from Tennessee appeared on behalf of persons "interested" in the defendants but stated that he had not had an opportunity to prepare the case or to familiarize himself with local procedure and therefore was unwilling to represent the defendants on such short notice. The problem was "resolved" when the court decided that the Tennessee lawyer would represent the defendants, with whatever help the local bar could provide. *See* United States v. Cronic, 446 U.S. 648, 659 (1984). Seven of the defendants were convicted and two of the original defendants

were acquitted at trial. As the Court in *Powell* noted, the case of the Scottsboro Boys represented a low point in the history of the American criminal justice system:

> The defendants, young, ignorant, illiterate, surrounded by hostile sentiment, hauled back and forth under guard of soldiers, and charged with an atrocious crime regarded with special horror in the community where they were to be tried, were thus put in peril of their lives within a few moments after counsel for the first time charged with any degree of responsibility began to represent them. 287 U.S. at 57–58.

75. Powell v. Alabama, 287 U.S. at 68–69.

76. Betts v. Brady, 316 U.S. 455 (1942).

77. Gideon v. Wainwright, 372 U.S. 335, 344 (1963).

78. *In re* Gault, 387 U.S. 1 (1967).

79. Argersinger v. Hamlin, 407 U.S. 25 (1972).

80. Davis v. California, 372 U.S. 353 (1963).

81. Mempa v. Rhay, 389 U.S. 128 (1967).

82. *Cronic*, 466 U.S. at 653; *see also* United States v. Ash, 413 U.S. 300, 307–8 (1973); *Argersinger*, 407 U.S. at 31–32; *Wainwright*, 372 U.S. at 343–45; *Zerbst*, 304 U.S. at 462–63; *Powell*, 287 U.S. at 68–69.

83. *See* MODEL CODE OF PROF'L RESPONSIBILITY Canon 15 (1908) (referring to the lawyer's obligation to give "entire devotion to the interest of the client, warm zeal in the maintenance and defense of his rights and the exertion of [the lawyer's] utmost learning and ability"); MODEL RULES OF PROF'L CONDUCT, Rule 1.3, comment 1 (1983) ("[a] lawyer should act with commitment and dedication to the interests of the client and with zeal in advocacy upon the client's behalf"); MODEL CODE OF PROF'L RESPONSIBILITY Canon 7 (1969) ("A Lawyer Should Represent a Client Zealously Within the Bounds of Law"); *see also* STANDARDS FOR CRIMINAL JUSTICE §4–1.1–4—8.6 (ABA, 2d ed. 1981).

84. *Cronic*, 466 U.S. at 653.

85. Walter Schaefer, *Federalism and State Criminal Procedure*, 70 HARV. L. REV. 1, 8 (1956).

86. *Cronic* and this case present the Court's first occasions to elaborate the appropriate standards for judging claims of ineffective assistance of counsel. In *Cronic*, the Court considered such claims in the context of cases "in which the surrounding circumstances [make] it so unlikely that any lawyer could provide effective assistance that ineffectiveness [is[properly presumed without inquiry into actual performance at trial." *Cronic*, 466 U.S. at 661. In *Cronic*, a young real estate lawyer with no jury trial experience was given 25 days to prepare for a mail fraud trial involving a complex, $9 million "check-kiting" scheme that the Government had taken four years to investigate. The Court found no ineffective assistance of counsel.

87. *Cronic* , 466 U.S. at 654. Under *Cronic,* prejudice is presumed when there has been a denial of the "right of the accused to require the prosecution's case to survive the crucible of meaningful adversarial testing." 466 U.S. at 656.

88. *See* Richard Klein, *The Emperor Gideon Has No Clothes: The Empty Promise of the Constitutional Right to Effective Assistance of Counsel,* 13 HASTINGS CONST. L. Q. 625, at 540–41 (1986) [hereinafter *The Emperor Gideon Has No Clothes*].

89. STANDARDS FOR CRIMINAL JUSTICE §4–4.1 (ABA, 2d ed. 1982 Supp.).

90. *Strickland,* 693 F.2d at 1251. Under the Fifth Circuit's analysis, first the defendant must prove that his "right to effective assistance of counsel was violated." Where defense counsel claims to have made a "strategic choice to channel his investigation into fewer than all plausible lines of defense," a defendant must prove that the assumptions underlying the strategic choice were unreasonable. *Id.* at 1256. Where defense counsel failed to conduct "a substantial investigation into plausible lines of defense for reasons other than strategic choice," the attorney will be held to have rendered ineffective assistance. *Id.* at 1257–58. *See also* STANDARDS FOR CRIMINAL JUSTICE, *supra* note 33.

91. *Strickland,* 466 U.S. at 694.

92. *Strickland,* 693 F.2d at 1262. The Fifth Circuit divided the burden of proving prejudice between the defendant and the state. The defendant must first show that counsel's deficient performance created not only "'a possibility of prejudice, but that [it] worked to his actual and substantial disadvantage.'" *Id.* at 1258 (quoting United States v. Frady, 456 U.S. 152, 170 (1982)). If the defendant carries that burden, the state must then prove that "counsel's ineffectiveness was harmless beyond a reasonable doubt." *Id.* The Court explicitly rejected a rule of *per se* prejudice, *see Strickland,* 693 F.2d at 1258–60, because in the case of ineffective assistance "the state is not responsible for the violation of the [defendant's] rights." *Id.* at 1260. I disagree with this analysis. Whether or not the state bears any responsibility for ineffective assistance of counsel—and perhaps it does, if prosecutors fail to bring concerns about deficient counsel to the attention of the trial judge (who has his/her own responsibilities, *see* Galia Benson-Amram, *Protecting the Integrity of the Court: Trial Court Responsibility for Preventing Ineffective Assistance of Counsel in Criminal Cases,* 29 N.Y.U. REV. L. & SOC. CHANGE 425 (2004))—the blameworthiness of the state is irrelevant. The prejudice is inherent in deficient representation. Moreover, in *Chapman v. California,* 386 U.S. 18, 23 and n.8 (1967), the Court noted that certain constitutional violations, including the denial of the right to counsel, can never be deemed harmless. In my view, the denial of effective assistance of counsel is equivalent to the denial of any counsel.

93. *See Strickland,* 466 U.S. at 712 (Justice Marshall, dissenting) ("I would thus hold that a showing that the performance of a defendant's lawyer departed from constitutionally prescribed standards requires a new trial regardless of whether the defendant suffered demonstrable prejudice thereby."); *see also* United States v.

Yelardy, 567 F.2d 864, 865, n. 1 (CA6), *cert. denied,* 439 U.S. 842 (1978); Beasley v. United States, 491 F.2d 687, 696 (CA6 1974); Commonwealth v. Badger, 482 Pa. 240, 243–244; 393 A.2d 642, 644 (1978).

94. United States v. DeCoster *[Decoster I],* 487 F.2d 1197, 1204 (D.C. Cir. 1973).

95. *Strickland,* 466 U.S. at 711 (Marshall, J., dissenting); *see also* United States v. Decoster (*Decoster II*), 624 F.2d 196–294 (*en banc*) (Bazelon, C.J., dissenting), *cert. denied,* 444 U.S. 944 (1979).

96. *Strickland,* 466 U.S. at 711 (Marshall, J., dissenting).

97. David L. Bazelon, *The Realities of Gideon and Argersinger,* 64 GEO. L.J. 811, 825 (1976).

98. Laurence Tribe, *Trial by Mathematical Precision and Ritual in the Legal Process,* 84 HARV. L. REV. 1329, 1391–92 (1971).

99. *Strickland,* 466 U.S. at 673.

100. *Id.* at 699 (commenting that "counsel understandably felt hopeless"). The Court goes on to say that nothing in the record indicates that "counsel's sense of hopelessness distorted his professional judgment" and counsel "could reasonably surmise from his conversations with respondent that character and psychological evidence would be of little help." I do not share this view.

101. Fla. Stat. Ann. §921.141(1) (1983 Supp.) ("Evidence may be presented as to *any matter the court deems relevant to sentence,* and shall include matters relating to any of the aggravating or mitigating circumstances enumerated in [the statute].") (emphasis added).

102. See, ANTHONY AMSTERDAM, TRIAL MANUAL V FOR THE DEFENSE OF CRIMINAL CASES (1988).

103. J.A., at 320–324.

104. Diggs v. Welch, 148 F.2d 667 (D.C. Cir., 1945) (holding that due process is violated where the circumstances surrounding a trial "shock[s] the conscience of the court and "ma[kes] the proceedings a farce and mockery of justice").

105. *Strickland,* 466 U.S. at 674 (quoting P.A., at A223–A225).

106. P.A., at 50–53.

107. *See Strickland,* 466 U.S. at 672, 699; P.A., at 54, 57.

108. P.A., at 62.

109. *Strickland,* 466 U.S. at 673.

110. *See* Amsterdam, *supra* note 102 (advising waiver of presentence report in less serious cases).

111. *Strickland,* 466 U.S. at 673.

112. *Id.* at 674.

113. *Id.* at 688–89.

114. *Id.* at 689; Gary Goodpaster, *The Trial for Life: Effective Assistance of Counsel in Death Penalty Cases,* 58 N.Y.U. L. REV. 299, 343 (1983).

115. *Strickland,* 466 U.S. at 688 (emphasis added).

116. *See id.* at 683, 686, 688; Cuyler v. Sullivan, 446 U.S. 335, 346 (1980).

117. *See Cronic,* 466 U.S. at 659.

118. *Id.; see also* Powell v. Alabama, 287 U.S. at 68–69.

119. *Cronic,* 466 U.S. at 659–60. The majority in *Cronic* offers *Powell v. Alabama* as such a case. *See Cronic,* 446 U.S. at 661. But, *Powell,* an alleged interracial rape case in the Jim Crow South 30 years before *Gideon,* is unlikely to ever happen again. It is unimaginable that an out-of-state lawyer would today be allowed to represent all defendants in a capital murder case only six days before trial. On the other hand, this Court has affirmed convictions where counsel was appointed in a capital case only three days before trial and the trial court denied counsel's request for additional time to prepare. Avery v. Alabama, 308 U.S. 444, 450–53 (1940); *see also* Chambers v. Maroney, 399 U.S. 42, 54 (1970) (refusing to "fashion a *per se* rule requiring reversal of every conviction following tardy appointment of counsel").

120. *Strickland,* 466 U.S. at 688.

121. *Id.* at 688. *See* STANDARDS FOR CRIMINAL JUSTICE, *supra* note 89.

122. *Strickland,* 466 U.S. at 689.

123. *See, e.g.,* MODEL CODE OF PROF'L RESPONSIBILITY (1908); MODEL CODE OF PROF'L RESPONSIBILITY (1969); STANDARDS FOR CRIMINAL JUSTICE (ABA, 2d ed. 1982 Supp.); MODEL RULES OF PROF'L CONDUCT (1983).

124. *Strickland,* 466 U.S. at 689. The majority concedes that improving the quality of legal representation is "a goal of considerable importance to the legal system" but believes this has nothing to do with the Sixth Amendment. *Id.* at 689.

125. *Id.* at 685, citing Adams v. United States *ex rel.* McCann, 317 U.S. 269, 275, 276 (1942).

126. *Strickland,* 466 U.S. at 689.

127. *Id.* at 689.

128. McMann v. Richardson, 397 U.S. 759, 771 n. 14 (1970).

129. *Cronic,* 466 U.S. at 654.

130. United States v. Ash, 413 U.S. 300, 308 (1973).

131. *Cronic,* 466 U.S. at 654; *see also* United States v. Decoster, 199 U.S. App. D.C. 359, 382, 624 F.2d 196, 219 (MacKinnon, J., concurring), *cert. denied,* 444 U.S. 944 (1979). As Justice MacKinnon stated in *Decoster:* "Assistance begins with the appointment of counsel, it does not end there. In some cases the performance of counsel may be so inadequate that, in effect, no assistance of counsel is provided. Clearly, in such cases, the defendant's Sixth Amendment right to 'have Assistance of Counsel' is denied." 199 U.S. App. D.C. 359, 382, 624 F.2d 196, 219.

132. Bazelon, *The Realities of Gideon and Argersinger, supra* note 97, at 818–19.

133. *Avery,* 308 U.S. at 446 (footnote omitted).

134. David L. Bazelon, *The Defective Assistance of Counsel,* 42 CINCINNATI. L. REV. 1, 4 (1973).

135. *Id.* at 3 (internal citations omitted).

136. *See Strickland*, 466 U.S. at 689 (directing trial courts to "indulge a strong presumption that counsel's conduct falls within the *wide range of reasonable professional assistance.*").

137. *See* Monroe H. Freedman, *Judge Frankel's Search for Truth*, 123 U. PA. L. REV. 1060, 1065 (1975):

> [The adversarial] system proceeds on the assumption that the best way to ascertain the truth is to present to an impartial judge or jury a confrontation between the proponents of conflicting views, assigning to each the task of marshalling and presenting the evidence for its side in as thorough and persuasive a way as possible. . . . The judge or jury is given the strongest case that each side can present, and is in a position to make an informed, considered, and fair judgment.

138. LEWIS, *supra* note 8 at 205.

139. *See, e.g.*, Barbara Levine, *Preventing Defense Counsel Error—An Analysis of Some Ineffective Assistance of Counsel Claims and Their Implications for Professional Regulation*, 15 U. TOLEDO L. REV. 1275, 1299 (1984) ("realistic, rough estimate" of "amount of poor trial lawyer performance ranges anywhere from 9% to 22%"). Ms. Levine sets out the "sparse" empirical data on the issue. *See id.* at 1295–1300.

140. Robert Cover & T. Alexander Aleinikoff, *Dialectical Federalism: Habeas Corpus and the Court*, 86 YALE L.J. 1035, 1086 (1977).

141. NORMAN LEFSTEIN, CRIMINAL DEFENSE SERVICES FOR THE POOR, 2 (1982).

142. *See, e.g.*, Bazelon, *The Defective Assistance of Counsel*, *supra* note 134, at 2 ("The adversary system assumes that each side has adequate counsel. This assumption probably holds true for giant corporations or well-to-do individuals, but . . . a great many—if not most—indigent defendants do not receive the effective assistance of counsel guaranteed them by the 6th Amendment."); *see also* Bazelon, *The Realities of Gideon and Argersinger*, *supra* note 97; Barbara Babcock, *Fair Play: Evidence Favorable to an Accused and Effective Assistance of Counsel*, 34 STAN. L. REV. 1133, 1163–65, 1173 (1982). Over the years, occasionally some of the members of this Court have called for the Court to articulate standards for effective assistance of counsel. *See, e.g.*, Romero v. United States, 459 U.S. 926 (1982) (White, J. dissenting from denial of cert.) (ineffectiveness case); Marzullo v. Maryland, 435 U.S. 1011 (1978) (White and Rehnquist, J.J., dissenting from denial of cert.) (ineffectiveness case).

143. *See* LEFSTEIN, *supra* note 141, at 8–24.

144. *See* Albert Alschuler, *The Defense Attorney's Role in Plea Bargaining*, 84 YALE L.J. 1179, 1182 (1975).

145. *See* THE AMERICAN BAR ASSOCIATION, THE NATIONAL LEGAL AID AND DEFENDER ASSOCIATION, GIDEON UNDONE! THE CRISIS IN INDIGENT

DEFENSE FUNDING, 1–3 (1982) (finding that inadequate funding leads to inadequate indigent representation).

146. See *Argersinger*, 407 U.S. at 34–35 (citing PRESIDENT'S COMMISSION ON LAW ENFORCEMENT AND ADMINISTRATION OF JUSTICE, THE CHALLENGE OF CRIME IN A FREE SOCIETY 128 (1967)).

147. William J. Brennan, Jr., *The Criminal Prosecution: Sporting Event or Quest for Truth?*, 1963 WASH. U. L.Q. 279, 280 (emphasis added).

148. *Strickland*, 466 U.S. at 687.

149. Woodson v. North Carolina, 428 U.S. 280, 305 (1976) (plurality opinion).

150. Associated Press, *Prison Population Sets Record*, N.Y. TIMES, Apr. 25, 1983, at B11 (reporting an increase of 42,915 inmates making the total 412,303 according to the Bureau of Justice Statistics). According to the Justice Department, the increase in prisoners was sparked by longer sentencing and more restricted parole laws. *See id.*

151. See Stuart Taylor, Jr., *Strict Penalties for Criminals: Pendulum of Feeling Swings*, N.Y. TIMES, Dec. 13, 1984, at A1 (noting that sentencing reforms have led to longer prison terms, prison overcrowding, and the increased arbitrary power of prosecutors). These sentencing measures were instituted to reduce the power of judges and parole boards and to increase sentences.

152. National Desk, *State Prisons Around Nation Scramble for Relief as Overcrowding Mounts*, N.Y. TIMES, Sept. 29, 1983, at A18 (reporting prisoners sleeping on the floor in at least 18 states and 40 states exceeding official housing capacity for inmates). As one commentator noted, "the public's desire for punishment . . . continues to exceed its willingness to pay for decently housing all the people it wants to imprison." Taylor, *supra* note 131, at A1.

153. See Edward A. Gargan, *New York Prison Population Hits a Record 30,000*, N.Y. TIMES, May 15, 1983, at A26 (reporting that 2,193 inmates were at Attica, a prison designed to hold 1,758).

154. See DEP'T OF JUSTICE, BUREAU OF JUSTICE STATISTICS, PRISON AND JAIL INMATES AT MIDYEAR 2004, 11 (2005) *available at* http://www.ojp.usdoj.gov/bjs/abstract/pjim04.htm (click on the Acrobat file to access the electronic publication)(visited October 17, 2007).

155. *Strickland*, 466 U.S. at 694.

156. Much of the history of the right to counsel comes from the National Legal Aid and Defender (NLADA) Web site, *available at* http://www.nlada.org/Civil/Civil_Library/document_search?batch_size%3Aint=20&nlada_weighted_searchable_text=history (click on "History of NLADA) (visited October 17, 2007); *see also* Note, *"Burdine v. Johnson": The Fifth Circuit Wakes Up, But the Supreme Court Refuses to Put the Sleeping Attorney Standard to Rest*, 39 HOUS. L. REV. 835 (2002); Green, *Lethal Fiction*, *supra* note 71, at 438–39 & n.12.

157. See, e.g., RICHARD KLEIN & ROBERT SPANGENBERG, THE INDIGENT DEFENSE CRISIS 10 (August 1993) (prepared for ABA Section on Criminal Justice

Ad Hoc Committee on the Indigent Defense Crisis) (discussing current crisis and noting that the ABA issued similar reports in 1979, 1982, and 1986); *see also id.* at 25 (finding "long-term neglect and under-funding of indigent defense have created a crisis of extraordinary proportions in many states throughout the country."").

158. *See* DEBORAH L. RHODE, ACCESS TO JUSTICE 122–30 (discussing the poor quality of indigent criminal defense) (2004); JOSHUA DRESSLER, UNDERSTANDING CRIMINAL PROCEDURE 597–98 (3d ed. 2002); Berger, *supra* note 51, at 59–64 (discussing the problem of incompetent defense lawyers); Bright, *Worst Lawyer, supra* note 11, at 1841–66 (discussing the pervasive inadequacy of counsel for the poor and the reasons for it); Stephen B. Bright, *Neither Equal Nor Just: The Rationing and Denial of Legal Services to the Poor When Life and Liberty Are at Stake,* 1997 ANN. SURV. AM. L. 783, 785–93 [hereinafter *Neither Equal Nor Just*] (discussing the resistance to *Gideon* at trial and appeal and the consequences for the poor accused); Donald A. Dripps, *Criminal Law: Ineffective Assistance of Counsel: The Case for an Ex Ante Parity Standard,* 88 J. CRIM. L. & CRIMINOLOGY 242, 245–51 (1997) (describing the "permanent crisis" in indigent defense); Richard Klein, *The Eleventh Commandment: Thou Shall Not Be Compelled to Render the Ineffective Assistance of Counsel,* 68 IND. L.J. 363 , 363–408 (1993) (discussing inadequate funding for court-appointed counsel and excessive caseloads in public defender offices).

159. *See generally* Abbe Smith, *Too Much Heart and Not Enough Heat: The Short Life and Fractured Ego of the Heroic, Empathic Public Defender,* 37 U.C. DAVIS L. REV. 1203 (2004) (discussing the sustaining motivations of defenders).

160. William J. Stuntz, *The Uneasy Relationship Between Criminal Procedure and Criminal Justice,* 107 YALE L.J. 1, 6–7, 65–67 (1997); *see also* Kim Taylor-Thompson, *Tuning Up Gideon's Trumpet,* 71 FORDHAM L. REV. 1461 (2003) (remarking that "[i]n hindsight, it is hard to imagine that the [*Gideon*] opinion could have missed the massive economic impact of providing counsel in all serious cases and that this price ticket threatened the meaningful implementation of the guarantee [of the right to counsel]").

161. *See* DEFENSE COUNSEL IN CRIMINAL CASES, *supra* note 52, at 1; *see also* Bob Sablatura, *Study Confirms Money Counts in County's Courts: Those Using Appointed Lawyers Are Twice as Likely to Serve Time,* HOUS. CHRON., Oct. 17, 1999, at 1. The Houston Chronicle's study examined 30,000 felony cases filed in Harris County, Texas, which includes Houston, in 1996.

Conviction rates for indigent defendants with court-appointed counsel and those who could afford to hire their own lawyers were about the same in state and federal court. Ninety percent of federal defendants and 75 percent of defendants in the most populous counties were found guilty regardless of the type of attorney. DEFENSE COUNSEL IN CRIMINAL CASES *supra* note 52, at 1.

Interestingly, average sentence lengths for defendants sent to jail or prison were shorter for those with publicly financed counsel than those with private counsel. In federal court those with publicly financed counsel were given just under five years on average, and those with private attorneys received just over five years. In large state courts, those with publicly financed counsel were sentenced to an average of two and a half years and those with private counsel to three years. *Id.*

162. *See* DEFENSE COUNSEL IN CRIMINAL CASES, *supra* note 52, at 1.

163. *See* Barbara L. Jones, *Minnesota's public defenders, Legal Aid face funding concerns again*, THE MINNESOTA LAWYER, Dec. 13, 2004, (reporting that a state budget shortfall would result in the lay-off of 140 lawyers from the State Public Defender, about a quarter of public defenders in the state). At the time of the proposed lay-offs, Minnesota public defenders were already averaging 800 cases a year, more than double the caseload recommended by ABA guidelines).

164. Jan Ackerman, *Justice on a Tight Budget; Commissioners Are courting Disaster by Cutting Budget of Overworked Public Defenders*, PITT. POST-GAZETTE, Feb. 4, 1996, at A1 (quoting a study done for the ABA by the Spangenberg Group, a consulting firm that specializes in indigent defense). The year before the funding cuts, an independent study had concluded that the public defender's office was in crisis because of chronic underfunding and "years of neglect."

165. *See* Dave Daley, *Defense Attorney Fears Poor Clients Will Be Hurt by Cuts*, MILWAUKEE JOURNAL, Mar. 16, 1995, at A18. Nearly $4 million was cut from the allocation for indigent criminal defense.

166. *See* Tom Schoenberg, *Court Seeks Budget Boost*, LEGAL TIMES, Apr. 26, 1999, at 6 (noting that in 1998 the court withheld payment of court-appointed lawyers for four months).

167. *See generally* Klein, *The Emperor Has No Clothes, supra* note 88, at 658–63; Richard Klein, *The Constitutionalization of Ineffective Assistance of Counsel*, 58 MD. L. REV. 1433 (1999).

168. *See* Paul M. Barrett, *Lawyer's Fast Work on Death Cases Raises Doubts About System*, WALL ST. J., Sept. 7, 1994, at A1. The lawyer, Joe Frank Cannon, was known for blundering his way through trials when he managed to stay awake. At least 10 clients received death sentences on his watch.

169. *See* COLE, *supra* note 5, at 84 (citing data from The Equal Justice Initiative, *A Report on Alabama's Indigent Defense System: Capital Cases*, 3–5 (March 1997)).

170. Pruett v. State, 574 So.2d 1342, 1357 (1990) (quoting State *ex rel.* Stephen v. Smith, 747 P.2d 816, 831 (Kan.1987) (companion case to *Pruett*). The defense lawyer was paid what amounted to five dollars an hour in the case.

171. *See* Luban, *supra* note 15, at 1734–35 (citing Margaret L. Steiner, *Special Project, Adequacy of Fact Investigation in Criminal Defense Lawyers' Trial Preparation*, 1981 ARIZ. ST. L.J. 523, 534, 537; Gary T. Lowenthal, *Theoretical Notes on Lawyer Competency and an Overview of the Phoenix Criminal Lawyer Study*,

1981 Ariz. St. L.J. 451n.23; Marty Lieberman, *Special Project, Investigation of Facts in Preparation for Plea Bargaining,* 1981 Ariz. St. L.J. 557, 576, 579 (1981).

172. *Luban, supra* note 15, at 1735 (citing Michael McConville & Chester L. Mirsky, *Criminal Defense of the Poor in New York City,* 15 NYU Rev. L. & Soc. Change 581 (1986–87)).

173. *See* Jonathan D. Casper, Criminal Courts: The Defendant's Perspective 35, tbl Vi-5 (1978).

174. *See generally* Standards for Criminal Justice, *supra* note 33.

175. *See* Bruce A. Green, *Criminal Neglect: Indigent Defense from a Legal Ethics Perspective,* 52 Emory L.J. 1169 (2003).

176. Berger, *supra* note 51, at 50; *see also* Jonathan D. Casper et al., *Procedural Justice in Felony Cases,* 22 Law & Soc'y Rev. 483, 498 (1988) (finding positive correlation between defendants' perception of fairness of criminal process and amount of time they spent with their lawyers).

177. Vanessa Merton, *What Do You Do When You Meet A "Walking Violation of the Sixth Amendment," If You're Trying to Put That Lawyer's Client in Jail?,* 69 Fordham L. Rev. 997, 1007–8 (2000).

178. *See* Linda Greenhouse, *Inmate Whose Lawyer Slept Gets New Trial,* N.Y. Times, June 4, 2002, at A16. The case, *Burdine v. Johnson,* 262 F.3d 336 (5th Cir. 2001) (*en banc*), *cert. denied,* 535 U.S. 1120 (2002), had a tortured history. Prior to the full court of the Fifth Circuit ruling in a 9-5 decision that Burdine's conviction be vacated, *see id.* at 262 F.3d 349) ("[T]he repeated unconsciousness of Burdine's counsel through not insubstantial portions of the critical guilt-innocence phase . . . warrants a presumption of prejudice"), a three-judge panel had overruled a district court decision granting habeas relief and ruled that sleeping counsel during a capital trial was insufficient to presume prejudice. *See* Burdine v. Johnson, 231 F.3d 950 (5th Cir. 2000). On June 19, 2003, Calvin Burdine pleaded guilty to capital murder and was sentenced to three life sentences. *See* Texas Lawyer, June 23, 2003, at 8. One of Burdine's lawyers, Danalynn Recer, who directs an indigent capital defense office, declared, "Today, the so-called 'sleeping lawyer' case was finally put to rest." *Id.*

179. *See* Matthew J. Fogelman, *Justice Asleep Is Justice Denied: Why Dozing Defense Attorneys Demean the Sixth Amendment and Should Be Deemed per se Prejudicial,* 26 J. Legal Prof. 67 (2001/2002); Jeffrey L. Kirchmeier, *Drink, Drugs, and Drowsiness: The Constitutional Right to Effective Assistance of Counsel and the Strickland Prejudice Standard,* 75 Neb. L. Rev. 425 (1996).

180. Rompilla v. Beard, 545 U.S. 374 (2005).

181. *Id.* at 377.

182. *Id.* at 387 (citing 1 ABA Standards for Criminal Justice 4–4.1 (2d ed. 1982 Supp.).

183. Wiggins v. Smith, 539 U.S. 510, 524 (2003) (quoting *Strickland*, 466 U.S. at 688). Both *Wiggins* and *Williams v. Taylor*, 529 U.S. 362 (2000), the other post-*Strickland* reversal on ineffectiveness grounds, found counsel ineffective for failing to investigate and put on mitigating evidence during the penalty phase of a capital case.

184. *Rompilla*, 545 U.S. at 387.

185. *See* Ruth Marcus, *Public Defender Systems Tried by Budget Problems*, Wash. Post, March 8, 1992, at A1 (recounting the facts of State v. Peart, 621 So.2d 7780 (La. 1993); *see also* Cole, *supra* note 5, at 83.

Note to the Reader Regarding Legal Citations

THE NONLAWYER READER may not be familiar with the format of many of the citations in the Endnotes. This brief note is intended to provide basic information for the reader to use in accessing the sources in question.

A legal citation provides a reference to a legal authority such as the Constitution, a court case, a statute, or an article in a legal periodical. This reference information indicates precisely where the legal authority may be found.

All reported court decisions are compiled into books organized by court and district or geographic region. A citation provides six pieces of information to locate the case in the appropriate book. First, the citation indicates the name of the case. Second, it indicates the volume number of the book in which the case may be found. Third is the name of the book (otherwise known as a "reporter"). Fourth, the page number in the reporter on which the case can be found is provided. Fifth, unless it is clear from the name of the reporter, the court that decided the case is indicated. Sixth, the citation indicates the year in which the court made the decision. For example: *Alden v. Maine*, 527 U.S. 706 (1999).

The name of the case is indicated first (Alden against the State of Maine). Next, the number 527 indicates the volume number of the book. U.S. is an abbreviation for the United States Reporter, which itself indicates that the case is a United States Supreme Court case. The number 706 is the page on which the case begins. Finally, 1999 is the year in which the Supreme Court decided *Alden v. Maine*. In the citation *Lewis v. Sacramento County*, 98 F.3d 434 (9th Cir. 1996), the case was published in the Federal Reporter, Third Series and the reference to "9th Cir." means that the case was decided by the Ninth Circuit Court of Appeals.

Citations to legal articles published in law reviews and journals similarly provide volume numbers of the review or journal in which the information is located, as well as the relevant page numbers and the year of publication. Citations to statutes provide the chapter or title of the statute book, the name of the collection of statutes, and the page where the law in question is located.

Readers who make their way to a law library to read cases or other cited materials should ask for assistance in locating the books from a reference librarian. These knowledgeable people are usually more than happy to help you.

About the Contributors

MICHAEL AVERY is a professor at Suffolk University Law School and a past president of the National Lawyers Guild. He was a civil rights and criminal defense lawyer for nearly 30 years before joining the Suffolk faculty in 1998. He is a co-author of *Police Misconduct: Law and Litigation*, a legal treatise concerning civil rights claims against law enforcement officers and agencies, and a co-author of *Handbook of Massachusetts Evidence*, the leading authority on evidence law in Massachusetts.

ERWIN CHEMERINSKY is the founding dean of the Donald Bren School of Law at the University of California, Irvine. He was previously the Alston & Bird Professor of Law and Political Science at Duke University. Prior to joining the Duke faculty in 2004, he spent 21 years as a professor at the University of Southern California Law School. Dean Chemerinsky is the author of six books, including a constitutional law treatise and casebooks in constitutional law and criminal procedure. He frequently argues appellate cases, including in the United States Supreme Court.

MARJORIE COHN is a professor at Thomas Jefferson School of Law and the President of the National Lawyers Guild. She is the author of *Cowboy Republic: Six Ways the Bush Gang Has Defied the Law* and co-author of *Cameras in the Courtroom: Television and the Pursuit of Justice*. Professor Cohn frequently publishes articles on contemporary issues of law and justice. Her Web site is at www.marjoriecohn.com.

TRACEY MACLIN teaches constitutional law and criminal procedure at Boston University School of Law. He has written many law review articles on the Fourth Amendment and has written more than a dozen amicus curiae briefs in the Supreme Court representing public interest organizations in Fourth Amendment cases.

EVA JEFFERSON PATERSON is a civil rights lawyer and the president and a co-founder of the Equal Justice Society, a national advocacy organization dedicated in part to advancing progressive and racially enlightened jurisprudence. One of the primary goals of EJS is to dismantle the intent standard enunciated in *Washington v. Davis* using strategy and tactics similar to those employed by Charles Hamilton Houston at Howard University Law School. Houston and his colleagues used social science to show the absurdity of the "separate but equal" doctrine adopted by the Supreme Court in *Plessy v. Ferguson.* Their work over several decades eventually persuaded the Court to overrule *Plessy* in *Brown v. Board of Education.*

JAMIN RASKIN is a professor of constitutional law at American University, where he directs the Program on Law and Government, and a state senator in Maryland, serving on the judiciary committee. He wrote the 2003 bestseller *Overruling Democracy: The Supreme Court versus the American People* and *We the Students,* which has been called "the bible of the new movement for constitutional literacy."

DAVID RUDOVSKY is a senior fellow at the University of Pennsylvania Law School. He is also a founding partner of Kairys, Rudovsky, Messing & Feinberg, a Philadelphia law firm specializing in civil rights and civil liberties litigation. Mr. Rudovsky has published widely in the criminal justice field and has litigated significant constitutional cases from trial to the United States Supreme Court. In 1986, he was awarded a MacArthur Fellowship for his work in criminal justice and civil liberties.

SUSAN K. SERRANO is the Director of Educational Development at the Center for Excellence in Native Hawaiian Law at the University of Hawai'i Law School, where she teaches an advanced legal writing and social justice course. She was the founding research director of the national Equal Justice Society and was a civil rights and legal services lawyer in San Francisco, California. Ms. Serrano has published widely on racial justice, civil rights, and Native Hawaiian rights.

ABBE SMITH is a professor at the Georgetown University Law Center, where she is the co-director of the Criminal Justice Clinic and the E. Barrett Prettyman Fellowship Program. Previously she was a public defender in Philadelphia for eight years and taught in the criminal defense clinic at Harvard Law School. In 2005–2006 she was a Senior Fulbright Scholar at the University of Melbourne Law School, in Australia. Professor Smith has written widely in the area of criminal law, legal ethics, juvenile justice, and clinical legal education and is the author of *Case of a Lifetime: A Lawyer's Struggle for Criminal Justice.*

Index